1,001 CCNA®
Routing and Switching
Practice Questions

FOR

DUMMIES®

A Wiley Brand

by Glen E. Clarke

FOR

DUMMIES®

A Wiley Brand

1,001 CCNA® Routing and Switching Practice Questions For Dummies®

Published by: **John Wiley & Sons, Inc.,** 111 River Street, Hoboken, NJ 07030-5774, www.wiley.com

Copyright © 2014 by John Wiley & Sons, Inc., Hoboken, New Jersey

Media and software compilation copyright © 2014 by John Wiley & Sons, Inc. All rights reserved.

Published simultaneously in Canada

No part of this publication may be reproduced, stored in a retrieval system or transmitted in any form or by any means, electronic, mechanical, photocopying, recording, scanning or otherwise, except as permitted under Sections 107 or 108 of the 1976 United States Copyright Act, without the prior written permission of the Publisher. Requests to the Publisher for permission should be addressed to the Permissions Department, John Wiley & Sons, Inc., 111 River Street, Hoboken, NJ 07030, (201) 748-6011, fax (201) 748-6008, or online at http://www.wiley.com/go/permissions.

Trademarks: Wiley, For Dummies, the Dummies Man logo, Dummies.com, Making Everything Easier, and related trade dress are trademarks or registered trademarks of John Wiley & Sons, Inc. and may not be used without written permission. CCNA is a registered trademark of Cisco Technology, Inc. All other trademarks are the property of their respective owners. John Wiley & Sons, Inc. is not associated with any product or vendor mentioned in this book.

For general information on our other products and services, please contact our Customer Care Department within the U.S. at 877-762-2974, outside the U.S. at 317-572-3993, or fax 317-572-4002. For technical support, please visit www.wiley.com/techsupport.

Wiley publishes in a variety of print and electronic formats and by print-on-demand. Some material included with standard print versions of this book may not be included in e-books or in print-on-demand. If this book refers to media such as a CD or DVD that is not included in the version you purchased, you may download this material at http://booksupport.wiley.com. For more information about Wiley products, visit www.wiley.com.

Library of Congress Control Number: 2013949068

ISBN 978-1-118-79429-6 (pbk); ISBN 978-1-118-79414-2 (ebk); ISBN 978-1-118-79424-1 (ebk)

Manufactured in the United States of America

10 9 8 7 6 5 4 3 2 1

Contents at a Glance

Table of Contents

Introduction

The popular CCNA popular certification tests your knowledge of networking concepts and day-to-day configuration of Cisco routers and switches. It is a great technical certification that can enhance your career and open doors to many IT careers. The Cisco CCNA certification is also the foundation of other Cisco certification tracks, such as the CCNP. The CCNA exams will test your knowledge of real-world networking concepts and Cisco features found on most networks today.

About This Book

1,001 CCNA Routing and Switching Practice Questions For Dummies is designed to be a practical practice exam guide that will help you prepare for the two CCNA exams. As the book title says, it includes 1,001 questions, organized by exam so that you can prepare for the ICND1 exam first, and then after passing it, you can prepare for the ICND2 exam.

This book has been designed to help you prepare for the style of questions you will receive on the CCNA exams. It also helps you understand the topics you can expect to be tested on for each exam. In order to properly prepare for the CCNA exams, I recommend that you:

- ✔ **Review a reference book:** *1,001 CCNA Routing and Switching Practice Questions For Dummies* is designed to give you sample questions to help you prepare for the style of questions you will receive on the real certification exam. However, it is not a reference book that teaches the concepts in detail. That said, I recommend that you review a reference book before attacking these questions so that the theory is fresh in your mind.

- ✔ **Get some practical, hands-on experience:** After you review the theory, I highly recommend getting your hands on some routers and switches, or using a simulator; practice configuring the router with each topic you are studying. The CCNA certification is a practical, hands-on certification: The more hands-on experience you have, the easier the exams will be.

- ✔ **Do practice test questions:** After you review a reference book and perform some hands-on work, attack the questions in this book to get you "exam ready"!

Conventions Used in This Book

Each chapter in this book has different elements that help you prepare to pass your CCNA certification exams. Each chapter holds the following features:

- ✔ **The Problems You'll Work On:** Each chapter opens with a quick introduction on what is covered in that chapter, along with a list of topics you can expect questions on for that chapter.

- ✔ **What to Watch Out For:** This area points out some important facts that you should not forget when preparing for the certification questions related to that chapter.

✔ **Network Diagrams:** CCNA certification exams are very hands-on focused; that said, network diagrams are used in the questions as often as possible so that you can analyze a specific situation and solve a problem!

Foolish Assumptions

I make a few assumptions about you as a reader:

✔ **You are interested in obtaining the CCNA Certification.** The sole purpose of this book is to help you prepare for the CCNA certification exams. This book is not a complete reference on the topic, but it presents a set of questions to help you prepare for the style and topic areas of CCNA!

✔ **You have Cisco equipment or a simulator.** It is important to ensure you have as much hands-on knowledge as possible when preparing for the CCNA exams. This book assumes you have been working with Cisco devices for some time and are familiar with the configuration of Cisco devices. If you are not, then try to get your hands on some equipment or a simulator and practice the configuration of each topic as you read through this book.

✔ **You will study hard and do as much hands-on work as possible.** The Cisco CCNA certification exams cover a lot of material. You most likely will need to read the reference material a few times to ensure that you understand the concepts before attempting the questions in this book. You should also experiment as much as possible on the actual devices after you read a particular topic. Be sure to run through the chapters in this book multiple times to test your knowledge over time.

How This Book Is Organized

I highly recommend preparing for one CCNA exam at a time (yes, there are two exams to take — ICND1 and ICND2). This book is divided into two parts. Part I covers the topics you need to know for the ICND1 exam, while Part II covers the topics you need to know to prepare for the ICND2 exam.

The following sections outline what you can find in each part.

Part I: ICND1 – Exam 100-101

In this part, you are presented with a number of questions, organized by topic, that prepare you for the types of questions you can expect on the ICND1 exam (exam 100-101). This part covers topics such as networking basics, TCP/IP, subnetting, introduction to the Cisco IOS, basic router configuration, and switch configuration. This part also covers the basics of routing and routing protocols, such as RIP and OSPF, as well as WANs and troubleshooting network communication.

Part II: ICND2 – Exam 200-101

Part II presents practice questions to help prepare you for the ICND2 exam (exam 200-101). This part covers questions on ICND2 topics, including switching technologies such as STP, Etherchannel, VLANs, VTP, IOS boot process and file management, router essentials and route summarization, RIP and OSPF, EIGRP, IP services, and Frame Relay and WAN technologies.

Beyond the Book

This book gives you plenty of CCNA questions to work on, but maybe you want to track your progress as you tackle the questions, or maybe you're having trouble with certain types of questions and wish they were all presented in one place where you could methodically make your way through them. You're in luck. Your book purchase comes with a free one-year subscription to all 1,001 practice questions online. You get on-the-go access any way you want it — from your computer, smartphone, or tablet. Track your progress and view personalized reports that show where you need to study the most. Study what, where, when, and how you want!

What you'll find online

The online practice that comes free with this book offers you the same 1,001 questions and answers that are available here. The beauty of the online questions is that you can customize your online practice to focus on the topic areas that give you the most trouble. So if you need help with wireless standards, then select questions related to this topic online and start practicing. Or, if you're short on time but want to get a mixed bag of a limited number of questions, you can specify the number of problems you want to practice. Whether you practice a few hundred problems in one sitting or a couple dozen, and whether you focus on a few types of problems or practice every type, the online program keeps track of the questions you get right and wrong so that you can monitor your progress and spend time studying exactly what you need.

You can access this online tool using a PIN code, as I describe in the next section. Keep in mind that you can create only one login with your PIN. Once the PIN is used, it's no longer valid; it also is nontransferable. So you can't share your PIN with other users after you've established your login credentials.

This product also comes with an online Cheat Sheet that helps you increase your odds of performing well on the CCNA exam. Check out the free Cheat Sheet at `www.dummies.com/ cheatsheet/1001ccnaroutingswitchingpracticequestions`. (No PIN required. You can access this info before you even register.)

How to register

Purchasing the book entitles you to one year of free access to the online, multiple-choice version of all 1,001 of this book's practice questions. To gain access, all you have to do is register. Just follow these simple steps:

1. **Find your PIN access code.**

   - **Print book users:** If you purchased a hard copy of this book, turn to the inside front cover to find your access code.

   - **E-book users:** If you purchased this book as an e-book, you can get your access code by registering your e-book at `dummies.com/go/getaccess`. Go to this website, find your book and click it, and answer the security question to verify your purchase. Then you'll receive an e-mail with your access code.

2. **Go to** `http://prep.dummies.com/proed/go/accesscode`.

3. **Enter your access code.**

4. **Follow the instructions to create an account and establish your personal login information.**

That's all there is to it! You can come back to the online program again and again — simply log in with the username and password you chose during your initial login. No need to use the PIN a second time.

If you have trouble with the PIN or can't find it, please contact Wiley Product Technical Support at 800-762-2974 or `http://support.wiley.com`.

Your registration is good for one year from the day you activate your PIN. After that time frame has passed, you can renew your registration for a fee. The website gives you all the important details about how to do so.

Extra content

A lot of extra content that you won't find in this book is available at `www.dummies.com`. Go online to find the following:

- **The Cheat Sheet for this book is at**

  `www.dummies.com/cheatsheet/1001ccnaroutingswitchingpracticequestions`.

- **Updates to this book, if we have any, are also available at**

  `www.dummies.com/extras/1001ccnaroutingswitchingpracticequestions`.

The Value of CCNA Certification

The Cisco CCNA certification is considered one of the premiere certifications for networking professionals who want to prove their competence to implement small to medium size networks. Earning the CCNA certification is hard but rewarding work: It tests your practical knowledge of configuring Cisco networks.

Cisco decided that someone looking to obtain a CCNA should take two exams, known as the *Interconnecting Cisco Network Devices* (ICND) exams: They include the ICND1 (100-101) and ICND2 (200-101) exams: The ICND1 comes first, and then after passing that exam, you proceed with the ICND2 exam to earn your CCNA certification.

If you have been working with Cisco network devices for some time and feel confident that you know all the material for both exams, you could take the single, accelerated CCNA exam (known as the CCNAX exam). Be sure you are up to the challenge of taking on *all* exam topics in one exam, though. There is no major cost benefit to doing the CCNAX exam; both the ICND1 and ICND2 exams are about half the price of the CCNAX exam.

Cisco also decided that if someone were to take the ICND1 exam and pass it, then he or she would earn the Cisco CCENT certification — the first Cisco certification of many Cisco certification paths.

That's right. Cisco has many different certification paths that IT professionals can take, such as the Routing and Switching path, the Security path, and the Wireless path. The CCENT/CCNA certification is the first certification exam in all the Cisco certification paths; as a result, it has become a very popular certification.

Obtaining the CCNA certification is your way of proving to employers and customers that you have the skills to manage Cisco devices in small- and medium-size network environments.

CCNA Exam Details

The CCNA certification is earned after you pass Cisco's ICND1 and ICND2 exams, which are numbered 100-101 and 200-101, respectively. You can schedule your exam appointment at any VUE testing center by calling one of the phone numbers listed below or by scheduling it online at www.vue.com/cisco/schedule.

- ✔ **United States:** 1-877-404-EXAM (3926)
- ✔ **Canada:** 1-877-404-3926
- ✔ **Other Countries:** For other parts of the world, check out VUE's website at www.vue.com/cisco/contact.

Each exam presents 40 to 50 questions and you will have approximately 90 minutes to complete each test. The exams are available English and Japanese languages.

In order to take the CCNA certification exams, you must be 18 years or older if you wish to take the exam without a parent's consent. If you are between 13 and 17 years old, you may still take the exam but only with a parent's consent.

If for some reason you do not pass an exam, Cisco requires that you wait six days before retaking it (five days from the day after your last exam). After passing the CCNA certification exam, your certification is valid for three years, at which point it will need to be renewed.

The following summarizes exam details you should know when you schedule your exam:

- ✔ **Exam Numbers:** 100-101 (ICND1) and 200-101 (ICND2)
- ✔ **Time:** 90 minutes each
- ✔ **Questions:** 40 to 50 questions each
- ✔ **Passing Score:** 804 (based on a scale of 300 to 1,000)
- ✔ **Test Provider:** Pearson VUE
- ✔ **Available Languages:** English, Japanese

What to Expect on the CCNA Exams

A big part of passing any certification exam is being as prepared as possible. This means knowing two things: what to expect on the exam as far as the technical content and understanding the style of exam questions.

Types of questions

The CCNA certification exams have a number of different style questions. Each style of question is designed to test you in a different way. For example, the multiple-choice questions are designed to test your knowledge level (the theory), while the simulation questions will test your hands-on skills — ensuring you can perform the task.

Following are some of the different types of question formats you will find on the CCNA certification exams:

- **Multiple-choice, single answer:** These types of question present you with a question and then list a number of choices as potential answers. You are required to select the best answer from the list of choices.

- **Multiple-choice, multiple answer:** These types of questions pose a single question that requires you to choose multiple answers from the list of choices. These types of questions normally specify "select all that apply" or may tell you how many items to select, such as "Select three."

- **Drag-and-drop:** These questions are a little more interactive and typically involve your dragging items from the right side of the screen and dropping them in the correct place on the left side of the screen. For example, you may be given a list of definitions on the right side of the screen and you need to drop the correct term onto the proper definition.

- **Fill-in-the-blank:** You may receive a fill-in-the-blank question that requires you to read a question and instead of selecting the correct answer from a list, you must type the correct answer without any kind of prompt.

- **Testlet:** A *testlet* is a group of questions to which the same scenario applies. You are first presented with the scenario and then given four or five multiple-choice questions to answer for that scenario.

- **Simlet:** A *simlet* is similar to testlet in the sense that you are given a scenario and have to answer multiple questions for that scenario. The difference: A simlet scenario is in the form of a simulation. With a simlet, you are asked multiple questions, and to answer the questions you need to use router commands to view the configuration of the router in the simulator.

- **Simulations:** Simulators are a popular type of question in Cisco exams. You are given a number of tasks that need to be performed in the simulator, and you are graded on how you handle your configuration within that simulator.

It is essential that you familiarize yourself with how to answer each of the question types described above. I recommend doing two things if you have never taken a Cisco exam. The first thing is to visit Cisco's website, where an exam tutorial shows what each question type looks like and how you should answer it. The URL for the exam tutorial is:

```
www.cisco.com/web/learning/wwtraining/certprog/training/cert_exam_
tutorial.html
```

The second thing you can do to help prepare for the style of questions is that when you actually begin your exam on test day, Cisco will ask if you would like to take the exam tutorial. I highly recommend doing the exam tutorial because it will give you a chance to see how to use the test engine. It only takes a few minutes to do the tutorial, and the time does not count against your 90-minute exam time. Again, you want to be as prepared as possible!

One last, critical point to make about the exam is this: You cannot mark questions and go back to them at a later time, like you can with Microsoft or CompTIA exams. Once you answer a question, you will not be able to change your answer after moving on to the next question.

Exam objectives

The CCNA certification is respected in the industry and coveted because it tests the exam candidate on basic networking concepts and the skills needed to configure Cisco devices in a network environment.

The following is a list of the major exam objectives that you will be tested on with each CCNA exam. For full details on the exam objectives, check out Cisco's website at www.cisco.com/web/learning/certifications/associate/ccna/index.html.

- ✔ **ICND1 (100-101):** Objectives for this test include

  - *Operation of IP Data Networks:* Covers topics such as networking devices, such hubs, switches, and routers. Know network models such as OSI and TCP/IP Internet model. Predict data flow between two systems given a scenario, and understand cable types.

  - *LAN Switching Technologies:* Know the switching concepts, such as collision domains and broadcast domains and the MAC address table. Know basic commands to configure a switch and VLANs.

  - *IP Addressing (IPv4/IPv6):* Know details of IPv4 addressing and subnetting. Also understand the different IPv6 address types.

  - *IP Routing Technologies:* Know the concepts of IP routing, including static routing and dynamic routing. Know RIP and OSPF routing protocols, and how to route between VLANs.

  - *IP Services:* Know how to configure DHCP and access control lists on a router. Be sure to understand NAT and how to configure NAT on the router.

  - *Network Device Security:* Understand security best practices with switches and routers. This includes port security, SSH, and password security.

  - *Troubleshooting:* Know how to troubleshoot all topics covered by ICND1, including ACLs, communication, DHCP, NAT, and IP addressing issues.

- ✔ **ICND2 (200-101):** Objectives for this test include

  - *LAN Switching Technologies:* Know LAN switching technologies, such as STP, RSTP, VLANs, and Etherchannels.

  - *IP Routing Technologies:* Know the basics of the IOS boot process and how to manage files. Know how to configure routering between VLANs and how to configure OSPF and EIGRP.

  - *IP Services:* Know high availability concepts such as FHRP, VRRP, and HSRP. Know how to configure and use Syslog and describe SNMP v2 and v3.

- *Troubleshooting:* Know how to troubleshoot switches and routers and each topic covered by ICND2. This includes troubleshooting RSTP, OSPF, EIGRP, and connectivity issues.

- *WAN Technologies:* Know the different WAN technologies such as T1, ISDN, DSL, Frame Relay, and VPN. Know how to configure a serial connection and Frame Relay on a router.

On Your Test Day

I have taken many certification exams over the years and have picked up some good habits along that testing process. (I am sure I have some bad habits as well, but I'll keep those to myself!) Here are some basic steps you should take to ensure that you are as prepared as possible for your exam.

Arriving at the test site

The first thing you want to do on test day is make sure that you show up at the testing center early so that you can familiarize yourself with the facility and do things like getting a drink and using the restroom before your exam starts.

Make sure that you bring two forms of ID: One must include a photo of you. Also note that Cisco requires the test center take a photo of you on test day; this photo is printed on your score card.

Getting lots of rest

Another habit I have learned over the years is that sometimes it is not best to cram any more information in your head the night before the exam. For most people, it is more effective to get a good night's sleep the night before the exam. Be sure to eat a filling breakfast, too, before heading out to take your exam.

Also, if you are a morning person, you may want to schedule the exam early in the day. I don't seem to do as well, I've noticed, if I schedule a post-lunchtime exam sitting. I seem to think clearer in the morning, so as a result, I make sure I schedule all my exams around 10 a.m.

Answering questions

When you are answering exam questions, always read them thoroughly and be sure you understand the question before looking at the choices. Always eliminate the obvious incorrect choices first, and then choose the best answer from the remaining choices. And remember that your first instinct is usually correct, so go with your gut if you are not 100% sure.

Part I
ICND 1 – Exam 100-101

1,001
Questions

In this part...

The only way to become proficient in networking is through a lot of practice. By having access to 1001 CCNA questions with different levels of difficulty you will be well on your way to achieving some level of proficiency. Every basic networking concept is included, and you will see a large variety of the types of questions that you can expect to encounter. By mastering these types of questions you will be well on your way to having a very solid CCNA foundation!

In this part, you are presented with a number of questions, organized by topic, that prepare you for the ICND1 exam (exam 100-101). The topics covered here include

- Networking basics
- TCP/IP, subnetting
- Introduction to the Cisco IOS
- Basic router configuration
- Switch configuration.

This part also covers the basics of routing and routing protocols, such as RIP and OSPF, as well as WANs and troubleshooting network communication.

Chapter 1

Networking Devices, Technologies, and Models

. . . .

A lthough the CCNA certification exams test you on some difficult and in-depth networking issues, the ICND1 exam also tests you on basic networking knowledge. For the ICND1 exam, you are expected to know the purpose of different network services, devices, cabling, and the OSI model. This chapter helps you prepare for those questions by testing you on basic networking concepts.

The Questions You'll Work On

In this chapter, you'll review questions concerning the following topics:

- ✔ Recognizing the purpose of networking services such as DHCP, DNS, NAT, and authentication services
- ✔ Understanding the difference between hubs, bridges, switches, and routers
- ✔ Understanding the OSI model and what devices and protocols run at each layer of the OSI model
- ✔ Knowing when to use a straight-through cable or a crossover cable
- ✔ Understanding the difference between a collision domain and a broadcast domain

What to Watch Out For

Don't let common mistakes trip you up; watch for the following when working with these questions:

- ✔ Straight-through cables are used to connect dissimilar devices, whereas crossover cables are used to connect similar devices. The one gotcha on this is that a crossover cable is used to connect a workstation to a router.
- ✔ Know the OSI model and what devices and protocols run at the different layers. Ensure that you know the difference between a layer-2 address and a layer-3 address.
- ✔ Hubs are layer-1 devices, whereas switches and bridges are layer-2 devices. A router is a layer-3 device.
- ✔ Web servers deliver HTML pages using HTTP as a delivery protocol. FTP is the Internet protocol for downloading files, SMTP is the Internet protocol for delivering e-mail, and POP3 and IMAP are Internet protocols for reading e-mail. An authentication server is responsible for verifying usernames and passwords before someone can gain network access.

Network Services

1–7 Choose the best answer(s).

1. Your manager asks you which service is responsible for translating the source IP address of a packet to the IP address of the public interface on the router.

    (A) DHCP

    (B) NAT

    (C) DNS

    (D) HTTP

2. You are troubleshooting a communication problem. You seem to be able to communicate with Glen's website by IP address, but not by the fully qualified domain name (`www.gleneclarke.com`). What is most likely the problem?

    (A) DHCP

    (B) NAT

    (C) DNS

    (D) HTTP

3. Which network service can be configured on your router that is responsible for assigning IP addresses to systems on the network?

    (A) DHCP

    (B) NAT

    (C) DNS

    (D) HTTP

4. What service on the network is responsible for converting the FQDN to an IP address?

    (A) Authentication server

    (B) DNS server

    (C) DHCP server

    (D) NAT

5. What service on the network is responsible for verifying username and passwords when the user attempts to log on?

    (A) Authentication server

    (B) DNS server

    (C) DHCP server

    (D) NAT

6. You are monitoring network traffic and you notice a number of DHCP discover messages on the network. Which of the following is the destination address of the DHCP discover message?

(A) 0F-1B-3C-2F-3C-2A

(B) FF-FF-FF-FF-FF-FF

(C) 192.168.4.5

(D) 192.168.0.0

7. When a client system boots up and requests an IP address, it first must send out which message?

(A) DHCP request

(B) DHCP discover

(C) DHCP response

(D) DHCP ACK

Network Devices and Communication

8–17 Choose the best answer(s).

8. What device is responsible for regenerating the signal so that the signal can travel a greater distance?

(A) Bridge

(B) Router

(C) Repeater

(D) Switch

(E) Hub

9. Which device filters traffic by looking at the destination address of the frame and then forwards the frame to the port that the destination system resides on?

(A) Hub

(B) Router

(C) Repeater

(D) Switch

10. Which of the following is a layer-3 device?

(A) Bridge

(B) Router

(C) Repeater

(D) Switch

(E) Hub

11.   A device that can send and receive information, but not at the same time, is said
      to be _____.

      (A)   Simplex

      (B)   Full duplex

      (C)   Multicast

      (D)   Half-duplex

12.   A message that is sent out on the network and is destined for all systems is known as a
      _____ message.

      (A)   Unicast

      (B)   Multicast

      (C)   Full duplex

      (D)   Broadcast

13.   A message that is sent out on the network and is destined for a group of systems is known as a
      _____ message.

      (A)   Unicast

      (B)   Multicast

      (C)   Full duplex

      (D)   Broadcast

14.   A group of systems that can receive one another's broadcast messages is known as a
      _____.

      (A)   Collision domain

      (B)   Active directory domain

      (C)   Fully qualified domain name

      (D)   Broadcast domain

15.   You are monitoring network traffic and notice that there is a large number of broadcast
      messages sent across the wire. You would like to separate your network into multiple broadcast
      domains. How can you do this? (Select two.)

      (A)   Switch

      (B)   VLANs

      (C)   Router

      (D)   Bridge

16. A group of systems that can have their data collide with one another is known as a
_____.

    (A)   Broadcast domain

    (B)   VLAN

    (C)   Collision domain

    (D)   Multicast

17. How many broadcast domains and collision domains are there in the diagram below?

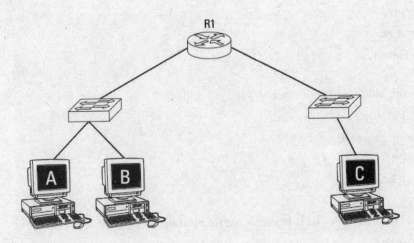

    (A)   1 broadcast domain and 5 collision domains

    (B)   2 broadcast domains and 3 collision domains

    (C)   1 broadcast domain and 3 collision domains

    (D)   2 broadcast domains and 5 collision domains

OSI Model and Network Standards

18–31 Choose the best answer(s).

18. Sue is having trouble understanding some network concepts and asks you to help identify address types. Which of the following is considered a layer-2 address?

    (A)   192.168.2.200

    (B)   `www.gleneclarke.com`

    (C)   COMPUTER1

    (D)   00-AB-0F-2B-3C-4E

19. You are troubleshooting communication to a network by looking at the link light on the switch. What layer of the OSI model are you troubleshooting when looking at a link light?

(A) Application

(B) Physical

(C) Network

(D) Data link

20. What layer of the OSI model is responsible for breaking the data into smaller segments?

(A) Data link

(B) Physical

(C) Network

(D) Transport

21. Which of the following is considered a layer-3 address?

(A) 192.168.2.200

(B) www.gleneclarke.com

(C) COMPUTER1

(D) 00-AB-0F-2B-3C-4E

22. What layer of the OSI model is responsible for routing and logical addressing?

(A) Network

(B) Physical

(C) Data link

(D) Transport

23. Which of the following are considered layer-2 devices? (Choose two.)

(A) Bridge

(B) Router

(C) Repeater

(D) Switch

(E) Hub

24. Which of the following are considered layer-1 devices? (Choose two.)

(A) Bridge

(B) Router

(C) Repeater

(D) Switch

(E) Hub

25. What is the application layer protocol for delivering e-mail across the Internet?

(A) FTP

(B) SNMP

(C) SMTP

(D) POP3

26. Which layer of the OSI model works with packets?

(A) Layer 1

(B) Layer 2

(C) Layer 3

(D) Layer 4

27. What is the application layer protocol for receiving e-mail over the Internet?

(A) FTP

(B) SMTP

(C) SNMP

(D) POP3

28. Which Gigabit Ethernet standard uses UTP cabling to reach 1000 Mbps?

(A) 1000BaseTX

(B) 1000BaseSX

(C) 1000BaseCX

(D) 1000BaseLX

29. Which 10 Gigabit Ethernet standard uses multimode fiber-optic cabling?

(A)   10GBaseLR

(B)   10GBaseER

(C)   10GBaseSR

(D)   1000BaseSX

30. Which of the following addresses does a router use to determine where a packet needs to be delivered? (Choose two.)

(A)   24.56.78.10

(B)   00-3B-4C-2B-00-AF

(C)   A layer-3 address

(D)   A layer-2 address

31. Which layer of the OSI model works with frames?

(A)   Layer 1

(B)   Layer 2

(C)   Layer 3

(D)   Layer 4

Network Cabling

32–38 Choose the best answer(s).

32. What type of cable would you use if you wanted to connect a system to an RJ-45 port on a switch?

(A)   Fiber

(B)   Crossover

(C)   Straight-through

(D)   Thinnet

33. You wish to network two systems by connecting a computer directly to another computer. Which type of cable would you use?

(A)   Fiber

(B)   Crossover

(C)   Straight-through

(D)   Thinnet

34. You need to create a crossover cable. What wires would you cross on one of the ends?

(A)   1 and 2 with 3 and 4

(B)   2 and 4 with 6 and 8

(C)   2 and 4 with 5 and 6

(D)   1 and 2 with 3 and 6

35. See figure below. You are trying to ping computer B from computer A and are unsuccessful. What is the problem?

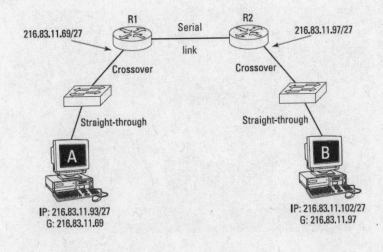

(A)   The IP address of R1 is on the wrong subnet.

(B)   The default gateway setting of computer B is incorrect.

(C)   The default gateway setting of computer A is incorrect.

(D)   The cable type between the switches and routers is incorrect.

(E)   The IP address of R2 is on the wrong subnet.

(F)   The cable type between the computers and switches is incorrect.

36. You are testing communication to a router and have decided to connect your workstation to the Fast Ethernet port of the router. What type of cable would you use?

(A)   Fiber

(B)   Crossover

(C)   Straight-through

(D)   Thinnet

37. You have a UTP cable that has been configured at both ends with the 568B standard. What type of cable is it?

(A)   Straight-through

(B)   Crossover

(C)   Rollover

(D)   Coax

38. You wish to create a crossover cable and have wired one end of the cable with the 568A standard, What standard should you use to wire the opposite end of the cable?

(A)   568B

(B)   568A

(C)   569B

(D)   569A

Chapter 2

Introduction to TCP/IP

• •

You have to be an expert at the TCP/IP protocol in order to pass the Cisco ICND1 and ICND2 exams. In order to prepare you for TCP/IP-related questions, this chapter reviews critical points such as IP addressing, protocols, and common ports. The next chapter builds off this and covers more advanced TCP/IP questions, but let's hit the basics first!

The Questions You'll Work On

In this chapter, you'll review questions concerning the following topics:

- ✔ Understanding IP addressing topics, such as the default address classes
- ✔ Recognizing the different protocols that make up the TCP/IP protocol suite, such as TCP, UDP, IP, ARP, and ICMP
- ✔ Demonstrating on the new ICND1 exam your knowledge of IPv6 and the different address types
- ✔ Knowing the common TCP and UDP ports that are used by applications
- ✔ Converting a binary value to a decimal value and vice versa

What to Watch Out For

Don't let common mistakes trip you up; watch for the following when working with these questions:

- ✔ There are three core address classes, known as class A, class B, and class C. Class A addresses have the first octet with a value that ranges from 1 to 127. Class B addresses have the first octet with a value that ranges from 128 to 191. Class C addresses have the first octet with a value that ranges from 192 to 223.
- ✔ Watch for the use of common protocols such as IP for logical addressing and routing. ICMP does error and status reporting, TCP is responsible for reliable delivery, UDP is responsible for unreliable delivery, and ARP is responsible for converting the logical address to the physical address.
- ✔ Know the port values used by common applications such HTTP (80), Telnet (23), SSH (22), HTTPS (443), FTP (21 and 20), SMTP (25), POP3 (110), and DNS (53).
- ✔ Know the IPv6 benefits and types of addresses. Link-local addresses are similar to APIPA addresses and start with FE80. Unique local addresses are similar to private IP addresses and start with FC00, and finally, global addresses are like public IP addresses and start with 2000. The IPv6 loopback address is ::1.

IP Addressing

39–54 Choose the best answer(s).

39. Which of the following are considered class A addresses? (Select all that apply.)

    (A) 129.45.10.15

    (B) 10.35.87.5

    (C) 131.15.10.12

    (D) 192.156.8.34

    (E) 121.59.87.32

    (F) 210.45.10.112

40. Sue is reviewing IP addressing basics and asks you which of the following is considered a class A private address.

    (A) 24.56.10.12

    (B) 192.168.0.5

    (C) 172.16.45.10

    (D) 10.55.67.99

41. What is the default subnet mask of a system with the IP address of 189.34.5.67?

    (A) 255.0.0.0

    (B) 255.255.0.0

    (C) 255.255.255.0

    (D) 255.255.255.255

42. What is the default subnet mask of a class C address?

    (A) 255.0.0.0

    (B) 255.255.0.0

    (C) 255.255.255.0

    (D) 255.255.255.255

43. Which of the following is a class B private address?

    (A) 24.56.10.12

    (B) 192.168.0.5

    (C) 172.16.45.10

    (D) 10.55.67.99

44. Are the systems of 201.45.3.56 and 201.45.5.20 on the same network?

(A) Yes

(B) No

45. Which of the following addresses are considered invalid addresses to assign to a host on the network? (Select all that apply.)

(A) 10.254.255.255

(B) 120.127.34.10

(C) 190.34.255.255

(D) 136.45.68.22

(E) 202.45.6.0

(F) 127.87.3.22

46. The decimal number of 137 is which of the following in binary?

(A) 10001001

(B) 10101001

(C) 11001001

(D) 10000101

47. Are the systems with the IP addresses of 121.56.78.10 and 121.45.6.88 on the same network?

(A) Yes

(B) No

48. What is the default subnet mask of 130.56.78.10?

(A) 255.0.0.0

(B) 255.255.0.0

(C) 255.255.255.0

(D) 255.255.255.255

49. Your system has an IP address of 131.107.45.10. Which of the following systems is on the same network as you?

(A) 131.56.10.12

(B) 130.107.45.10

(C) 131.107.22.15

(D) 113.107.45.11

50. Which of the following addresses are considered invalid addresses to assign to a host on the network? (Select all that apply.)

(A) 216.83.11.255

(B) 12.34.0.0

(C) 10.34.15.22

(D) 131.107.0.0

(E) 127.15.34.10

(F) 189.56.78.10

51. The binary number of 01101101 is which of the following decimal values?

(A) 101

(B) 109

(C) 135

(D) 143

52. Which class address always has the value of the first bits in the IP address set to 110?

(A) Class A

(B) Class B

(C) Class C

(D) Class D

53. Which class address always has the first two bits of the IP address set to 10?

(A) Class A

(B) Class B

(C) Class C

(D) Class D

54. Which IP address class always has the first bit in the address set to 0?

(A) Class A

(B) Class B

(C) Class C

(D) Class D

TCP/IP Protocols

55–71 Choose the best answer(s).

55. Which protocol is responsible for converting the logical address to a physical address?

(A) TCP

(B) IP

(C) ICMP

(D) ARP

56. The ARP request is sent to which of the following layer-2 destination addresses?

(A) FF-FF-FF-FF-FF-FF

(B) 192.168.0.255

(C) 00-FF-00-FF-00-FF

(D) 00-00-00-00-00-00

57. What are the three phases of the TCP three-way handshake?

(A) ACK/SYN, SYN, ACK

(B) SYN, ACK/SYN, ACK

(C) ACK/SYN, ACK, SYN

(D) SYN, ACK, SYN/ACK

58. Which of the following does TCP use to guarantee delivery?

(A) Source and destination IP address

(B) Source and destination port

(C) Sequence numbers and acknowledgements

(D) Sequence numbers and ports

59. What TCP/IP protocol is responsible for logical addressing and routing functions?

(A) TCP

(B) IP

(C) ICMP

(D) UDP

60. Which transport layer protocol is responsible for unreliable delivery?

(A) TCP

(B) IP

(C) ICMP

(D) UDP

61. Which TCP/IP protocol is responsible for error and status reporting?

(A) TCP

(B) IP

(C) ICMP

(D) UDP

62. The router looks at which field in the IP header to decide where to send the packet?

(A) Source IP address

(B) Destination IP address

(C) Source MAC address

(D) Destination MAC address

63. What flags are set on the second phase of the three-way handshake?

(A) FIN/SYN

(B) ACK/FIN

(C) ACK/SYN

(D) ACK/RST

64. Which flag is set in a TCP packet that indicates a previous packet was received?

(A) PSH

(B) FIN

(C) ACK

(D) RST

65. You wish to allow echo request messages to pass through the firewall. What ICMP type is used in an echo request message?

(A) 0

(B) 8

(C) 3

(D) 11

66. Which of the following are fields found in the IP header? (Select all that apply.)

  (A) Sequence number

  (B) Destination port

  (C) Source IP address

  (D) Type

  (E) Time to Live

  (F) SYN flag

67. Which of the following are considered application layer protocols?

  (A) TCP

  (B) IP

  (C) FTP

  (D) ICMP

68. Which transport layer protocol is responsible for reliable delivery?

  (A) UDP

  (B) ICMP

  (C) IP

  (D) TCP

69. What ICMP type is used by the echo reply message?

  (A) 0

  (B) 3

  (C) 5

  (D) 8

70. The security administrator for your network has asked that you block ping messages from entering your network. What protocol would you block?

  (A) ICMP

  (B) IP

  (C) TCP

  (D) UDP

71. Which TCP flag is responsible for dropping a connection at any point in time?

  (A) PSH

  (B) FIN

  (C) ACK

  (D) RST

IPv6

72–78 Choose the best answer(s).

72. Which of the following is the IPv6 equivalent to 127.0.0.1?

(A) ::127

(B) 127::1

(C) ::1

(D) FE80::

73. Your manager has been hearing a lot about IPv6 addressing, and asks you which of the following statements are true about IPv6 unicast addresses? (Select two.)

(A) A link-local address starts with FE00.

(B) A global address starts with 2000.

(C) The loopback address is 127::1.

(D) When an interface is assigned a global address, it is allowed only one IP6 address.

(E) The loopback address is ::1.

74. Which of the following is an example of an IPv6 link-local address?

(A) ff00::f407:622c:a0ce:90cc

(B) fe80::f407:622c:a0ce:90cc

(C) fe08::f407:622c:a0ce:90cc

(D) 2001::f407:622c:a0ce:90cc

75. Your manager has asked you what some of the benefits of transitioning from IPv4 to IPv6 are. (Select two.)

(A) IPSec is optional

(B) No broadcast messages

(C) A 64-bit address scheme

(D) Telnet passwords are encrypted

(E) Automatic configuration

76. Your manager is evaluating IPv6 transitioning technologies and is wondering which IPv6 tunneling method encapsulates the IPv6 data into an IPv4 user datagram to travel over the Internet and can pass through NAT devices.

(A) 6-to-4

(B) Dynamic IP

(C) Teredo

(D) Dual stack

77. You are evaluation how you are going to slowly transition to IPv6. What three techniques can be used to allow migrating from IPv4 to IPv6? (Choose three.)

    (A) Broadcast addressing

    (B) Translation between IPv6 and IPv4

    (C) Multicast to unicast translation

    (D) Use of dual-stack routing

    (E) Use tunneling protocols

78. What IPv6 address type is similar to an IPv4 private IP address and starts with FC00?

    (A) Global address

    (B) Loopback address

    (C) Link-local address

    (D) Unique local address

TCP/IP Ports

79–83 Choose the best answer(s).

79. SMTP uses which of the following ports?

    (A) UDP 53

    (B) TCP 21

    (C) TCP 23

    (D) TCP 25

80. FTP uses which of the following ports?

    (A) 25

    (B) 23

    (C) 21

    (D) 53

81. Which of the following represents the port used by POP3?

    (A) 21

    (B) 110

    (C) 143

    (D) 443

82. Which of the following are true statements about TCP ports? (Select all that apply.)

(A) FTP uses TCP ports 21 and 20.

(B) FTP uses TCP ports 11 and 12.

(C) HTTP uses TCP port 53.

(D) HTTP uses TCP port 80.

(E) SMTP uses TCP port 53.

(F) SMTP uses TCP port 25.

83. Which of the following are true statements about ports? (Select all that apply.)

(A) DHCP uses UDP 67/68.

(B) DHCP uses TCP 67/68.

(C) SNMP uses UDP 161.

(D) DNS uses UDP 25.

(E) SNMP uses TCP 161.

(F) DNS uses UDP 53.

Troubleshooting

84–85 Choose the best answer(s).

84. Sue is unable to surf the Internet and calls you over to her desk to troubleshoot. You use ipconfig on the system and notice the following IP configuration. What is the problem?

```
Local Area Network Connection:
IPv4 Address…. … .: 169.254.34.56
Subnet Mask… …. .: 255.255.0.0
Default Gateway… …:
```

(A) The DNS server is down.

(B) The subnet mask is incorrect.

(C) The router is down.

(D) The DHCP server is down.

85. Bob is unable to surf the Internet and calls you over to his desk to troubleshoot. You use ipconfig on the system and notice the following IP configuration. What should you do?

```
Local Area Network Connection:
IPv4 Address.... ... .: 192.19.210.79
Subnet Mask... .... .: 255.255.255.0
Default Gateway... ...: 192.19.0.1
```

   (A)   Change his IP address to 169.254.210.79.

   (B)   Change his IP address to 192.19.0.79.

   (C)   Change his subnet mask to 255.0.0.0.

   (D)   Remove his default gateway setting.

Chapter 3

Subnetting and VLSM

• •

*B*oth the Cisco ICND1 and the ICND2 certification exams expect you to have a sound knowledge of subnetting and variable length subnet masks. Make sure you understand subnetting before attempting this chapter so that you can get the most out of these questions and apply your knowledge. When you're familiar with IP addressing and subnetting, then dive into this chapter and have lots of fun with it as each question presents you with a mathematical challenge!

The Problems You'll Work On

In this chapter, you'll review questions concerning the following topics:

- ✔ Determining the number of subnet bits to use to create the desired number of subnets
- ✔ Determining the number of host bits required to support the desired number of systems on a subnet
- ✔ Calculating the network ID, broadcast address, and range of valid addresses based on given criteria
- ✔ Determining the optimal subnet mask to use with the goal of reserving address space

What to Watch Out For

Don't let common mistakes trip you up; watch for the following when working with these questions:

- ✔ To calculate the number of networks, the formula is $2^{\text{subnet bits}}$ = number of networks. For example, if you have three subnet bits, the formula gives you $2^3 = 8$ subnets. To calculate the number of systems supported on a network, use this formula: $2^{\text{host bits}} - 2$ = number of valid addresses.

- ✔ When solving subnetting questions, always determine the increment value and then calculate all the network IDs. Once you have all the network IDs calculated, determine the network to which the question applies, and then determine the answer. For example, if asked for the third valid address or the broadcast address, determine the network ID first and then figure out the third valid address or the broadcast address.

- ✔ Variable length subnet masks (VLSM) do not follow the concept of classes, but instead determine how many host bits are needed to support the number of hosts on the subnet. VLSM allows for each subnet to have a different subnet mask as each subnet supports a different number of hosts.

Subnetting

86–119 Choose the best answer(s).

86. You are designing the IPv4 address scheme for the network. How do you calculate the broadcast address of a subnet?

 (A) Set all host bits to 0

 (B) Set all host bits to 1

 (C) Set all network bits to 0

 (D) Set all subnet bits to 1

87. Your manager would like you to subnet the 129.65.0.0 network into six different networks. What is your new subnet mask?

 (A) 255.224.0.0

 (B) 255.255.192.0

 (C) 255.255.224.0

 (D) 255.255.255.224

88. What is the subnet mask of 135.44.33.22/20?

 (A) 255.255.192.0

 (B) 255.255.240.0

 (C) 255.255.224.0

 (D) 255.255.248.0

89. You are designing the IP address scheme for your network and you need to subnet the 142.65.0.0 network into 12 different networks. What is your new subnet mask?

 (A) 255.255.240.0

 (B) 255.255.192.0

 (C) 255.255.224.0

 (D) 255.255.248.0

90. How many host bits are needed in order to support 1,010 systems on the network?

    (A) 12

    (B) 10

    (C) 11

    (D) 14

91. How many masked bits are needed in order to create at least 20 subnets?

    (A) 3

    (B) 4

    (C) 5

    (D) 6

92. You are designing your IPv4 address scheme. How do you calculate the network ID of a subnet?

    (A) Set all host bits to 0.

    (B) Set all host bits to 1.

    (C) Set all network bits to 1.

    (D) Set all subnet bits to 0.

93. How many hosts can exist on a network with the address of 180.45.10.20/20?

    (A) 1,024

    (B) 4,096

    (C) 4,094

    (D) 1,022

94. How many subnet bits do you need to create 6 networks?

    (A) 3

    (B) 4

    (C) 5

    (D) 6

95. Which option on the Cisco router indicates that you can use the first and last subnets of a subnetted network?

    (A) VLSM

    (B) ip subnet-zero

    (C) RIPv1

    (D) RIPv2

96. Which of the following subnet masks matched to the CIDR notation is correct?

    (A)   255.255.255.224 = /27

    (B)   255.255.192.0 = /19

    (C)   255.255.240.0 = /27

    (D)   255.255.255.192 = /28

97. You are designing a network with subnets of variable sizes. In the figure below, identify two problems with the design.

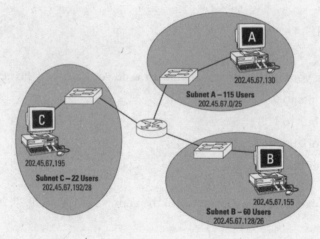

    (A)   Subnet A does not have enough addresses.

    (B)   Subnet B does not have enough addresses.

    (C)   Subnet C does not have enough addresses.

    (D)   Computer A is assigned an incorrect address.

    (E)   Computer B is assigned an incorrect address.

    (F)   Computer C is assigned an incorrect address.

98. Your system uses the IP address of 145.68.23.45/25. How many systems are supported on your network?

    (A)   126

    (B)   128

    (C)   64

    (D)   62

99. The Fast Ethernet port on a router is assigned the IP address of 131.107.16.1/20. How many hosts can exist on the subnet?

(A) 4,096

(B) 4,094

(C) 1,048,574

(D) 1,022

100. You want to assign your serial interface the third valid IP address in the second subnet of 192.168.2.0/26. Which IP address would you use?

(A) 192.168.2.3

(B) 192.168.2.35

(C) 192.168.2.64

(D) 192.168.2.67

101. You are designing the IP address scheme for a branch office that needs to support 92 systems on the network. What should your subnet mask be?

(A) 255.255.255.240

(B) 255.255.255.128

(C) 255.255.255.248

(D) 255.255.255.192

102. What is the minimum number of host bits needed to support 510 hosts on the network?

(A) 12

(B) 7

(C) 9

(D) 14

103. You wish to subnet 137.15.0.0 in order to support 8,190 hosts on each network. You wish to use the smallest subnet size to support this number of hosts. What will be the new subnet mask?

(A) 255.255.255.224

(B) 255.255.192.0

(C) 255.255.240.0

(D) 255.255.224.0

104. How many hosts can exist on a network with the address of 201.10.20.30/27?

(A) 28

(B) 30

(C) 32

(D) 64

105. With the goal of preserving addresses, which of the following subnet masks would you use to create a subnet of up to 60 hosts?

(A)   255.255.255.224

(B)   255.255.255.192

(C)   255.255.255.252

(D)   255.255.255.248

106. You have a system whose IP address is correctly configured for 198.45.6.87/27. You are now responsible for assigning an IP address to the router. Which of the following IP addresses should be assigned to the router?

(A)   198.45.6.95

(B)   198.45.6.62

(C)   198.45.6.64

(D)   198.45.6.94

107. What is the network ID for the third subnet of 220.55.66.0/27?

(A)   220.55.66.32

(B)   220.55.66.96

(C)   220.55.66.60

(D)   220.55.66.64

108. The 24.60.32.20/11 address is located in which of the following subnets?

(A)   24.32.0.0

(B)   24.64.0.0

(C)   24.96.0.0

(D)   24.16.0.0

109. You need to assign the fourth valid IP address of 107.53.100.10/12 to the Fast Ethernet port on the router. What address would you use?

(A)   107.53.0.4

(B)   107.53.100.4

(C)   107.0.0.4

(D)   107.48.0.4

110. A network administrator is working with the 195.34.56.0 network, which has been subnetted into 8 networks. Which of the following two addresses can be assigned to hosts on the same subnet? (Select two.)

(A) 195.34.56.35

(B) 195.34.56.14

(C) 195.34.56.76

(D) 195.34.56.58

(E) 195.34.56.98

(F) 195.34.56.129

111. Using the network diagram shown in the figure below and having the goal of making the best use of your IP address space, which of the following represents the address scheme you would apply to the Toronto office?

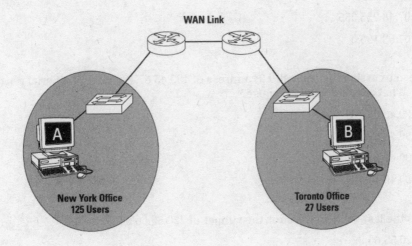

(A) 199.11.33.160/31

(B) 199.11.33.0/25

(C) 199.11.33.128/27

(D) 199.11.33.0/31

(E) 199.11.33.160/30

(F) 199.11.33.128/28

112. What is the network ID of 190.53.159.150/22?

(A) 190.53.132.0

(B) 190.53.144.0

(C) 190.53.152.0

(D) 190.53.156.0

113. Which of the following statements are true of 205.56.34.53/28? (Choose three.)

(A) The network is not subnetted.

(B) The first valid address of the subnet is 205.56.34.26.

(C) The network ID of the subnet is 205.56.34.48.

(D) The first valid address of the subnet is 205.56.34.65.

(E) The last valid address of the subnet is 205.56.34.55.

(F) The network is subnetted.

(G) The last valid address of the subnet is 205.56.34.47.

(H) The broadcast address of the subnet is 205.56.34.63.

114. What is the broadcast address of 107.50.100.10/12?

(A) 107.63.255.255

(B) 107.50.255.255

(C) 107.48.255.255

(D) 107.53.156.0

115. You need to assign the last valid IP address of 199.45.67.139/26 to the Serial port on your router. What address would you use?

(A) 199.45.67.128

(B) 199.45.67.126

(C) 199.45.67.191

(D) 199.45.67.190

116. What is the last valid address for the subnet of 220.55.66.64/27?

(A) 220.55.66.32

(B) 220.55.66.94

(C) 220.55.66.62

(D) 220.55.66.64

117. Which of the following addresses exists on the same network, knowing that all systems have a subnet mask of 255.255.255.240? (Select two.)

(A) 195.34.56.7.14

(B) 195.34.56.7.30

(C) 195.34.56.7.38

(D) 195.34.56.7.55

(E) 195.34.56.7.17

(F) 195.34.56.7.69

118. Which of the following statements are true of 190.88.122.45/19? (Choose three.)

(A) The network is not subnetted.

(B) The first valid address of the subnet is 190.88.122.1.

(C) The network ID of the subnet is 190.88.122.0.

(D) The first valid address of the subnet is 190.88.96.1.

(E) The last valid address of the subnet is 190.88.96.254.

(F) The network is subnetted.

(G) The last valid address of the subnet is 190.88.255.254.

(H) The broadcast address of the subnet is 190.88.127.255.

119. Which of the following subnet masks would you typically use on a WAN interface to make the best use of address space?

(A) 255.255.255.224

(B) 255.255.255.192

(C) 255.255.255.252

(D) 255.255.255.248

VLSM

120–123 Choose the best answer(s).

120. Which IP feature allows you to use different subnet masks on different subnets within the network?

(A) IP Subnet Zero

(B) RIPv1

(C) VLSM

(D) RIPv2

121. You are connecting two of your office locations together over a WAN link. Each office has a router with an IP address assigned. What should your subnet mask be in order to leverage the best use of address space?

(A) 255.255.255.0

(B) 255.255.255.192

(C) 255.255.255.224

(D) 255.255.255.252

122. Your organization network diagram is shown in the figure below. Your company has the class C address range of 199.11.33.0. You need to subnet the address into three subnets and make the best use of the available address space. Which of the following represents the address scheme you would apply to the New York office?

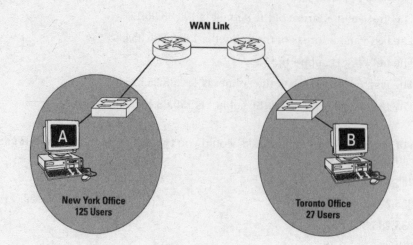

(A)   199.11.33.160/31

(B)   199.11.33.0/25

(C)   199.11.33.128/27

(D)   199.11.33.0/31

(E)   199.11.33.160/30

(F)   199.11.33.128/28

123. Using the network diagram shown in the figure below and having the goal of making the best use of your IP address space, which of the following represents the address scheme you would apply to the WAN link?

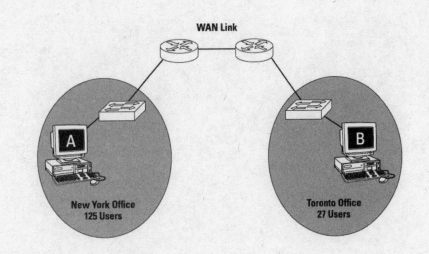

(A)   199.11.33.160/31

(B)   199.11.33.0/25

(C)   199.11.33.128/27

(D)   199.11.33.0/31

(E)   199.11.33.160/30

(F)   199.11.33.128/28

Chapter 4

Introduction to Cisco IOS

· ·

When preparing for the Cisco CCNA certification, you will be tested on a number of advanced topics, but before you get there it is important that you have a sound foundation. This chapter is designed to test you on the basics of the Cisco IOS and prepare you for related questions you will find on the ICND1 exam.

The Problems You'll Work On

In this chapter, you'll review questions concerning the following topics:

- ✔ Recognizing the different port types found on a Cisco device and their purpose
- ✔ Understanding the different types of memory and what is stored there
- ✔ Navigating the Cisco IOS
- ✔ Grasping the basics of the Cisco device boot process
- ✔ Comprehending the information outputted from the show version command

What to Watch Out For

Don't let common mistakes trip you up; watch for the following when working with these questions:

- ✔ Cisco devices will have different types of ports, but the most common are the console (CON) port and the auxiliary (AUX) port. The console port is used for local administration, whereas the auxiliary port is used to connect a modem to a router and to remotely manage the router.

- ✔ Serial ports are used to connect to a WAN environment by connecting to an external CSU/DSU. Serial ports can also be used to connect two routers directly together with a back-to-back serial cable. In this example, one router will act as the DCE device and the other will act as the DTE device (specified on each end of the cable). The DCE device will need to specify the clock rate command.

- ✔ There are different types of memory on the Cisco device. Flash memory is used to store the Cisco IOS; NVRAM is used to store the startup configuration; RAM or VRAM is used to store the running configuration; and ROM is used to store the POST routines, bootstrap program, and mini-IOSes, such as ROMMON, which you can use to troubleshoot problems with the real IOS.

Device Ports

124–138 Express the given number in scientific notation.

124. Which of the following represents a purpose for the serial port on a Cisco router?

(A) To connect to the LAN

(B) To connect the console port

(C) To connect to the WAN

(D) To connect a modem

125. Which of the following port identifiers are used to reference a Fast Ethernet port? (Select two.)

(A) s0/0

(B) f0/0

(C) con 0

(D) aux 0

(E) fa0/0

126. What type of cable is used to connect to the console port?

(A) Crossover

(B) Straight-through

(C) Null modem

(D) Rollover

127. Your manager notices an AUX port on the back of the Cisco router and asks what it is used for. How would you reply?

(A) To connect a CSU/DSU

(B) To connect an external Ethernet interface

(C) To connect an internal Ethernet interface

(D) To connect a modem

128. You are performing a security audit on the network devices and have verified that the console port has a password configured. What other port should you verify has a password?

(A) FastEthernet0/0

(B) FastEthernet0/1

(C) AUX

(D) Serial0/0/0

129. You are configuring the DCE end of a point-to-point serial link between two routers. What extra command is typed on the DCE end of the link?

(A) `clock rate 64000`

(B) `encapsulation hdlc`

(C) `ip address w.x.y.z`

(D) `no shutdown`

130. The external CSU/DSU connects to which port on the router?

(A) FastEthernet0/0

(B) Con 0

(C) Aux 0

(D) Serial0/0/0

131. What type of module can be purchased to install an internal CSU/DSU into the router?

(A) WNA

(B) WCI

(C) WIC

(D) WAC

132. You are trying to assign an IP address to the LAN port on the router and get the following message on the screen.

```
Router(config)#interface e0
        ^

% Invalid input detected at '^' marker.
```

You use the show version command to try to identify the problem. The output is displayed below. What is the problem?

```
Cisco 2811 (MPC860) processor (revision 0x200) with 60416K/5120K bytes
of memory

Processor board ID JAD05190MTZ (4292891495)

M860 processor: part number 0, mask 49

2 FastEthernet/IEEE 802.3 interface(s)

4 Low-speed serial(sync/async) network interface(s)

239K bytes of NVRAM

62720K bytes of processor board System flash (Read/Write)

Configuration register is 0x2102

Router>
```

This means:

(A) The interface is disabled.

(B) The interface type specified does not exist.

(C) You are at the wrong prompt.

(D) The interface is already configured.

Memory Types

133–138 Express the given number in scientific notation.

133. Where is the running configuration stored?

(A) NVRAM

(B) VRAM

(C) ROM

(D) Flash

134. Which of the following are stored in ROM on the Cisco device?

 (A) Startup config

 (B) POST

 (C) Bootstrap

 (D) IOS

 (E) ROMMON

 (F) Running config

135. What type of memory is shown here?

 (A) VRAM

 (B) NVRAM

 (C) ROM

 (D) Flash

136. Which commands can you use to save the running configuration to the startup configuration? (Select two.)

 (A) `copy startup-config running-config`

 (B) `save running-config startup-config`

 (C) `save running-config`

 (D) `copy running-config startup-config`

 (E) `write`

137. When the Cisco router starts up, where does it find the Cisco IOS?

(A) NVRAM

(B) RAM

(C) ROM

(D) Flash

138. When you first boot up the Cisco router, where does it locate the startup configuration?

(A) NVRAM

(B) RAM

(C) ROM

(D) Flash

IOS Basics

139–150 Express the given number in scientific notation.

139. You are connected to your switch and wish to remotely administer the Cisco router. Which command would you use?

(A) `telnet`

(B) `enable`

(C) `connect`

(D) `rdp`

140. You are at the global configuration prompt and wish to configure a communication protocol for remote access to the router. What command would you type?

(A) `line vty 0 4`

(B) `line ssh 0`

(C) `line telnet 0 4`

(D) `line telnet 0`

141. What command would you use to navigate from priv exec mode to user exec mode?

(A) `disable`

(B) `shutdown`

(C) `enable`

(D) `exit`

142. You wish to get help on which parameters exist on the ping command. How would you get a list of parameters?

  (A) `help ping`

  (B) `ping ?`

  (C) `? ping`

  (D) `?? ping`

143. What is the command to move to priv exec mode from user exec?

  (A) `router>enable`

  (B) `router#enable`

  (C) `router(config)#enable`

  (D) `router#disable`

144. Which of the following prompts represents global configuration mode?

  (A) `router#`

  (B) `router(config)#`

  (C) `router>`

  (D) `router(global)#`

145. What is the default router name if a name is not assigned to the router during initial configuration?

  (A) R1

  (B) switch

  (C) router

  (D) default

146. What command would you use to navigate to global configuration mode?

  (A) `>config terminal`

  (B) `#setup`

  (C) `>enable`

  (D) `#config terminal`

147. What types of actions can an administrator perform at this IOS prompt? (Select two.)

```
R1(config-if)#
```

(A) Show running-config

(B) Disable the interface

(C) Show the IOS version

(D) Change the hostname

(E) Assign an IP address

148. You wish to run the initial configuration dialog. What command would you use?

(A) install

(B) dialog

(C) setup

(D) initdialog

149. Under what conditions would the initial configuration dialog appear?

(A) When there is no running-config

(B) When there is no startup-config

(C) When you type initdialog

(D) When you type setup

150. You have connected a computer to the console port of a brand new router. What will the router display on the screen after it is powered on?

(A) router>

(B) POST errors

(C) The option to enter initial configuration

(D) router#

Boot Process

151–156 Express the given number in scientific notation.

151. What is the purpose of the POST?

(A) Locate the IOS in flash memory.

(B) Locate the IOS in ROM.

(C) Verify that hardware is functioning.

(D) Apply the startup configuration.

152. You have rebooted your Cisco switch and it displays an amber light on the system LED during POST. What does this indicate?

(A) A failure during POST

(B) System booted without fault

(C) A successful POST

(D) Failed communication with router

153. What happens when a router starts up and it does not have a startup configuration file?

(A) The router prompts for a password.

(B) The router prompts to enter setup mode.

(C) The router applies a default configuration.

(D) The router goes into global configuration mode.

154. Which of the following best describes ROMMON?

(A) A limited operating system used to troubleshoot startup and password recovery

(B) Storage area to hold the startup configuration

(C) Used to store the Cisco IOS

(D) Storage area to hold the running configuration

155. Which of the following best identifies the boot order of a Cisco device?

(A) Bootstrap loads IOS from flash; POST; apply startup configuration to running config.

(B) Bootstrap loads IOS from flash; apply startup configuration to running config; POST.

(C) POST; apply startup configuration to running config; bootstrap loads IOS from flash.

(D) POST; bootstrap loads IOS from flash; apply startup configuration to running config.

156. What keystroke is used to access the ROMMON prompt in order to bypass the password?

(A) Ctrl-Alt-Del

(B) Ctrl-Del

(C) Ctrl-Enter

(D) Ctrl-Break

IOS Version Information

157–161 Express the given number in scientific notation.

157. Using this output of the show version command, how many Fast Ethernet ports exist on the router?

```
Cisco 2811 (MPC860) processor
(revision 0x200) with 60416K/5120K bytes of memory
Processor board ID JAD05190MTZ (4292891495)
M860 processor: part number 0, mask 49
2 FastEthernet/IEEE 802.3 interface(s)
4 Low-speed serial(sync/async) network interface(s)
239K bytes of NVRAM
62720K bytes of processor board System flash (Read/Write)
Configuration register is 0x2102
Router>
```

(A) 49

(B) 2

(C) 1

(D) 4

158. Using the output below, what version of the Cisco IOS is running?

```
Router>show version
Cisco IOS Software, 2800 Software (C2800NM-ADVIPSERVICESK9-M), Version
12.4(15)T1, RELEASE SOFTWARE (fc2)
Technical Support:http://www.cisco.com/techsupport
Copyright (c) 1986-2007 by Cisco Systems, Inc.
Compiled Wed 18-Jul-07 06:21 by pt_rel_team
```

(A) 2800

(B) 12.4

(C) 15

(D) T1

159. Your manager is wondering how many Fast Ethernet ports are on the router. What command would you use to find that out?

(A) show help

(B) show modules

(C) show fastethernet

(D) show version

160. You wish to verify the version of the Cisco IOS you are running. What command would you use?

(A) Show IOS

(B) Show memory

(C) Show version

(D) Show software

161. You wish to view the current value of the configuration register. What command would you use?

(A) show reg

(B) show version

(C) show flash

(D) show config

Chapter 5

Basic Router Configuration

• •

The Cisco CCNA certification exams — in particular, the ICND1 exam — will test you on the basic configuration of a Cisco router. This chapter is designed to test you on the basics of router configuration, including interface configuration, global configuration commands, and basic troubleshooting of the interfaces. Be very familiar with the configuration commands, and also make note of the troubleshooting scenarios that are presented in this chapter (or any chapter): They are the types of questions you can expect on the CCNA exams!

The Problems You'll Work On

In this chapter, you'll review questions concerning the following topics:

- ✔ Viewing and altering the command history
- ✔ Understanding basic router configuration settings
- ✔ Configuring Fast Ethernet and serial interfaces
- ✔ Configuring different types of passwords on the Cisco router
- ✔ Troubleshooting interface problems

What to Watch Out For

Don't let common mistakes trip you up; watch for the following when working with these questions:

- ✔ Know basic configuration commands such as changing the console time-out, history size, and the hostname of the router.
- ✔ Be aware of the prompt at which you are typing each command.
- ✔ You can erase the configuration of a device by erasing the startup-config and then reloading the router.
- ✔ Know your show commands, such as show interfaces. The show interfaces command and the show ip interface brief command are used to display the status of the interfaces, whereas the show controllers command can be used to view whether a serial interface is a DTE or DCE device. Specifically know how to view the status of an interface and know the meaning of an interface status such as "Serial0/2/0 is down, line protocol is down".

Configuring Interfaces

162–172 Express the given number in scientific notation.

162. You wish to disable the Fast Ethernet interface on your router. What command would you use?

(A) router(config-if)#shutdown

(B) router(config-if)#disable

(C) router(config)#shutdown interface F0/0

(D) router(config)#disable interface F0/0

163. Which of the following are encapsulation protocols that can be used on a serial link for a Cisco router? (Select all that apply.)

(A) IPX

(B) PPP

(C) PPTP

(D) HDLC

(E) RIP

164. You would like to configure the Fast Ethernet port on your router for full duplex. What commands would you use?

(A) Use the following commands:

R1#config term

R1(config)#interface f0/0

R1(config-if)#duplex full

(B) Use the following commands:

R1#config term

R1(config)#interface f0/0

R1(config-if)#duplex half

(C) Use the following commands:

R1#config term

R1(config)#interface f0/0

R1(config-if)#set full duplex

(D) Use the following commands:

R1#config term

R1(config)#interface f0/0

R1(config-if)#set half duplex

165. You wish to enable the Fast Ethernet port on the router. What command would you use?

(A) R1(config-if)#undo shutdown

(B) R1(config-if)# enable

(C) R1(config-if)#no shutdown

(D) R1(config-if)#no disable

166. Which of the following layer-2 protocols are supported encapsulation protocols on the serial link of a Cisco device? (Select two.)

(A) PPP

(B) RIP

(C) OSPF

(D) HDLC

167. Which of the following commands would you use to assign an IP address to the Fast Ethernet interface on the router?

(A) router(config-if)#ip address 10.0.0.1

(B) router(config)#ip address 10.0.0.1 255.0.0.0

(C) router(config-if)#ip address 10.0.0.1 255.0.0.0

(D) router(config)#ip address 10.0.0.1

168. When looking at the interface fastethernet 0/1 command, what is the port number for the interface?

(A) 0

(B) 1

(C) 2

(D) 3

169. In a point-to-point serial link between two routers, which router sets the clock rate?

(A) AUI

(B) DTE

(C) BNC

(D) DCE

170. Which of the following are additional commands needed to configure a serial interface over what is needed when configuring an Ethernet interface? You are configuring the DCE device on a serial link. (Select all that apply.)

(A) clock rate 64000

(B) description WAN link

(C) encapsulation hdlc

(D) ip address dhcp

171. After disabling the serial interface using the shutdown command, which of the following represents the output displayed on the console as a result of your action?

    (A) serial0/0 is administratively down, line protocol is administratively down

    (B) serial0/0 is down, line protocol is down

    (C) serial0/0 is administratively down, line protocol is down

    (D) serial0/0 is down, line protocol is administratively down

172. What command do you use on the interface to assign an IP address to the interface automatically via DHCP?

    (A) R1(config)#ip address dhcp

    (B) R1(config)#ip dhcp address

    (C) R1(config-if)#ip dhcp address

    (D) R1(config-if)#ip address dhcp

Basic Configuration

173–186 Express the given number in scientific notation.

173. Which of the following commands would you use to change the hostname on the router?

    (A) router>hostname R1

    (B) router(config-if)#hostname R1

    (C) router#hostname R1

    (D) router(config)#hostname R1

174. Which of the following password types are encrypted in the configuration by default?

    (A) enable password

    (B) enable secure password

    (C) enable secret

    (D) enable encrypted password

175. You are at the following prompt. What command would you type first to change the name of the router?

Router (config-if)#

    (A) hostname

    (B) exit

    (C) disable

    (D) enable

176. Which of the following command-sets would you use to configure a password on the console port of the router?

(A) Use the following commands:

```
enable

password myConPass

login
```

(B) Use the following commands:

```
enable

config term

line con 0

password myConPass

login
```

(C) Use the following commands:

```
enable

config term

line con 0

password myConPass
```

(D) Use the following commands:

```
enable

config term

password myConPass

login
```

177. You are looking to create a username for Tom to log on to the router. What command would you use?

(A) r1(config)# `username tom password P@ssw0rd`

(B) r1# `username tom password P@ssw0rd`

(C) r1> `username tom password P@ssw0rd`

(D) r1(config-if)# `username tom password P@ssw0rd`

178. You wish to view a list of commands recently used on the router, what command would you use?

(A) `show history`

(B) `show commands`

(C) `show all`

(D) `show my commands`

179. You would like to encrypt all passwords configured on the router. What command would you use?

(A) `enable password-encryption`

(B) `service password-encryption`

(C) `encrypt-password all`

(D) `encrypt-passwords`

180. You have made changes to your Cisco router and would like to verify the changes before saving them. What command would you use?

(A) `show startup-config`

(B) `show memory`

(C) `show running-config`

(D) `show flash`

181. You are administering a Cisco router. When you have a typo in the command name, you have to wait for the router to do a DNS lookup before getting control of the console again — an annoying problem. What command would fix it?

(A) `disable dns`

(B) `no ip domain lookup`

(C) `ip domain lookup`

(D) `no dns lookup`

182. You would like the console to time out after a minute and 45 seconds of inactivity. What command would you use?

(A) `exec-timeout 1 45`

(B) `exec-timeout 1:45`

(C) `no exec-timeout 1 45`

(D) `no exec-timeout 1:45`

183. What command can be used to modify the history size on the Cisco router?

(A) `R1#terminal history size 30`

(B) `R1(config)#terminal history size 30`

(C) `R1(config)#history size 30`

(D) `R1#history size 30`

184. After creating a user named Bob, you would like to ensure that the console port prompts for username and password. What command would you use?

(A) r1(config-line)# `login`

(B) r1(config-line)# `enable login`

(C) r1(config-line)# `login local`

(D) r1(config-line)# `logon`

185. Which of the following banner types is the first to be displayed?

(A) Login

(B) MOTD

(C) Exec

(D) Logout

186. You would like to delete the configuration on your router and start with a clean configuration. Which two commands would you use? (Select two.)

(A) `delete startup-config`

(B) `reload`

(C) `restart`

(D) `erase startup-config`

(E) `format-router`

Basic Troubleshooting

187–199 Express the given number in scientific notation.

187. A network technician is having trouble connecting two routers across the serial ports. One router is a Cisco router, whereas the other router is from a different manufacturer. You have loaded HDLC on both routers. What should you do?

(A) Ensure the subnet mask on the serial ports is 255.255.255.252.

(B) Change the frame size on the serial interfaces.

(C) Use PPP as the serial link protocol.

(D) Change the buffer size on the serial interfaces.

188. You would like to verify the status of one of your interfaces. What command would you use?

(A) `show interfaces`

(B) `show ip route`

(C) `show router`

(D) `show f0/0 status`

189. You are having trouble communicating with networks that are connected to your FastEthernet0/0 port. You use the command shown below to view the status of the links. What can you do to solve the problem?

```
R1>show ip interface brief
Interface              IP-Address    OK? Method Status
FastEthernet0/0        23.0.0.1      YES manual administratively down
FastEthernet0/1        unassigned    YES manual up
Serial0/2/0            24.0.0.1      YES manual up
Serial0/3/0            unassigned    YES manual administratively down
```

(A) Configure an encapsulation protocol.

(B) Assign an IP address.

(C) Configure it to use DHCP.

(D) Enable the interface.

190. Which of the following commands is used to display a table (output shown below) indicating the IP assigned to each interface and the status of the interface?

```
Interface              IP-Address    OK? Method Status
FastEthernet0/0        23.0.0.1      YES manual up
FastEthernet0/1        unassigned    YES manual up
Serial0/2/0            24.0.0.1      YES manual up
Serial0/3/0            unassigned    YES manual administratively down
```

(A) show ip interfaces

(B) show ip table

(C) show ip interface brief

(D) show ip table brief

191. Which of the following commands display information on the IOS version? (Select three.)

(A) show version

(B) show IOS

(C) show hardware

(D) show flash

(E) show running-config

192. You are troubleshooting communication issues between router R1 and R2. The physical cabling is connected as shown in the figure below, as well as the IP address range. You use the show command displayed in the figure to identify the problem. Why are the routers not communicating?

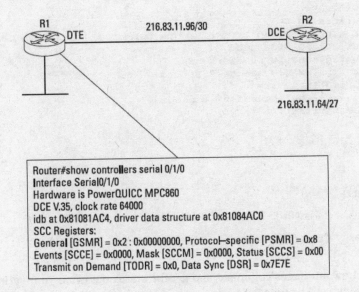

(A) The IP range for the serial ports is incorrect.

(B) The serial interface is using half-duplex.

(C) The serial port has the wrong cable connected.

(D) The serial interface is using the wrong subnet mask.

193. You need to find out if the serial port on your router is acting as the DCE device in the point-to-point link with another router. What command do you need to use?

(A) `show ip interface brief`

(B) `show interfaces`

(C) `show interface serial0/0`

(D) `show controllers serial0/0`

194. You are troubleshooting communication across a serial port and use the show interfaces command to get the output displayed below. What is the problem?

```
Serial0/2/0 is down, line protocol is down
```

(A) The clock rate is not set.

(B) An encapsulation protocol has not been set.

(C) Check the physical connection.

(D) You are using PPP.

195. Sue, a network administrator in your office, has configured the router with the commands shown below. What is the order of the passwords that would need to be supplied if she connects to the console port on the router to make changes?

```
Router>enable
Router#config term
Enter configuration commands, one per line.  End with CNTL/Z.
Router(config)#hostname R1
R1(config)#enable password cisco
R1(config)#enable secret P@ssw0rd
R1(config)#line vty 0 4
R1(config-line)#password telnetpass
R1(config-line)#
```

(A) P@ssw0rd

(B) cisco

(C) telnetpass / Cisco

(D) telnetpass / P@ssw0rd

(E) telnetpass / Cisco / P@ssw0rd

196. You use the show interfaces command and get the status below on your serial port. Which layer of the OSI model has a problem?

```
Serial0/2/0 is up, line protocol is down
```

(A) Layer-1

(B) Layer-2

(C) Layer-3

(D) Layer-4

197. Jeff configures the router with the commands shown below. What is the order of the passwords that he would need to use when connecting to the console port of the router to make changes?

```
Router>enable
Router#config term
Enter configuration commands, one per line.  End with CNTL/Z.
Router(config)#hostname R1
R1(config)#enable password cisco
R1(config)#enable secret P@ssw0rd
R1(config)#line con 0
R1(config-line)#password conpass
R1(config-line)#
```

(A) P@ssw0rd

(B) cisco

(C) conpass / Cisco

(D) conpass / P@ssw0rd

(E) conpass / Cisco / P@ssw0rd

198. Using the output below from the show interfaces command, what is most likely the problem?

```
Serial0/2/0 is up, line protocol is down
```

(A) There is no physical link.

(B) A protocol or clock rate has not been set.

(C) You need to configure the router as the DCE device.

(D) You need to configure the router as the DTE device.

199. Tom configures the router with the commands shown below. What is the order of the passwords that he would need to enter when connecting to the console port of the router to make changes?

```
Router>enable
Router#config term
Enter configuration commands, one per line.  End with CNTL/Z.
Router(config)#hostname R1
R1(config)#enable password cisco
R1(config)#enable secret P@ssw0rd
R1(config)#line con 0
R1(config-line)#password conpass
R1(config-line)#login
```

(A) P@ssw0rd

(B) cisco

(C) conpass / Cisco

(D) conpass / P@ssw0rd

(E) conpass / Cisco / P@ssw0rd

Chapter 6

Managing Cisco Devices

• •

*T*o help you manage Cisco devices day-to-day, you need to understand a few basic topics. The ICND1 exam expects you to know how to back up and restore the Cisco IOS and configuration files to and from a TFTP server. You are also expected to know how to use the Cisco Discovery Protocol to identify other Cisco devices on the network and details about those devices, and to understand how to remotely connect to a device via telnet and manage your telnet sessions. This chapter tests on these issues and more.

The Problems You'll Work On

In this chapter, you'll review questions concerning the following topics:

- ✔ Backing up and restoring the Cisco IOS and configuration files to and from a TFTP server
- ✔ Knowing how to control which IOS image file the Cisco device will use on startup
- ✔ Understanding the purpose of CDP and its default values
- ✔ Knowing how to alter CDP settings such as the CDP timer and the CDP hold timer
- ✔ Comprehending the requirements to use telnet for remote administration and how to manage your telnet session

What to Watch Out For

Don't let common mistakes trip you up; watch for the following when working with these questions:

- ✔ You must know the syntax for the copy command (copy <source> <destination>) to perform backup and restores of your IOS image and configuration files. For example, **copy flash TFTP** would back up your IOS to a TFTP server, but **copy TFTP running-config** would restore your running configuration from a TFTP server.
- ✔ Know the ports used by the protocols discussed in this chapter. Telnet uses TCP port 23, SSH uses TCP port 22, and TFTP uses UDP port 69.
- ✔ The Cisco Discovery Protocol is a Cisco proprietary protocol used to discover information about neighboring (directly connected) Cisco devices. Know that the CDP advertisements are sent out every 60 seconds (known as the CDP timer) and stored for 180 seconds (known as the hold timer) by the receiving Cisco device. You can change the CDP timer and hold timer with the global configuration commands of **cdp timer** and **cdp holdtimer**. You can also use the show cdp command to view the configuration of CDP.

Backup and Remote

200–212 Express the given number in scientific notation.

200. Which of the following connectionless application layer protocols is used to transfer Cisco IOS images and configuration files to a backup location?

(A) TFTP

(B) FTP

(C) Telnet

(D) SSH

201. Your coworker would like to back up the router configuration to a TFTP server. What command would you use to back up your running configuration to a TFTP server?

(A) `backup running-config tftp`

(B) `copy running-config tftp`

(C) `backup tftp running-config`

(D) `copy tftp running-config`

202. A few weeks ago, you backed up your router configuration to a TFTP and now you wish to restore the configuration back to your router. What command would you use?

(A) `backup running-config tftp`

(B) `copy running-config tftp`

(C) `backup tftp running-config`

(D) `copy tftp running-config Copy flash tftp`

203. Susan types the preceding command on her company router. What is the command's purpose?

(A) To back up the IOS image to a server

(B) To back up the router running configuration to a server

(C) To back up the router startup configuration to a server

(D) To back up the routing table to a server

204. Which of the following command associations are true? (Select two.)

    (A)   Restore the config⇨`copy running-config tftp`

    (B)   Back up the IOS⇨`copy tftp flash`

    (C)   Replace the IOS⇨`copy tftp flash`

    (D)   Replace the IOS⇨`copy flash tftp`

    (E)   Back up the IOS⇨`copy flash tftp`

205. In the figure below, what is the purpose of address 192.168.1.3?

```
R2#copy running-config tftp
Address or name of remote host []? 192.168.1.3
Destination filename [R2-confg]? R2-Backup-Config

!! [OK - 459 bytes]
459 bytes copied in 3.006 secs (0 bytes/sec)
R2#
```

    (A)   It is the address of the router to use to reach the TFTP server.

    (B)   It is the IP address of the device whose running-config you wish to back up.

    (C)   It is the address of the TFTP server to copy the running configuration to.

    (D)   It is the address of the TFTP server to copy the running configuration from.

206. Which of the following commands allows you to view the filename of your IOS?

    (A)   `show IOS`

    (B)   `show flash`

    (C)   `show filename`

    (D)   `show ios filename`

207. What happens if you are copying a new IOS image to flash memory and there is not enough available space due to space used by your existing IOS file?

    (A)   The old IOS file is deleted to make room.

    (B)   The copy operation fails.

    (C)   The copy operation succeeds but with no data in the file.

    (D)   The old file is renamed.

208. You are looking to create a backup copy of your Cisco IOS to a TFTP server. What command would you use?

(A) `backup flash tftp`

(B) `copy IOS tftp`

(C) `backup tftp flash`

(D) `copy flash tftp`

209. What port does TFTP use?

(A) TCP 23

(B) UDP 69

(C) TCP 21

(D) UDP 21

(E) TCP 69

(F) TCP 22

210. You have three IOS image files in flash memory. What command would you use to control which IOS is used when the router starts up?

(A) `boot startup`

(B) `startup`

(C) `boot system`

(D) `load image`

211. You are having issues with your router, which currently does not have network access or an IOS. What protocol could you use to transfer an IOS image to the router?

(A) xmodem

(B) tftp

(C) ftp

(D) snmp

212. What command would you use to ensure that the Cisco router loads the IOS image file of c2800nm-advipservicesk9-mz.124-15.T1.bin from flash memory?

(A) `boot system tftp c2800nm-advipservicesk9-mz.124-15.T1.bin`

(B) `boot startup flash c2800nm-advipservicesk9-mz.124-15.T1.bin`

(C) `boot system flash c2800nm-advipservicesk9-mz.124-15.T1.bin`

(D) `boot startup tftp c2800nm-advipservicesk9-mz.124-15.T1.bin`

Cisco Discovery Protocol (CDP)

213–226 Express the given number in scientific notation.

213. You need to identify other Cisco devices on the network; which Cisco protocol do you use?

    (A)   Spanning Tree Protocol

    (B)   Point-to-Point Protocol

    (C)   Cisco Discovery Protocol

    (D)   Discovery Device Protocol

214. You are connected to the console port of router R3 shown in the figure below. When you use CDP to display other network devices that have been discovered, what devices will you see?

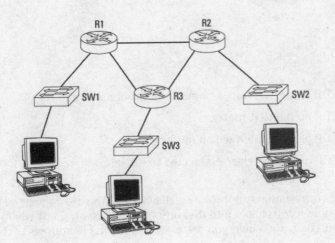

    (A)   R1, R2, SW1, SW2, SW3

    (B)   R2, SW3

    (C)   R1, R2, SW2

    (D)   R1, R2, SW3

215. Which of the following statements are true in regards to CDP? (Select three.)

    (A)   CDP is a Cisco proprietary protocol.

    (B)   CDP is an industry standard protocol.

    (C)   CDP runs at the network layer.

    (D)   CDP runs at the data link layer.

    (E)   CDP discovers all devices on the network.

    (F)   CDP discovers directly connected devices.

216. You are the network administrator for the network shown in the figure below. Your manager would like to ensure that CDP advertisements are not sent out to the Internet from router HO1, but they should be sent to the Toronto and Boston routers. What should you do?

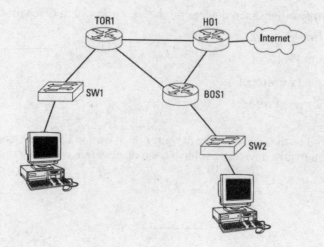

(A) Disable CDP on the interfaces connected to routers R1 and R2.

(B) Disable CDP on the HO1 router.

(C) Disable CDP on each interface on router R1.

(D) Disable CDP on the interface connected to the Internet.

217. You are the network administrator for a small network. You are connected to the console port on a switch and would like to telnet into the router on the network, but you forget the IP address of the router. What command could you use to determine the IP address of the router?

(A) `show ip interface brief`

(B) `show cdp neighbors detail`

(C) `show cdp`

(D) `show ip neighbors`

218. There is a switch on the network called NY-SW1. What command would you use on the router to determine the model number of that switch?

(A) `show cdp entry NY-SW1`

(B) `show cdp`

(C) `show cdp NY-SW1`

(D) `show cdp protocol NY-SW1`

219. The frequency at which CDP messages are sent out is known as the _____.

(A) CDP hold timer

(B) CDP stat

(C) CDP interval

(D) CDP timer

220. By default, how frequently does a Cisco device send out CDP advertisements?

(A) 30 seconds

(B) 60 seconds

(C) 120 seconds

(D) 180 seconds

221. You wish to view only the IP addresses of neighboring devices; what command do you use?

(A) `show cdp entry * protocol`

(B) `show cdp neighbors`

(C) `show cdp neighbors detail`

(D) `show cdp`

222. By default, when a Cisco device receives a CDP message, how long does it store the CDP information locally?

(A) 30 seconds

(B) 60 seconds

(C) 120 seconds

(D) 180 seconds

223. You would like to alter the amount of time that CDP information is stored on a Cisco device. What command should you use?

(A) `cdp timer`

(B) `cdp store`

(C) `cdp holdtime`

(D) `cdp retain`

224. What command do you use to disable CDP on the serial interface?

(A) `disable cdp`

(B) `cdp disable`

(C) `no disable cdp`

(D) `no cdp enable`

225. You would like to alter the frequency at which CDP sends out advertisements to every 90 seconds. What command would you use?

   (A)   `R1#cdp timer 90`

   (B)   `R1(config)#cdp 90`

   (C)   `R1#cdp 90`

   (D)   `R1(config)#cdp timer 90`

226. Your manager is concerned that hackers can discover information about the network via CDP and asks you to disable CDP on your router. What command would you use?

   (A)   `disable cdp`

   (B)   `no cdp run`

   (C)   `no cdp enable`

   (D)   `no disable cdp`

Telnet

227–237 Express the given number in scientific notation.

227. You have telnetted into a switch on the network from your router and now wish to suspend your telnet session. How do you do this?

   (A)   suspend

   (B)   pause

   (C)   Ctrl-Shift-6, then X

   (D)   Ctrl-Alt-Del

228. Which of the following IOS commands is used to connect to VTY ports on a Cisco device?

   (A)   `telnet`

   (B)   `login`

   (C)   `cdp`

   (D)   `connect`

   (E)   `resume`

229. What port does Telnet use?

   (A)   TCP 23

   (B)   UDP 23

   (C)   TCP 21

   (D)   UDP 21

   (E)   TCP 25

   (F)   TCP 22

230. Which of the following secure protocols should be used instead of Telnet for remote administration of the Cisco device?

(A)   HTTPS

(B)   VPN

(C)   IPSEC

(D)   SSH

231. What port does SSH use?

(A)   TCP 23

(B)   UDP 23

(C)   TCP 21

(D)   UDP 21

(E)   TCP 25

(F)   TCP 22

232. Which of the following represent characteristics of telnet with Cisco devices? (Select two.)

(A)   Traffic is encrypted

(B)   Traffic is unencrypted

(C)   No longer supported on Cisco devices

(D)   Should be used instead of SSH

(E)   Requires configuration on the destination device

233. Your network has been up and running for a few months. Two days ago, Bob, the network administrator, assigned an IP address to the switch. Why would an IP address be assigned to the switch?

(A)   For remote management

(B)   To allow the switch to forward traffic based on layer-3 address

(C)   To allow the switch to forward traffic based on layer-2 address

(D)   To allow devices connected to the switch to communicate

234. You have suspended a Telnet session and wish to reconnect to that session again; what command do you use?

(A)   `reconnect <IP Address>`

(B)   `resume <Device ID>`

(C)   `reconnect <Device ID>`

(D)   `resume <IP Address>`

235. What command do you use to determine if you have any suspended Telnet sessions?

    (A)   `show sessions`

    (B)   `show users`

    (C)   `show suspensions`

    (D)   `show suspended users`

236. Your manager would like you to monitor who is remotely connected to the router via Telnet. What command would you use?

    (A)   `show sessions`

    (B)   `show suspensions`

    (C)   `show users`

    (D)   `show suspended users`

237. You are having trouble telnetting into one of your Boston switches from the New York office. You have no problem telnetting into the switch when you are in the Boston office. What is most likely the solution?

    (A)   Enable routing on the switch.

    (B)   Configure a static route on the router in New York.

    (C)   Configure a default gateway on the switch.

    (D)   Configure a default gateway on the New York router.

Chapter 7

Advanced Router Topics

. . . .

C hapter 8 presents questions on some fun topics for the Cisco ICND1 (CCENT) certification exam. This chapter introduces questions related to configuring DNS name
resolution, DHCP services, and network address translation. It is important to note that the
new version of the ICND1 exam includes objectives on password recovery procedures and
access lists.

The Problems You'll Work On

In this chapter, you'll review questions concerning the following topics:

- ✔ Resolving hostnames
- ✔ Configuring DHCP service
- ✔ Implementing NAT
- ✔ Recovering passwords
- ✔ Configuring access lists (ACLs)

What to Watch Out For

Don't let common mistakes trip you up; watch for the following when working with these
questions:

- ✔ You can resolve names you use on the router either by viewing the hostname table
  on the router or by querying DNS. Use the `IP Host` command to add a hostname to
  the hostname table on the router. To view the hostname table, use the `show hosts`
  command.

- ✔ To configure DHCP on your router, you need to use the `IP dhcp pool` command to
  create an address pool. After you create the address pool, you specify the network
  range of addresses to give out with the `network` command.

- ✔ There are two types of NAT – static NAT and overloading. Static NAT associates a
  single public address to a single private address, while overloading is the concept that
  all private addresses translate to the one public address.

- ✔ Access lists are used to control the traffic entering or leaving the network. To filter by
  the source IP address of a packet, you should configure standard access lists; to filter
  by the source and destination IP address, source and destination port, and protocol,
  on the other hand, use extended access lists.

Hostname Resolution

238–245 Choose the best answer(s).

238. You try to ping the Boston router and get the error shown in the figure below. What should you do to allow the ping to work?

```
NY-R1>ping BOS-R1
Translating "BOS-R1"...domain server (255.255.255.255)
% Unrecognized host or address or protocol not running.
```

    (A)   Add the entry to the NAT translation table

    (B)   Add the entry to the hostname table

    (C)   Add the entry to the MAC address table

    (D)   Change the encapsulation protocol

239. What command displays the hostname table on a router?

    (A)   `show ip hosts`

    (B)   `show ip names`

    (C)   `show names`

    (D)   `show hosts`

240. To configure your router to query a DNS server, what command do you use?

    (A)   `ip name-server 23.0.0.10`

    (B)   `name-server 23.0.0.10`

    (C)   `ip dns 23.0.0.10`

    (D)   `ip domain 23.0.0.10`

241. You have decided to remove the entry for the Boston router from your hostname table. What command would you use?

    (A)   `NY-R1(config)#no ip host BOS-R1`

    (B)   `NY-R1#no ip host BOS-R1`

    (C)   `NY-R1#no host BOS-R1`

    (D)   `NY-R1(config)#no host BOS-R1`

242. What command would you use to resolve the BOS-R1 router to the IP address of 15.10.0.5?

(A) `host BOS-R1 15.10.0.5`

(B) `ip BOS-R1 15.10.0.5`

(C) `ip name BOS-R1 15.10.0.5`

(D) `ip host BOS-R1 15.10.0.5`

243. Which command has created the output shown in the figure below?

```
Default Domain is not set
Name/address lookup uses domain service
Name servers are 255.255.255.255

Codes: UN - unknown, EX - expired, OK - OK, ?? - revalidate
       temp - temporary, perm - permanent
       NA - Not Applicable None - Not defined

Host      Port  Flags      Age Type  Address(es)
BOS-R1    None  (perm, OK)  0  IP    24.0.0.2
NY-R1#
```

(A) `show systems`

(B) `show hosts`

(C) `show ip dhcp`

(D) `show ip arp`

244. When administering your Cisco router, it tries to do a DNS query every time you have a typo in a command. How can you disable this?

(A) `ip domain lookup`

(B) `no ip domain lookup`

(C) `no hosts lookup`

(D) `hosts lookup disabled`

245. You have configured your router for a name server, but you still find that names are not being resolved. What command would you execute?

(A) `ip domain-lookup`

(B) `no ip domain-lookup`

(C) `ip routing`

(D) `ip name server-lookup`

Configuration of DHCP Service

246–252 Choose the best answer(s).

246. Which of the following DHCP commands would you use to specify that the address pool is to configure the default gateway on client computers?

(A) NY-R1(dhcp-config)#default-gateway 23.0.0.1

(B) NY-R1(dhcp-config)#default-router 23.0.0.1

(C) NY-R1#default-router 23.0.0.1

(D) NY-R1#default-gateway 23.0.0.1

247. Clients are no longer receiving IP addresses from the DHCP server running on your Cisco router. You suspect the DHCP service may have been shut down. How can you start it?

(A) start dhcp

(B) net start dhcp

(C) ip start dhcp

(D) service dhcp

248. You have configured the DHCP service on your router as a backup DHCP service. You wish to stop the DHCP service so that addresses are not being handed out till you need the service. What command would you use to stop the service?

(A) no dhcp

(B) no service dhcp

(C) no dhcp service

(D) no services-dhcp

249. You want to create configure DHCP on your router to give out IP addresses for the second subnet of 192.168.3.0/27. The addresses should be leased to clients for 7 days. What commands would you use?

(A) Use the following:

NY-R1(config)#ip dhcp pool NY_Network

NY-R1(dhcp-config)#network 192.168.3.64 255.255.255.224

NY-R1(dhcp-config)#lease 7 0 0

(B) Use the following:

NY-R1(config)#dhcp pool

NY-R1(dhcp-config)#network 192.168.3.32 255.255.255.224

NY-R1(dhcp-config)#lease 7 0 0

(C)   Use the following:

NY-R1(config)#ip dhcp pool NY_Network

NY-R1(dhcp-config)#network 192.168.3.32 255.255.255.224

NY-R1(dhcp-config)#lease 7 0 0

(D)   Use the following:

NY-R1(config)#ip dhcp pool NY_Network

NY-R1(dhcp-config)#lease 0 7 0

250.   You are monitoring DHCP usage on your router. What command would you use to see how many DHCP related messages the router has received?

(A)   show dhcp

(B)   show ip dhcp server statistics

(C)   show dhcp statistics

(D)   show ip dhcp

251.   You are administering the DHCP service on your Cisco router and would like to look at the DHCP leases, What command would you use?

(A)   show ip dhcp leases

(B)   show dhcp

(C)   show ip dhcp binding

(D)   show dhcp leases

252.   To view a list of IP addresses given to clients on the network by your Cisco router DHCP service, what command do you use?

(A)   show binding

(B)   show ip dhcp binding

(C)   show ip translations

(D)   show ip dhcp translations

Implementing NAT

253–262 Choose the best answer(s).

253.   Which of the following implements NAT overload?

(A)   FAT

(B)   SNAT

(C)   PAT

(D)   JAT

254. Your manager has asked what would be a good use of static NAT.

(A) Share a single public IP address to all internal systems

(B) For internal clients to surf the Internet

(C) To allow DHCP to assign the address

(D) For publishing an internal system to the Internet

255. You wish to create an access list to be used for NAT as the inside addresses that will be permitted to use NAT. What command would you use to create the access list?

(A) NY-R1(config)#Access-list 16 permit 10.0.0.0 0.255.255.255

(B) NY-R1(config)#Access-list 16 permit 10.0.0.0 255.0.0.0

(C) NY-R1>Access-list 16 permit 10.0.0.0 255.0.0.0

(D) NY-R1>Access-list 16 permit 10.0.0.0 0.255.255.255

256. Your serial port is connected to the WAN environment, with your Fast Ethernet port connected to the LAN. When configuring NAT, how would you configure the serial port?

(A) NY-R1(config-if)#ip nat inside

(B) NY-R1(config)#ip nat inside

(C) NY-R1(config)#ip nat outside

(D) NY-R1(config-if)#ip nat outside

257. What mechanism does NAT overloading use to allow one public IP address to be mapped to multiple systems?

(A) NAP

(B) TAM

(C) NAC

(D) PAT

258. You have created access list 1 that lists the IP addresses for NAT usage. What command would you use to configure the router so that those addresses can use NAT?

(A) NY-R1(config)#nat access list 1

(B) NY-R1(config)#ip nat interface serial 0/0 overload

(C) NY-R1(config)#ip nat inside source list 1 interface serial 0/0 overload

(D) NY-R1(config)#ip nat inside source list 1

259. What type of NAT maps a single public address to all internal addresses?

(A) Overloading

(B) Static

(C) Internal

(D) Public

260. Your serial port is connected to the WAN environment, with your Fast Ethernet port connected to the LAN. When configuring NAT, how would you configure the Fast Ethernet port?

(A) NY-R1(config-if)#ip nat outside

(B) NY-R1(config-if)#ip nat parallel

(C) NY-R1(config-if)#ip nat public

(D) NY-R1(config-if)#ip nat inside

261. What command can you use to view the NAT translation table?

(A) show ip nat

(B) show nat

(C) show nat translations

(D) show ip nat translations

262. Looking at the figure below, which of the following would be used to configure NAT on the router? Assume the IP addresses are already assigned to the interfaces.

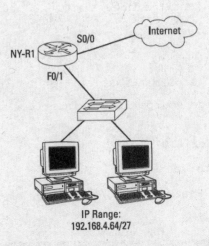

IP Range:
192.168.4.64/27

(A) Use the following commands:

NY-R1(config)#Access-list 1 permit 192.168.4.64 255.255.255.224

NY-R1(config)#ip nat inside source list 1 interface serial 0/0 overload

NY-R1(config)#interface Serial0/0

NY-R1(config-if)#ip nat outside

NY-R1(config-if)#interface FastEthernet0/1

NY-R1(config-if)#ip nat inside

(B) Use the following commands:

NY-R1(config)#Access-list 1 permit 192.168.4.64 0.0.0.31

NY-R1(config)#ip nat inside source list 1 interface serial 0/0 overload

NY-R1(config)#interface Serial0/0

NY-R1(config-if)#ip nat inside

NY-R1(config-if)#interface FastEthernet0/1

NY-R1(config-if)#ip nat outside

(C) Use the following commands:

NY-R1(config)#Access-list 1 permit 192.168.4.64 0.0.0.31

NY-R1(config)#ip nat inside source list 1 interface Fast Ethernet 0/1 overload

NY-R1(config)#interface Serial0/0

NY-R1(config-if)#ip nat outside

NY-R1(config-if)#interface FastEthernet0/1

NY-R1(config-if)#ip nat inside

(D) Use the following commands:

NY-R1(config)#Access-list 1 permit 192.168.4.64 0.0.0.31

NY-R1(config)#ip nat inside source list 1 interface serial 0/0 overload

NY-R1(config)#interface Serial0/0

NY-R1(config-if)#ip nat outside

NY-R1(config-if)#interface FastEthernet0/1

NY-R1(config-if)#ip nat inside

Password Recovery

263–268 Choose the best answer(s).

263. What keystroke interrupts the boot sequence on a Cisco router in order to implement password-recovery procedures?

(A) Ctrl-Alt-Delete

(B) Ctrl-Break

(C) Fn-F4

(D) Fn-Break

264. What is the default configuration register on most Cisco routers?

    (A) 0x2142

    (B) 0x2100

    (C) 0x2102

    (D) 0x2202

265. You wish to view the current configuration register value on a Cisco router, what command would you use?

    (A) `show register`

    (B) `show password`

    (C) `show version`

    (D) `show ip register`

266. After you have recovered the password on a Cisco device, what command would you use to set the configuration register back to the default?

    (A) `config-register 0x2102`

    (B) `config-register 0x2142`

    (C) `config-register 0x2100`

    (D) `config-register 0x1102`

267. When you need to recover a password, what bit number do you manipulate in the configuration register?

    (A) 1

    (B) 4

    (C) 6

    (D) 8

268. What is the new configuration register value after you configure it to bypass the loading of NVRAM?

    (A) 0x2142

    (B) 0x2100

    (C) 0x2102

    (D) 0x2202

Access Control Lists (ACLs)

269–275 Choose the best answer(s).

269. Extended access lists use what range for access list numbers?

(A) 1-99

(B) 200-299

(C) 100-199

(D) 300-399

270. Your manager has asked you to block traffic from the system with the IP address of 192.168.5.100. You have configured an access list using the commands show in the figure below, but now no traffic from any system can pass through the interface. Why?

```
config term
access-list 1 deny host 192.168.5.100

interface s0/0
ip access-group 1 in
```

(A) Access lists have an implied deny all at the bottom.

(B) You need a subnet mask in the access list command.

(C) You should have used ip access-class instead of ip access-group.

(D) You should have used a permit instead of deny.

271. What type of access control list only allows you to filter traffic by the source IP address?

(A) Extended

(B) Standard

(C) Basic

(D) Advanced

272. What type of access control list allows you to filter by source and destination IP address, source and destination port, and protocol?

(A) Advanced

(B) Basic

(C) Extended

(D) Standard

273. You would like to ensure that only systems on the 216.83.11.64/26 subnet can telnet into your router. What commands would you use?

(A) Use the following:

```
access-list 20 permit 216.83.11.64 0.0.0.63

line vty 0 4

access-class 20 in
```

(B) Use the following:

```
access-list 20 permit 216.83.11.64 255.255.255.192

line vty 0 4

access-class 20 in
```

(C) Use the following:

```
access-list 20 permit 216.83.11.64 0.0.0.63

line vty 0 4

access-group 20 in
```

(D) Use the following:

```
access-list 20 permit 216.83.11.64 255.255.255.192

line vty 0 4

access-group 20 in
```

274. You have created a standard access list # 20 that permits a group of IP addresses. You would like to use this access list to control who can telnet into the router. What command would you use on the telnet ports?

(A) `access-class 20 in`

(B) `access-group 20 in`

(C) `allow 20 in`

(D) `allow telnet 20 in`

275. What is the result of the access list in the figure below?

```
access-list 100 deny ip host 192.168.10.50 192.168.2.0 0.0.0.255
access-list 100 deny tcp host 192.168.10.50 host 3.3.3.3 80
access-list 100 permit ip any any
```

(A) It denies the 192.168.10.50 system from accessing the 192.168.2.0 network, denies the system of 192.168.10.50 from accessing the website on 3.3.3.3, and permits all others.

(B) It denies the 192.168.2.0 network from accessing the 192.168.10.50 system, denies the system of 192.168.10.50 from accessing the website on 3.3.3.3, and permits all others.

(C) It denies the 192.168.10.50 system from accessing the 192.168.2.0 network, all systems from accessing the website on 3.3.3.3, and permits all others.

(D) It denies the 192.168.10.50 system from accessing the 192.168.2.0 network, all systems from accessing the website on 3.3.3.3, and denies all others.

Chapter 8

Static Routing

•••

*T*his chapter tests you on the basics of IP routing and static routes. The ICND1 certification exam expects you to know the basics of configuring a router and also the basics of managing the routing table through static routing. This chapter also gives example questions on topics such as the gateway of last resort (GWLR) and router on a stick — a new topic for ICND1!

The Problems You'll Work On

In this chapter, you'll review questions concerning the following topics:

- Understanding routing concepts
- Configuring static routing
- Configuring the gateway of last resort
- Configuring router on a stick

What to Watch Out For

Don't let common mistakes trip you up; watch for the following when working with these questions:

- A static route is one that is manually added to the router's routing table. You can use the `ip route` command to add a static route to the routing table. You can delete a route from the routing table using the `no ip route` command. When troubleshooting routing issues, use the `show ip route` command to view the routing table.

- Routes have an administrative distance associated with them which indicates the trustworthiness of the knowledge of the route. The lower the administrative distance, the more trustworthy the knowledge is.

- The gateway of last resort (GWLR) feature can be configured on your router so that your router will forward all packets that it has no destination route for to a different router. To configure the GWLR, you use the ip route command to add a route to the 0.0.0.0 network.

- You can connect a switch to a router and have the router route traffic through the VLANs using the router on a stick feature. In order to configure router on a stick, you would create sub-interfaces on the router and enable dot1q as the tagging protocol, along with the VLAN ID, for each sub-interface. You would then configure the switch to use the port with the connection to the router as a trunk port so that it can carry all the VLAN traffic across the port.

Introduction to Routing and Communication

276–284 Choose the best answer(s).

276. What type of memory stores the routing table on Cisco routers?

(A)   ROM

(B)   NVRAM

(C)   Flash

(D)   RAM

277. Computer A is sending data to computer B on a remote network. Looking at the location of the packet in transit in the figure below, which of the following statements are true? (Select as many as apply.)

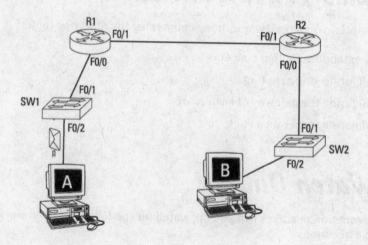

(A)   The destination IP address is that of Computer B.

(B)   The destination IP address is that of router R1.

(C)   The destination MAC address is that of the switch.

(D)   The source MAC address is that of router R1.

(E)   The destination MAC address is that of router R1.

278. When a router receives a packet what does it do? (Select two.)

(A)   Determines if a destination route exists in the routing table and what the next hop is

(B)   Determines if a destination MAC address appears in the routing table

(C)   Looks at the destination IP address in the packet

(D)   Filters traffic based on destination MAC address

279. What routes exist by default on your router?

(A) Static routes

(B) Dynamic routes

(C) Connected routes

(D) Gateway of last resort route

280. Which of the following represents one of the downfalls of static routes?

(A) They are shared automatically with neighboring routers.

(B) They are shared automatically with the entire network.

(C) They are manually configured by the router administrator.

(D) They generate network traffic to broadcast knowledge of the route.

281. Which of the following represents an advantage of static routing?

(A) Less administrative burden over dynamic routing

(B) No network bandwidth is being used by protocols sharing routing tables

(C) Easier to configure on the network than dynamic routing

(D) Uses a higher administrative distance than dynamic routing protocols

282. You are the administrator for router R1 and have configured a static route to the 216.83.11.0 network. Your company has loaded RIPv1 on all the routers on the network, and router R2 shares knowledge of a route to the 216.83.11.0 network with a RIP update. Which route will your router use?

(A) The default route

(B) The static route

(C) The RIPv1 route

(D) The GWLR

283. Which of the following two actions must a router do with an incoming packet in order to send it to its destination? (Choose two.)

(A) Determine if a route exists in the routing table

(B) Look at the source IP address of the packet

(C) Determine if an entry exists in the MAC address table

(D) Look at the destination IP address of the packet

284. What is the process called that the IP protocol uses to determine if the system it is trying to communicate with is on a different network?

(A) Routing

(B) ANDing

(C) NATing

(D) Switching

Configuring Static Routes

285–294 Choose the best answer(s).

285. What is the command to delete a static route?

(A) no ip route

(B) route delete

(C) delete route

(D) ip route delete

286. Your manager has disabled routing on the router by mistake. What command could you use to enable routing again?

(A) ip routing

(B) no ip routing

(C) enable routing

(D) no disable routing

287. What is the result of the following commands being entered on the route?

```
RouterA>enable
RouterA#config term
RouterA(config)#ip route 217.56.33.48 255.255.255.240 26.10.20.2
```

(A) Any data destined for the 26.10.20.2/28 network is forwarded to the IP address of 217.46.33.48.

(B) Any data destined for the 217.46.33.48/28 network is forwarded to the IP address of 26.10.20.2.

(C) Any data destined for the 217.46.33.0/28 network is forwarded to the IP address of 26.10.20.2.

(D) Any data destined for the 26.10.20.0/28 network is forwarded to the IP address of 217.46.33.48.

288. You have configured static routing on your router and would like to remove an entry from the routing table. What command would you use?

(A) `delete 27.0.0.0 255.0.0.0`

(B) `disable 27.0.0.0 255.0.0.0`

(C) `no ip route 27.0.0.0 255.0.0.0 26.0.0.2`

(D) `undo route 27.0.0.0 255.0.0.0`

289. What command adds a static route?

(A) `ip route 35.0.0.0 22.0.0.1`

(B) `route add 35.0.0.0 255.0.0.0 22.0.0.1`

(C) `route add 35.0.0.0 22.0.0.1`

(D) `ip route 35.0.0.0 255.0.0.0 22.0.0.1`

290. You type the following command into the router. Which of the following statements is true as a result of the command?

```
Ip route 200.45.7.0 255.255.255.224 22.202.33.10 10
```

(A) Packets destined for 200.45.7.98 will be forwarded to 22.202.33.10.

(B) The command configures a GWLR of 22.202.33.10.

(C) Packets destined for 200.45.7.45 will be forwarded to 22.202.33.10.

(D) The administrative distance to the destination network is 10.

291. You are the administrator for a small network made up of two routers. What is a quick method you can use to configure routing between all networks?

(A) Build static routes to all unknown routes on each router.

(B) Configure the GWLR on both routers to point to one another.

(C) Configure NAT overload on the first router and Static NAT on the second router.

(D) Configure access lists to allow traffic to route between the networks.

292. Your routers are running the RIP routing protocol and you type the following command. What is the outcome of typing this command?

```
Ip route 0.0.0.0 0.0.0.0 55.12.4.38
```

(A) If there is no matching destination network in the routing table, the router will send the packet to 55.12.4.38.

(B) You have configured RIP to broadcast knowledge of the 55.12.4.38 network.

(C) You have configured a connected route to forward traffic to 55.12.4.38.

(D) You have configured Gateway of Last Resort so that if there is a packet destined for the 55.0.0.0 network, then the router will forward it on to 0.0.0.0.

293. You are the administrator for router R1. Looking at the figure below, what command would you use to add a static route the missing network?

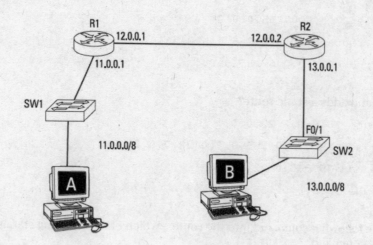

(A) ip route 12.0.0.0 255.0.0.0 12.0.0.1

(B) ip route 12.0.0.0 255.0.0.0 11.0.0.1

(C) ip route 13.0.0.0 255.0.0.0 12.0.0.1

(D) ip route 13.0.0.0 255.0.0.0 12.0.0.2

294. Tom, one of the network administrators in your office, types the following command into the router. Which of the following statements is true as a result of the command?

```
Ip route 200.45.7.64 255.255.255.224 22.202.33.10 10
```

(A) Packets destined for 200.45.7.98 will be forwarded to 22.202.33.10.

(B) The command configures a GWLR of 22.202.33.10.

(C) Packets destined for 200.45.7.89 will be forwarded to 22.202.33.10.

(D) The hop count to the destination network is 10.

Gateway of Last Resort

295–298 Choose the best answer(s).

295. You are considering configuring default routes on your routers. Which of the following are benefits of default routes? (Select two.)

(A) They allow communication to networks not appearing in the routing table.

(B) The routes never go down.

(C) The routes will take first priority.

(D) The routing table size is kept to a minimum.

(E) They are used to forward traffic from the Internet to your internal network.

296. Which of the following describes the gateway of last resort?

   (A) It is the address of the device on the network that converts FQDNs to IP addresses.

   (B) The address that your router will forward a packet to when it does not have a route for that packet.

   (C) It is the address of the device that translates private addresses to public addresses.

   (D) It is the address of the router that shares routing table information on the network.

297. Your manager asks you what the purpose of a default route is on the router. What would you say?

   (A) The default route takes precedence over the static route.

   (B) The default route takes precedence over the RIPv2 routes.

   (C) The default route is used when there is no other route to the destination.

   (D) The default route takes precedence over the RIPv1 route.

298. You would like to configure the GWLR to forward traffic to your ISP_s router, which uses the IP address of 145.66.77.99. What command would you use?

   (A) `ip route 145.66.77.99 255.255.255.255 0.0.0.0`

   (B) `ip route 145.66.77.99 255.255.0.0 0.0.0.0`

   (C) `ip route 145.66.77.99 255.255.0.0 145.66.77.99`

   (D) `ip route 0.0.0.0 0.0.0.0 145.66.77.99`

Troubleshooting Connectivity

299–305 Choose the best answer(s).

299. What command is used to view your routing table?

   (A) `ip route show`

   (B) `show ip route`

   (C) `show route table`

   (D) `table route show`

300. What does the following entry in the routing table signify?

S* 0.0.0.0 [1/0] via 56.0.0.1

(A) DNS server

(B) Gateway of last resort

(C) NAT-enabled router

(D) Address of the DHCP enabled router

301. Using the following output, how will data be sent to 26.13.45.222?

```
ROUTER87#show ip route
Codes: C - connected, S - static, I - IGRP, R - RIP, …
(Additional codes omitted for briefness)
Gateway of last resort is not set
S 29.0.0.0 [1/0] via 26.0.0.2
C 26.0.0.0/8 is directly connected, Serial0/0/0
C 25.0.0.0/8 is directly connected, FastEthernet0/1
```

(A) It will be sent out Fast Ethernet0/1

(B) It will be sent to 26.0.0.2

(C) It will be sent out Serial 0/0/0

(D) It will be sent out Serial 0/0/1

302. You are configuring router on a stick. Which of the following commands would create a sub-interface on the router?

(A) `create sub-interface 20`

(B) `sub-interface fa0/0.20`

(C) `interface fa0/0.20`

(D) `config sub-interface 20`

303. Using the following output, how will data be sent to 29.66.84.2?

```
ROUTER87#show ip route
Codes: C - connected, S - static, I - IGRP, R - RIP, …
(Additional codes omitted for briefness)
Gateway of last resort is not set
S 29.0.0.0 [1/0] via 26.0.0.2
C 26.0.0.0/8 is directly connected, Serial0/0/0
C 25.0.0.0/8 is directly connected, FastEthernet0/1
```

(A) Data will be sent out Serial0/0/0.

(B) Data will be sent out FastEthernet0/1.

(C) Data will be sent out Serial0/0/1.

(D) Data will be sent to 26.0.0.2.

304. Using the following output, how will data be sent to 25.33.200.2?

```
ROUTER87#show ip route
Codes: C - connected, S - static, I - IGRP, R - RIP, …
(Additional codes omitted for briefness)
Gateway of last resort is not set
S 29.0.0.0 [1/0] via 26.0.0.2
C 26.0.0.0/8 is directly connected, Serial0/0/0
C 25.0.0.0/8 is directly connected, FastEthernet0/1
```

(A) Data will be sent out FastEthernet0/1

(B) Data will be sent out Serial0/0/0

(C) Data will be sent out Serial0/0/1

(D) Data will be sent to 26.0.0.2

305. Using the output shown below, which resulted from the show ip route command, what is the hop count to reach the 29.0.0.0 network?

```
S 29.0.0.0 [1/5] via 26.0.0.2
```

(A) 1

(B) 5

(C) 26

(D) 29

Router on a Stick

306–307 Choose the best answer(s).

306. Which of the following statements are true in order to get traffic to route between the two VLANs in the figure below? (Select two.)

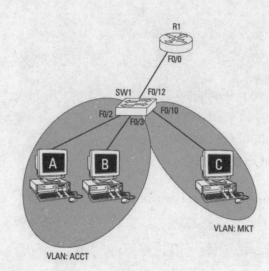

(A) Do nothing.

(B) Configure F0/12 on SW1 for trunk mode.

(C) Configure F0/0 on R1 for trunk mode.

(D) Configure sub-interfaces on SW1.

(E) Configure sub-interfaces on R1.

307. You are configuring router on the stick so the router will route traffic between VLAN 10 and VLAN 20. You configure the sub-interfaces with the following commands. During testing, you notice that the router is not routing between the VLANs. What is missing?

```
interface fa0/0.20
ip address 192.168.20.1 255.255.255.0
interface fa0/0.10
ip address 192.168.10.1 255.255.255.0
```

(A) You need to configure each sub-interface as a trunk port.

(B) You need to configure a different subnet mask on each interface.

(C) You need to enable dot1q and specify the VLAN on each interface.

(D) You need to configure both interfaces for the same network ID.

Administrative Distances

308–313 Choose the best answer(s).

308. The router will use the route that has the _____ administrative distance.

(A) highest

(B) lowest

309. Your router receives knowledge of a network via RIPv2 that it already has a static route to. Which pathway will be used?

(A) The static route entry

(B) The RIPv2 entry

(C) The default route entry

(D) The packet will be denied

310. What is the administrative distance of RIPv1?

(A) 1

(B) 100

(C) 120

(D) 0

311. What is the administrative distance of a connected route?

(A) 1

(B) 100

(C) 120

(D) 0

312. Which routing feature has an administrative distance of 120?

(A) Static

(B) Connected

(C) RIP

(D) OSPF

313. What is the administrative distance of a static route?

(A) 1

(B) 100

(C) 120

(D) 0

Chapter 9

Dynamic Routing Protocols

• •

*I*n the previous chapter, you were exposed to static routing, which involved manually adding routes to the router's routing table. This can be a long, involved, tedious task when working with large networks. That said, dynamic routing protocols can be loaded on the router so that the routers on the network exchange routing table information in order to build up the routing table. This chapter presents practice questions that test your knowledge of two routing protocols you must be familiar with for the ICND1 exam — RIP and OSPF.

The Problems You'll Work On

In this chapter, you'll review questions concerning the following topics:

✔ Understanding dynamic routing protocols

✔ Configuring RIP and RIPv2

✔ Grasping the basics of configuring OSPF

What to Watch Out For

Don't let common mistakes trip you up; watch for the following when working with these questions:

✔ To display your routing table, use the show ip route command. To view routing protocol details, you use the show ip protocols command.

✔ Distance vector routing protocols send the entire routing table in an update at regular intervals to neighboring routers, while link state routing protocols are aware of the entire network topology and the state of the links. Distance vector routing protocols use the hop count metric, while link state uses the availability of the link and bandwidth.

✔ RIP is an example of a distance vector routing protocol. To enable RIPv1, you use the router rip command to navigate to the router prompt and then enable RIP on each network interface with the network command. If you wish to use RIPv2, you then type the version 2 command at the router prompt.

✔ When troubleshooting RIP, you can turn on RIP debugging with the debug ip rip command. Be sure to turn off all debugging, when you finish troubleshooting, with the no debug all command.

Introduction to Dynamic Routing Protocols

314–329 Choose the best answer(s).

314. When a router receives a routing table update for a route it does not have in its routing table, what does it do?

(A) Adds the route to the MAC address table

(B) Adds the route to the ARP cache

(C) Adds the route to the routing table

(D) Adds the route as the GWLR

315. Which of the following protocols are distance vector routing protocols supported by multiple vendors and not just Cisco?

(A) OSPF

(B) RIP

(C) IGRP

(D) EIGRP

316. Which of the following protocols are link state routing protocols? (Select all that apply.)

(A) EIGRP

(B) RIP

(C) IGRP

(D) OSPF

317. Which routing protocol is limited to 15 hops?

(A) OSPF

(B) IGRP

(C) RIP

(D) EIGRP

318. A _____ routing protocol is a routing protocol that knows only about how many hops away a network is

(A) Distance vector

(B) Layer 2

(C) Link state

(D) Layer 4

319. Dynamic routing protocols run at what layer of the OSI model?

(A) Layer 1

(B) Layer 2

(C) Layer 3

(D) Layer 4

320. Which of the following is true of distance vector routing protocols? (Select two.)

(A) Routers share routing table with all other routers on the network

(B) Routers share routing table with neighboring routers

(C) Updates are only sent every 60 seconds

(D) Maintains multiple tables in memory — one for neighboring routers, one to store the entire topology, and final table is the routing table.

(E) Sends entire routing table as an update

321. Which of the following are true statements about RIPv2? (Select three.)

(A) It is a classless routing protocol

(B) Maximum hop count of 15

(C) Sends updates with broadcast

(D) RIPv2 supports authentication

(E) Has a high administrative distance than RIPv1

322. (True/False): RIPv1 is an example of a classless routing protocol.

(A) True

(B) False

323. How frequently does RIPv2 send out routing updates?

(A) Every 15 seconds

(B) Every 180 seconds

(C) Every 30 seconds

(D) Every 60 seconds

324. Which of the following is true of a distance vector routing protocol? (Select two.)

(A) Uses a topology table to determine whom to send updates to

(B) Sends periodic updates

(C) Updates routing table based on updates received from neighboring routers

(D) Sends entire routing table to all routers on the network

(E) Uses the shortest path first algorithm to determine best route

325. OSPF is an example of a _____ routing protocol.

    (A)   Layer 2

    (B)   Distance vector

    (C)   Link state

    (D)   Layer 4

326. Which of the following is true regarding link state routing protocols? (Select two.)

    (A)   Routers share routing table information with all other routers on the network

    (B)   Routers share routing table information with neighboring routers

    (C)   Updates are only sent every 60 seconds

    (D)   Maintains multiple tables in memory — one for neighboring routers, one to store the entire topology, and final table is the routing table.

    (E)   Sends entire routing table as an update

327. Your router receives an update for a route from both RIP and OSP   (F)   Which route will the router add to its routing table?

    (A)   RIP

    (B)   OSPF

    (C)   Neither

    (D)   Both

328. What does the term "routing by rumor" refer to?

    (A)   Broadcasting all routes to neighboring routers

    (B)   Broadcasting all routes to all routers

    (C)   Broadcasting static routes to neighboring routers

    (D)   Sharing routes learned from one neighbor to other neighboring routers

329. Which of the following represents a downfall of distance vector routing protocols over link state?

    (A)   Convergence time

    (B)   Sends updates to all routers

    (C)   Updates are triggered based off events

    (D)   Updates are delivered using unicast communication

Configuring RIP and RIPv2

330–341 Choose the best answer(s).

330. Your manager is thinking about upgrading from RIPv1 to RIPv2 and asks about the benefit of RIPv2. What would you say?

(A) Supports a maximum of 30 hops

(B) Sends updates every 90 seconds

(C) Is classful

(D) Supports VLSM

331. Which routing protocol sends the entire routing table to neighboring routers every 30 seconds?

(A) OSPF

(B) RIP

(C) IGRP

(D) EIGRP

332. You wish to see how RIP has been configured on the router. What command would you use?

(A) RouterA#show ip config

(B) RouterA#show protocols

(C) RouterA#show rip protocols

(D) RouterA#show ip protocols

333. When looking at the routing table, how do you know which entries have been learned through RIP?

(A) The entry with code R

(B) The entry with code C

(C) The entry with code RIP

(D) The entry with code 1

334. What version of RIP supports VLSM?

(A) RIPv1

(B) RIPv2

(C) RIPv8

(D) RIPv9

335. What command enables RIP debugging?

(A) `rip debug`

(B) `debug rip`

(C) `debug ip rip`

(D) `enable debug`

336. You need to configure RIPv2 on your router. Which of the following commands would do this?

(A) Use the following commands:

`R1>router rip`

`R1>network 25.0.0.0`

`R1>network 26.0.0.0`

`R1>version 2`

(B) Use the following commands:

`R1(config)#router rip`

`R1(config-router)#network 25.0.0.0`

`R1(config-router)#network 26.0.0.0`

`R1(config-router)#version 2`

(C) Use the following commands:

`R1(config)#router rip 2`

`R1(config-router)#network 25.0.0.0`

`R1(config-router)#network 26.0.0.0`

(D) Use the following commands:

`R1(config)#router rip version 2`

`R1(config-router)#network 25.0.0.0`

`R1(config-router)#network 26.0.0.0`

337. What is the default administrative distance for RIP?

(A) 90

(B) 100

(C) 120

(D) 150

338. You have three interfaces on the router: one configured for the 27.0.0.0/8, while the other two interfaces are configured with 29.1.0.0/16 and 29.2.0.0/16. If you want to use RIPv2, which of the following represents the least number of commands you would need to use?

(A) Use the following commands:

```
RouterA>enable
RouterA#config term
RouterA(config)#enable rip
RouterA(config)#network 27.0.0.0
RouterA(config)#network 29.0.0.0
RouterA(config)#version 2
```

(B) Use the following commands:

```
RouterA>enable
RouterA#config term
RouterA(config)#router rip
RouterA(config-router)#network 27.0.0.0
RouterA(config-router)#network 29.1.0.0
RouterA(config-router)#network 29.2.0.0
```

(C) Use the following commands:

```
RouterA>enable
RouterA#config term
RouterA(config)#router rip
RouterA(config-router)#network 27.0.0.0
RouterA(config-router)#network 29.1.0.0
RouterA(config-router)#network 29.2.0.0
RouterA(config-router)#version 2
```

(D) Use the following commands:

```
RouterA>enable
RouterA#config term
RouterA(config)#router rip
RouterA(config-router)#network 27.0.0.0
RouterA(config-router)#network 29.0.0.0
RouterA(config-router)#version 2
```

339. Which of the following is true about RIPng?

   (A) You need to enable RIPng on each interface.

   (B) RIPng uses broadcast traffic to share routing information.

   (C) RIPng is classful.

   (D) RIPng supports up to 30 hops.

340. You want to disable sending RIP messages on interface serial 0/1. Which of the following commands would you use?

   (A) RouterA(config)#passive-interface serial 0/1

   (B) RouterA(config-router)#passive-interface serial 0/1

   (C) RouterA#passive-interface serial 0/1

   (D) RouterA>passive-interface serial 0/1

341. When RIP has multiple routes to a destination with the same hop count, what will it do?

   (A) RIP uses the one with the administrative distance of 120.

   (B) RIP will load-balance the links to that destination.

   (C) RIP uses the second route in the table.

   (D) RIP uses the first route in the table.

Basics of Configuring OSPF

342–351 Choose the best answer(s).

342. What is the administrative distance of OSPF?

   (A) 110

   (B) 90

   (C) 120

   (D) 115

343. Which of the following would be used as the OSPF router ID if all were configured?

   (A) Highest IP address assigned to a loopback interface

   (B) Highest IP address assigned to a physical interface

   (C) Lowest IP address assigned to a loopback interface

   (D) Lowest IP address assigned to a physical interface

344. What type of OSPF router connects one or more areas to the backbone network?

   (A) BR

   (B) IR

   (C) ASBR

   (D) ABR

345. You are troubleshooting OSPF configuration. What command would you use to verify your configuration?

(A) `show ospf`

(B) `show ip ospf`

(C) `show interfaces`

(D) `show controllers`

346. When configuring OSPF on your router, you have specified an interface to be part of area 0. What is the area known as?

(A) Backbone

(B) Branch network

(C) Exterior network

(D) Internet

347. You need to configure OSPF on your router. Which of the following most accurately depicts the commands used?

(A) Use the following commands:

    router ospf 1

    network 192.168.1.0 255.255.255.0 area 0

(B) Use the following commands:

    router ospf 1

    network 192.168.1.0 0.0.0.255 area 0

(C) Use the following commands:

    router ospf

    network 192.168.1.0 0.0.0.255 area 0

(D) Use the following commands:

    router ospf

    network 192.168.1.0 0.0.0.255

348. You want to configure your router for OSPF and run it on interfaces that are on the 192.168.1.0 network. Which of the following commands would you use?

(A) Use the following:

    router ospf 1

    network 192.168.1.0 0.0.0.255 area 0

(B) Use the following:

    router ospf 1

    network 192.168.1.0 255.0.0.0 area 0

(C) Use the following:

```
router ospf

network 192.168.1.0 0.0.0.255 area 0
```

(D) Use the following:

```
router ospf 1

network 192.168.1.0 255.255.255.255 area 0
```

349. When troubleshooting OSPF, which of the following commands would you use? (Select two.)

(A) `show cdp neighbors`

(B) `show ip protocols`

(C) `show mac-address-table`

(D) `show`

(E) `show ip ospf neighbor`

350. Which of the following commands enables an OSPFv3 process?

(A) `router ospf 5`

(B) `ospf 5`

(C) `ipv6 ospf 5`

(D) `ipv6 router ospf 5`

351. Which of the following commands would you use to change the router ID of an OSPF router?

(A) Use the following:

```
Router rip

Router-id 8.8.8.8
```

(B) Use the following:

```
Router config

Router-id 8.8.8.8
```

(C) Use the following:

```
Router ospf 1

Set Router id 8.8.8.8
```

(D) Use the following:

```
Router ospf 1

Router-id 8.8.8.8
```

Chapter 10

Introduction to Switching

· ·

*W*e have come to the point in the book where we are going to switch directions (pardon the pun) and move away from routing as a topic and focus more on a network switch. This chapter is designed to test your knowledge of the fundamentals of network switches. This chapter is acting as more of a primer for the next chapter because it tests you on topics such as the purpose of a switch, the flow of communication, and basic configuration of the switch.

The Problems You'll Work On

In this chapter, you'll review questions concerning the following topics:

- ✔ Understanding the fundamentals of a Cisco switch
- ✔ Understanding the pathway to communication and addressing
- ✔ Looking at basic switch configurations, such as IP address and gateway assignment

What to Watch Out For

Don't let common mistakes trip you up; watch for the following when working with these questions:

- ✔ A switch is a layer-2 device that filters traffic based off the destination MAC address. The switch uses a MAC address table, which lists the MAC address of the systems connected and what port those systems are connected to. The switch can populate the MAC address table dynamically by looking at the source address of a received frame. Administrators can manually add entries to the MAC address table as well.

- ✔ The mode button on the front of the switch toggles the display mode, which changes the meaning of the LEDs on the front of the switch. For example, if you are in status display mode, a blinking light means traffic is being transmitted on that port. But if the display mode is set to speed, then a blinking light on a port means you are running at 1 Gbps.

- ✔ Know the pathway of communication for the exams! When a message is sent between two systems, the source and destination IP addresses in the message stay the same each step of the way, but the source and destination MAC addresses change each step of the way.

Introduction to Cisco Switches

352–359 Choose the best answer(s).

352. Bob calls complaining that he cannot access the network. When you look at the switch, you notice the port he is connected to is displaying an amber light. What does this mean?

(A) The IP address on the switch is incorrect.

(B) The default gateway setting on the switch is incorrect.

(C) The default gateway setting on Bob's station is incorrect.

(D) The port has been disabled.

353. After powering on the Cisco switch you notice that the System LED is green. What does this indicate?

(A) The system started without problems and is operational.

(B) There is a power problem.

(C) There is a problem with the default VLAN.

(D) There were POST errors.

354. The switch has the display mode set to Status and port 4 is blinking green. What does this indicate?

(A) There is a link

(B) Waiting for traffic to be sent

(C) The port is running in full duplex

(D) Data is being transmitted

355. After powering on the Cisco switch, you notice that the System LED is amber. What does this indicate?

(A) The system started without problems and is operational.

(B) There is a power problem.

(C) There is a problem with the default VLAN.

(D) There were POST errors.

356. You wish to verify which ports on the switch are running in full duplex mode. How would you do this?

   (A)   Switch the display mode to duplex and watch for a solid green light on the different ports.

   (B)   Switch the display mode to duplex and watch for an amber light on the different ports.

   (C)   Switch the display mode to duplex and watch for no light on the different ports.

   (D)   Switch the display mode to duplex and watch for a flashing green light on the different ports.

357. When your switch is set to the display mode of speed, what does the LED for a 1 Gbps port look like?

   (A)   Flashing amber

   (B)   Solid amber

   (C)   Solid green

   (D)   Flashing green

358. The switch display mode is set to duplex and you have a computer connected to port number 4 with no light displaying on the port. What is the problem?

   (A)   There is no link.

   (B)   No traffic is being sent.

   (C)   The port is running in half duplex.

   (D)   The port is running in full duplex.

359. You have the display mode set to speed on your 10/100/1000 switch. Three of the ports are not displaying a light. What does this indicate?

   (A)   Ports are running at 1000 Mbps.

   (B)   Ports are running at 100 Mbps.

   (C)   Ports are running at 10 Mbps.

   (D)   No data is being transmitted.

Understanding Switch Functionality

360–378 Choose the best answer(s).

360. A switch is an example of a layer-___ device.

   (A)   1

   (B)   2

   (C)   3

   (D)   4

361. Which of the following protocols does a Cisco switch use for loop avoidance?

(A) CDP

(B) VTP

(C) STP

(D) PDC

362. When a switch receives a frame, what address does it look to in order to determine where to forward the frame?

(A) The destination MAC address

(B) The source MAC address

(C) The destination IP address

(D) The source IP address

363. Which of the following descriptions matches a collision domain?

(A) A group of systems that can have their data collide with one another

(B) A group of systems that receive one another's broadcast messages

(C) A group of systems between two firewalls

(D) A system that filters traffic by source IP address

364. Which of the following are considered core services offered by a switch? (Select three.)

(A) Filtering and forwarding

(b) Loop avoidance

(C) Address translation

(D) IP address assignment

(E) Address learning

(F) Name resolution

365. Which of the following descriptions matches a broadcast domain?

(A) A group of systems that receive one another's broadcast messages

(B) The area between two firewalls

(C) A group of systems that can have their data collide with one another

(D) A network device that shares a single IP address via port address translation

366. Looking at the figure below, what does the switch do when it receives a frame destined for the MAC address of 00d0.bc8a.2766?

```
Switch#show mac-address-table
          Mac Address Table
-------------------------------------------------

Vlan    Mac Address      Type        Ports
----    -----------      --------    -----

 1      0009.7c57.5674   DYNAMIC     Fa0/2
 1      0010.11d9.d001   DYNAMIC     Fa0/1
 1      00d0.bc8a.2766   DYNAMIC     Fa0/12
```

(A)   It forwards the frame to port 1.

(B)   It forwards the frame to port 2.

(C)   It will flood the frame.

(D)   It forwards the frame to port 12.

367. What does a switch do with a frame it receives that is destined for a MAC address that is not stored in the MAC address table?

(A)   Broadcasts the frame

(B)   Floods the frame

(C)   Sends the frame to the address of FF-FF-FF-FF-FF-FF

(D)   Stores it until the destination MAC is in the MAC address table

368. Your manager is wondering what the benefit of switches over hubs are. What would you say?

(A)   Hubs filter traffic and only send the traffic to the destination port, while a switch sends all traffic to all ports.

(B)   Switches filter traffic and only send the traffic to the destination port, while a hub sends all traffic to all ports.

(C)   Hubs segment the traffic.

(D)   Switches use a single collision domain for all ports.

369. How many collision domains exist on a 24 port hub versus a 24 port switch?

(A) Hub – 1 collision domain / switch – 24 collision domains

(B) Hub – 24 collision domain / switch – 1 collision domains

(C) Hub – 48 collision domain / switch – 24 collision domains

(D) Hub – 24 collision domain / switch – 48 collision domains

370. Which of the following does the switch use to populate the MAC address table on the switch?

(A) The source MAC address of the frame

(B) The destination MAC address of the frame

(C) The source IP address of the frame

(D) The destination IP address of the frame

371. Looking at the figure below, how many collision domains and broadcast domains are there?

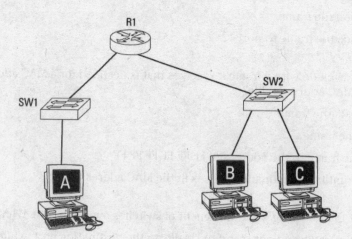

(A) 2 broadcast domains, 5 collision domains

(B) 2 collision domains, 4 broadcast domains

(C) 1 broadcast domain, 5 collision domains

(D) 1 broadcast domain, 4 collision domains

372. You have three switches connected together with crossover cables. How many broadcast domains exist?

(A) 3

(B) 1

(C) 6

(D) 2

373. You have linked two switches together with a straight-through cable but cannot seem to communicate between the two switches. What is the solution?

   (A)   Use a console cable.

   (B)   Connect a router between the two switches.

   (C)   Use a crossover cable.

   (D)   Connect a bridge between the two switches.

374. Which switch operation mode waits to receive the first 64 bytes of the frame before forwarding the frame on to its destination?

   (A)   Store-and-forward

   (B)   Cache and deliver

   (C)   Fragment-free

   (D)   Cut-through

375. What is the general term for data received and processed by a switch?

   (A)   Frame

   (B)   Packet

   (C)   Segment

   (D)   Payload

376. Which switch operation mode waits until the entire frame is received before forwarding the frame on to its destination?

   (A)   Store-and-forward

   (B)   Cache and deliver

   (C)   Fragment-free

   (D)   Cut-through

377. Looking at the figure below, what does the switch do when it receives a frame destined for the MAC address of 00d0.bc8a.2788?

```
Switch#show mac-address-table
          Mac Address Table
-------------------------------------------------

Vlan    Mac Address        Type        Ports
----    -----------        --------    -----

  1     0009.7c57.5674     DYNAMIC     Fa0/2
  1     0010.11d9.d001     DYNAMIC     Fa0/1
  1     00d0.bc8a.2766     DYNAMIC     Fa0/12
```

(A) It forwards the frame to port 1.

(B) It forwards the frame to port 2.

(C) It will flood the frame.

(D) It forwards the frame to port 12.

378. Which switch operation mode starts forwarding the frame off to its destination as soon as the destination MAC address is received?

(A) Store-and-forward

(B) Cache and deliver

(C) Fragment-free

(D) Cut-through

Understanding Data Flow

379–381 Choose the best answer(s).

379. When a packet is sent from a system on your network to a system on another network, which of the following is true of the packet as it is passed to your router from your system?

(A) Destination IP Address: your_router / Destination MAC Address: your_router

(B) Destination IP Address: the_remote_system / Destination MAC Address: your_router

(C) Destination IP Address: your_router / Destination MAC Address: the_remote_system

(D) Destination IP Address: the_remote_system / Destination MAC Address: the_remote_system

380. Computer A is sending a message to computer B. Looking at the figure below, which of the following are true of the message as it travels between R2 and SW2? (Select three.)

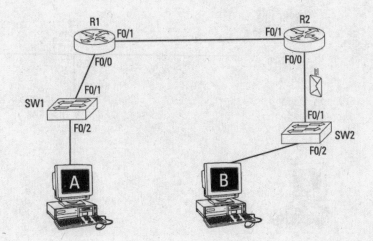

(A) The destination IP address is that of router R2.

(B) The destination MAC is that of Computer B.

(C) The source MAC address is that of router R1.

(D) The source MAC address is that of Computer A.

(E) The destination IP address is that of Computer B.

(F) The destination MAC is that of SW2.

(G) The source MAC is that of R2.

381. Computer A is sending a message to computer B. Looking at the figure below, which of the following are true of the message as it travels between R1 and R2? (Select three.)

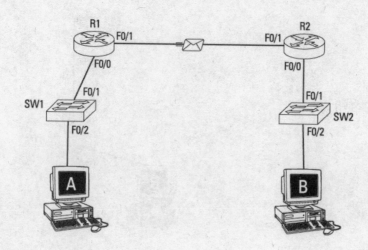

(A) The destination IP address is that of router R2.

(B) The source IP address is that of Computer A.

(C) The source MAC address is that of router R1.

(D) The source MAC address is that of Computer A.

(E) The destination IP address is that of Computer B.

(F) The destination MAC is that of Computer B.

Basic Switch Configuration

382–389 Choose the best answer(s).

382. Which of the following commands is used to change the name of the switch?

(A) Switch#hostname NY-SW1

(B) Switch(config)#hostname NY-SW1

(C) Switch(config)#name NY-SW1

(D) Switch#name NY-SW1

383. You wish to display your MAC address table. What command do you use?

(A) Switch(config)# show mac-address-table

(B) Switch(config-if)# show mac-address-table

(C) Switch# view mac-address-table

(D) Switch# show mac-address-table

384. Your manager has asked you to telnet into one of the switches in the Las Vegas office, but you cannot seem to connect. You can telnet into the switch when you are in the Las Vegas office, but you cannot seem to telnet when you are on a remote network. What could be the problem?

(A)   No Telnet password assigned to the switch

(B)   No default gateway address assigned on the switch

(C)   No default gateway address assigned on your router

(D)   No Telnet password assigned on your router

385. Which of the following commands are used to assign an IP address to the switch?

(A)   Use the following commands:

NY-SW1(config)#`interface f0/1`

NY-SW1(config-if)#`ip address 23.0.0.25 255.0.0.0`

(B)   Use the following commands:

NY-SW1(config)#`ip address 23.0.0.25 255.0.0.0`

(C)   Use the following commands:

NY-SW1(config)#`interface vlan1`

NY-SW1(config-if)#`ip address 23.0.0.25 255.0.0.0`

(D)   Use the following commands:

NY-SW1(config)#`line vty 0 4`

NY-SW1(config-if)#`ip address 23.0.0.25 255.0.0.0`

386. Which of the following commands assigns a default gateway address to your switch?

(A)   Switch(config-if)# `ip default-gateway 24.0.0.1`

(B)   Switch# `ip default-gateway 24.0.0.1`

(C)   Switch(config)# `ip default-gateway 24.0.0.1`

(D)   Switch(config)#`default-gateway 24.0.0.1`

387. How long does a dynamic entry stay in the MAC address table?

(A)   300 seconds from time added to table

(B)   60 seconds from last time used

(C)   60 seconds from time added to table

(D)   300 seconds from last time used

388. While looking at the figure below, what does the type of dynamic mean?

```
Switch#show mac-address-table
          Mac Address Table
-------------------------------------------------

Vlan    Mac Address        Type        Ports
----    -----------        --------    -----

  1     0009.7c57.5674     DYNAMIC     Fa0/2
  1     0010.11d9.d001     DYNAMIC     Fa0/1
  1     00d0.bc8a.2766     DYNAMIC     Fa0/12
```

(A) The administrator has programmed the address.

(B) CDP has populated the address.

(C) The switch has learned the address based off traffic received.

(D) RIP has added the address.

389. You would like to change the amount of time an entry stays in the MAC address table on the switch to 400. What command would you use?

(A) `mac-address-table 400`

(B) `aging-time 400`

(C) `aging-time set-table 400`

(D) `mac-address-table aging-time 400`

Chapter 11

Basic Switch Configuration

• •

This chapter is designed to help you prepare for the hands-on type of questions you will see on the ICND1 exam as it relates to day-to-day configuration of the switch and its ports. This chapter tests you on topics such as configure port speeds, duplex settings, and disabling ports. You also see questions surrounding topics such as VLANs and port security.

The Problems You'll Work On

In this chapter, you'll review questions concerning the following topics:

- ✔ Configuring port speed and duplex settings
- ✔ Enabling and disabling ports
- ✔ Understanding port security and how to configure and troubleshoot port security
- ✔ Understanding and configuring VLANs

What to Watch Out For

Don't let common mistakes trip you up; watch for the following when working with these questions:

- ✔ Know how to look at the output of related show commands (such as show interface) and identify problems when looking at the configuration. For example, you should be able to tell the duplex setting, speed, and whether the port has been disabled.

- ✔ Know how to configure the speed and duplex settings on a port. You can use the speed command to configure the speed of the port or the duplex command to configure the duplex setting on the port.

- ✔ Know there are multiple steps to configuring port security. You first must make sure that the port is in access mode, and then you can configure the port security settings, such as the maximum number of addresses, the MAC address, and the action to perform upon address violation. Be sure to know this very well!

- ✔ Know how to configure port security with the sticky option, which learns the MAC address of the system connected to the port, instead of making you type the MAC address.

- ✔ Know how to create VLANs and configure an interface to be part of a VLAN. Always know the show commands to go with verifying your configuration.

Configuring Ports

390–397 Choose the best answer(s).

390. Your manager would like a port description configured to port number 5 on the switch labeling the port as being used by the file server. What set of commands would you use?

    (A) Use the following commands:

        Switch#`interface f0/5`

        Switch#`description File Server Port`

    (B) Use the following commands:

        Switch#`config term`

        Switch(config)#`interface f0/5`

        Switch(config-if)#`description File Server Port`

    (C) Use the following commands:

        Switch#`config term`

        Switch(config)#`description File Server Port`

    (D) Use the following commands:

        Switch> `description File Server Port`

391. Jeff has disabled all of the unused ports on the switch. You would like to enable port 12. What command would you use?

    (A) `disable shutdown`

    (B) `enable port`

    (C) `no shutdown`

    (D) `enable no shutdown`

392. You wish to configure port 8 on the switch to negotiate its speed with the connecting system. What command would you use?

    (A) `speed auto`

    (B) `speed 100`

    (C) `speed 10`

    (D) `speed 1000`

393. You wish to configure port number 8 for full duplex. What command would you use?

    (A) `duplex all`

    (B) `duplex half`

    (C) `duplex auto`

    (D) `duplex full`

394. You would like to configure all 24 ports on the switch for 100 Mbps. Which of the following represents the best way to do this?

- (A) Use the following commands:

  Switch(config)#`interface range f0/1 - 24`

  Switch(config-if-range)#`speed 100`

- (B) Navigate to each port and use the following command on each port:

  `speed 100`

- (C) Use the following commands:

  Switch(config)#`interface f0/1 - 24`

  Switch(config-if-range)#`speed 100`

- (D) Use the following command:

  Switch(config)#`speed 100 interface f01 - 24`

395. Which command sets the port speed to 100 Mbps?

- (A) switch(config)#`speed 100`
- (B) switch#`speed 100`
- (C) switch>`speed 100`
- (D) switch(config-if)#`speed 100`

396. What command would you use first to configure a setting on multiple ports on the switch?

- (A) Use the `speed` command
- (B) Use the `duplex` command
- (C) Use `select ports` command
- (D) Use the `interface range` command

397. You need to disable ports 6 to 12 on your switch. What commands would you use?

- (A) Use the following commands:

  Switch(config)#`interface range f0/6 - 12`

  Switch(config-if-range)#`no shutdown`

- (B) Use the following commands:

  Switch#`interface range f0/6 - 12`

  Switch#`shutdown`

- (C) Use the following commands:

  Switch#`shutdown interface range f0/6 - 12`

- (D) Use the following commands:

  Switch(config)#`interface range f0/6 - 12`

  Switch(config-if-range)#`shutdown`

Troubleshooting Switch Configuration

398–409 Choose the best answer(s).

398. What command shows you MAC addresses associated with each port on the switch?

(A) `show vlan`

(B) `show port-security addresses`

(C) `display mac-address-table`

(D) `show mac-address-table`

399. Looking at the figure below, what is the duplex setting of the port set to?

```
FastEthernet0/8 is administratively down, line protocol is down (disabled)
   Hardware is Lance, address is 0002.1604.3605 (bia 0002.1604.3605)
   Description: File Server Port
   MTU 1500 bytes, BW 100000 Kbit, DLY 1000 usec,
       reliability 255/255, txload 1/255, rxload 1/255
   Encapsulation ARPA, loopback not set
   Keepalive set (10 sec)
   Half-duplex, 100Mb/s
   input flow-control is off, output flow-control is off
   ARP type: ARPA, ARP Timeout 04:00:00

(output has been omitted for briefness)
```

(A) Full duplex

(B) Half duplex

(C) Simplex

(D) No duplex

400. What command was used to create the output displayed in the figure below?

```
FastEthernet0/8 is administratively down, line protocol is down (disabled)
   Hardware is Lance, address is 0002.1604.3605 (bia 0002.1604.3605)
   Description: File Server Port
   MTU 1500 bytes, BW 100000 Kbit, DLY 1000 usec,
       reliability 255/255, txload 1/255, rxload 1/255
   Encapsulation ARPA, loopback not set
   Keepalive set (10 sec)
   Half-duplex, 100Mb/s
   input flow-control is off, output flow-control is off
   ARP type: ARPA, ARP Timeout 04:00:00

(output has been omitted for briefness)
```

(A) `show interface f0/5`

(B) `show vlan`

(C) `show ip interface brief`

(D) `show interface f0/8`

401. You wish to view the speed that port number 5 is using. What command would you use?

(A) `show speed`

(B) `show speed interface f0/5`

(C) `show interface f0/5`

(D) `show f0/5`

402. Looking at the figure below, what is the speed of the port set to?

```
FastEthernet0/8 is administratively down, line protocol is down (disabled)
  Hardware is Lance, address is 0002.1604.3605 (bia 0002.1604.3605)
  Description: File Server Port
  MTU 1500 bytes, BW 100000 Kbit, DLY 1000 usec,
     reliability 255/255, txload 1/255, rxload 1/255
  Encapsulation ARPA, loopback not set
  Keepalive set (10 sec)
  Half-duplex, 100Mb/s
  input flow-control is off, output flow-control is off
  ARP type: ARPA, ARP Timeout 04:00:00

(output has been omitted for briefness)
```

(A) 10 Mbps

(B) 1000 Mbps

(C) 100 Mbps

(D) 10 Gbps

403. You are administering a 24-port switch that is divided into 4 VLANs. How many collision domains exist?

(A) 48

(B) 24

(C) 8

(D) 4

404. You are administering a 24-port switch that is divided into 4 VLANs. How many broadcast domains exist?

(A) 48

(B) 24

(C) 8

(D) 4

405. Which of the following commands would you use to enable a port on the switch?

(A) shutdown

(B) enable

(C) no shutdown

(D) no disable

406. You are having trouble connecting to port 8 on the switch. You view the status of the port (shown in the figure below). What command would allow the port to function properly?

```
FastEthernet0/8 is administratively down, line protocol is down (disabled)
   Hardware is Lance, address is 0002.1604.3605 (bia 0002.1604.3605)
   Description: File Server Port
   MTU 1500 bytes, BW 100000 Kbit, DLY 1000 usec,
       reliability 255/255, txload 1/255, rxload 1/255
   Encapsulation ARPA, loopback not set
   Keepalive set (10 sec)
   Half-duplex, 100Mb/s
   input flow-control is off, output flow-control is off
   ARP type: ARPA, ARP Timeout 04:00:00

(output has been omitted for briefness)
```

(A) no shutdown

(B) shutdown

(C) ip address 12.0.0.10 255.0.0.0

(D) no cdp run

407. Looking at the figure below, what is the bandwidth of the port set to?

```
FastEthernet0/8 is administratively down, line protocol is down (disabled)
   Hardware is Lance, address is 0002.1604.3605 (bia 0002.1604.3605)
   Description: File Server Port
   MTU 1500 bytes, BW 100000 Kbit, DLY 1000 usec,
       reliability 255/255, txload 1/255, rxload 1/255
   Encapsulation ARPA, loopback not set
   Keepalive set (10 sec)
   Half-duplex, 100Mb/s
   input flow-control is off, output flow-control is off
   ARP type: ARPA, ARP Timeout 04:00:00

(output has been omitted for briefness)
```

(A) 100 Kbps

(B) 1000 Kbps

(C) 100000 Kbps

(D) 1000 Mbps

408. When you connect the workstation to port 6, you can ping three other systems on the network, but you cannot seem to connect to the file server. You verify that others can connect to the file server, but you cannot connect to those other systems as well. What could be the problem?

(A) Wrong default gateway address.

(B) NAT is misconfigured.

(C) The port used by the workstation is disabled

(D) You are in a different VLAN than the file server.

409. You have a workstation connected to port 10 on the switch, but for some reason you cannot ping any other system on the network. You view the configuration of the port and get the output display in the figure below. What is likely the problem?

```
FastEthernet0/10 is administratively down, line protocol is down (disabled)
   Hardware is Lance, address is 0002.1604.3605 (bia 0002.1604.3605)
   Description: File Server Port
   MTU 1500 bytes, BW 100000 Kbit, DLY 1000 usec,
      reliability 255/255, txload 1/255, rxload 1/255
   Encapsulation ARPA, loopback not set
   Keepalive set (10 sec)
   Half-duplex, 100Mb/s
   input flow-control is off, output flow-control is off
   ARP type: ARPA, ARP Timeout 04:00:00

(output has been omitted for briefness)
```

(A) You are using the wrong IP address.

(B) The port is disabled.

(C) The speed is 100 Mbps.

(D) ARPA is not being used.

Port Security

410–419 Choose the best answer(s).

410. What Cisco switch feature will allow you to control which systems can connect to a port on the switch?

(A) VTP

(B) Port Security

(C) VLANs

(D) STP

411. What option allows you to configure a static MAC address on the switch by using the MAC of the connected system?

(A) static

(B) dynamic

(C) sticky

(D) usemac

412. Why would a network administrator configure Port Security on the switch?

(A) To filter packets by layer-3 addresses

(B) To translate private addresses to public addresses

(C) To prevent loops on the network

(D) To prevent unauthorized access to the network

413. Which of the following violation modes would block traffic not coming from the correct MAC address, but allow traffic from the specified MAC address?

(A) shutdown

(B) restrict

(C) disable

(D) disconnect

414. Which of the following actions disables the port when an address violation occurs?

(A) disable

(B) shutdown

(C) disconnect

(D) restrict

415. What command was used to create the output displayed in the figure below?

```
Port Security               : Enabled
Port Status                 : Secure-down
Violation Mode              : Shutdown
Aging Time                  : 0 mins
Aging Type                  : Absolute
SecureStatic Address Aging  : Disabled
Maximum MAC Addresses       : 1
Total MAC Addresses         : 1
Configured MAC Addresses    : 1
Sticky MAC Addresses        : 0
Last Source Address:Vlan    : 0000.0000.0000:0
Security Violation Count    : 0
```

(A) `show interface f0/6`

(B) `show port-security interface f0/6`

(C) `show vlan`

(D) `show ip interface brief`

416. What mode must you place the interface into before you are able to configure Port Security on the interface?

(A) Access

(B) Trunk

(C) Dynamic

(D) Workstation

417. You are having trouble with a system connecting to port 5 on the switch. You want to see if the port has been configured for Port Security. What command do you use?

(A) `show mac-address-table`

(B) `show vlan`

(C) `show port-security interface f0/5`

(D) `show running-config`

418. What command was used to create the output displayed in the figure below?

```
                          Secure Mac Address Table
      ------------------------------------------------------------
      Vlan   Mac Address      Type              Ports
      ----   -----------      -----             ------
      1      1111.2222.3333   SecureConfigured  FastEthernet0/6
      ------------------------------------------------------------


      (output has been omitted for briefness)
      Switch#
```

(A) show mac-address-table

(B) show port-security address

(C) show ip interface brief

(D) show interface f0/8

419. What are the three actions that you can configure when an address violation occurs? (Select three.)

(A) restrict

(B) disable

(C) shutdown

(D) disconnect

(E) protect

Configuring VLANs

420–427 Choose the best answer(s).

420. Your manager has heard a lot about the VLAN feature available on switches and is wondering what the benefit is. What would your response be?

(A) To create communication boundaries

(B) Filters traffic based off layer-3 address

(C) Filters traffic based off layer-4 address

(D) Used to prevent loops on the network

421. Which of the following switch features would you use to create multiple broadcast domains?

(A) STP

(B) VTP

(C) CDP

(D) VLANs

422. You wish to view the VLAN configuration on the switch. What command do you use?

(A) `show port-security addresses`

(B) `show vlan`

(C) `show mac-address table`

(D) `show interfaces`

423. You are troubleshooting communication problems and suspect that a port is in the wrong VLAN. What command can you use to verify the VLANs that exist and what ports exist in each VLAN?

(A) `show vlan`

(B) `display all vlan`

(C) `show all vlan`

(D) `display vlans`

424. Which of the following protocols are used to carry VLAN traffic between switches? (Choose two.)

(A) VTP

(B) STP

(C) 802.1q

(D) ISL

(E) IGRP

425. What command would you use on a port to specify that it is allowed to carry all VLAN traffic across the port?

(A) `switchport mode trunk`

(B) `switchport mode vlan`

(C) `switchport mode access`

(D) `switchport mode vlanaccess`

426. Which of the following commands is used to create a VLAN name Floor1?

(A) `new vlan Floor1`

(B) `vlan Floor1`

(C) `create vlan Floor1`

(D) `vlan 2 name Floor1`

427. Which of the following commands is used to place port 6 in VLAN 2?

   (A)   Use the following commands:

       Switch(config)#`interface f0/6`

       Switch(config-if)#`switchport access`

   (B)   Use the following commands:

       Switch(config)# `switchport access vlan 2`

   (C)   Use the following commands:

       Switch(config)#`interface f0/6`

       Switch(config-if)#`switchport access vlan 2`

   (D)   Use the following commands:

       Switch(config)#`interface f0/8`

       Switch(config-if)#`switchport access vlan 2`

Chapter 12

Troubleshooting Network Communication

....

Knowing how to configure a Cisco router and switch is only a small portion of what you need to know in order to pass both the ICND1 and the ICND2 exams. A big part of each exam is ensuring you know how to troubleshoot problems with communication and the configuration. This chapter presents a number of common troubleshooting scenarios testing your knowledge of different commands and your ability to identify problems.

The Problems You'll Work On

In this chapter, you'll review questions concerning the following topics:

- ✔ Using commands to help troubleshoot and diagnose network related problems
- ✔ Troubleshooting connectivity issues
- ✔ Using show commands to troubleshoot configuration issues
- ✔ Using debug commands to diagnose a problem

What to Watch Out For

Don't let common mistakes trip you up; watch for the following when working with these questions:

- ✔ Troubleshoot layer-1 and layer-2 characteristics of the network first when you're having connectivity issues. When troubleshooting layer 1, ensure that you are using the correct cables and that they are properly connected to the ports by checking for a link light. When troubleshooting layer 2, ensure that the data link protocol is set (Ethernet, PPP, or HDLC) and verify related settings, such as the clock rate.
- ✔ After verifying the physical aspect of the network, you can then check the logical aspect, such as the network layer (layer 3). When troubleshooting layer 3, verify the IP address configuration and routing table information.
- ✔ Ensure you know the different show commands, such as `show ip route`, `show interfaces`, `show ip interface brief`, and `show cdp neighbors detail`. Many ICND1 exam questions test your knowledge about how to troubleshoot using the `show` commands.

Troubleshooting Commands

428–432 Choose the best answer(s).

428. You are troubleshooting communication to another device. What is the result of the command being executed in the figure below?

```
NY-R1>ping 24.0.0.2

Type escape sequence to abort.
Sending 5, 100-byte ICMP Echos to 24.0.0.2, timeout is 2 seconds:
!!!!!
```

(A) The pings were unsuccessful.

(B) The pings were successful.

(C) The traceroute was unsuccessful.

(D) The ARP cache is empty.

429. What are the results of the command executing in the figure below?

```
NY-R1>ping 24.0.0.5

Type escape sequence to abort.
Sending 5, 100-byte ICMP Echos to 24.0.0.5, timeout is 2 seconds:
.....
```

(A) The pings were unsuccessful.

(B) The pings were successful.

(C) The traceroute was unsuccessful.

(D) The ARP cache is empty.

430. You are troubleshooting communication problems on a network on the other side of the country. What command do you use to identify at what point in the communication pathway there is a failure?

(A) `show ip arp`

(B) `ping ip_address`

(C) `telnet ip_address`

(D) `traceroute ip_address`

431. What command would you use to test VTY port configuration?

(A) `traceroute`

(B) `nslookup`

(C) `ping`

(D) `telnet`

432. You are testing connectivity to a system on a remote network. Using the output shown in the figure below, what is the default gateway setting of this workstation?

```
C:\>tracert 25.0.0.10

Tracing route to 25.0.0.10 over a maximum of 30 hops:

  1    13 ms      9 ms      7 ms     23.0.0.1
  2    13 ms     13 ms      8 ms     24.0.0.2
  3    19 ms     18 ms     23 ms     25.0.0.10

Trace complete.
```

(A) 23.0.0.1

(B) 24.0.0.2

(C) 25.0.0.10

(D) 25.0.0.1

Troubleshooting Connectivity Issues

433–444 Choose the best answer(s).

433. You are connecting a switch to a router. What type of cable should you use?

(A) Straight-through

(B) Console

(C) Serial

(D) Crossover

434. You have your workstation connected to port 6 on the switch, but are unable to communicate on the network. What should you do first?

(A) Use `ipconfig`.

(B) Ping another system.

(C) Check the routing table.

(D) Verify your cable is connected properly.

435. You are connecting two switches together. What type of cable should you use?

(A) Straight-through

(B) Console

(C) Serial

(D) Crossover

436. You receive the following output when looking at the show interfaces command. What should you check?

```
Serial0/2/0 is down, line protocol is down
```

(A) Check the physical aspects of the link, such as the cable.

(B) Check that the IP address is set.

(C) Check that the data link protocol is configured.

(D) Verify that a route is defined to the remote network.

437. You are the network administrator for a small network running three VLANs on a switch. You have connected a workstation to port 8 on the switch and assigned it a valid IP address for that network. You try to communicate with another system on the network, but are unable to. What could be the problem?

(A) You have the wrong IP assigned.

(B) CDP is running on the switch.

(C) STP is blocking communication between the VLANs.

(D) You are connected to a port in a different VLAN than the other system.

438. Looking at the figure below, Computer A is initiating communication to Computer B and sends out an ARP request. Which device responds with the ARP reply message?

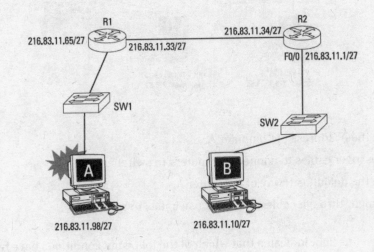

(A) SW1

(B) R1

(C) R2

(D) Computer B

439. You are the network administrator for a company that has users located in different offices. The network configuration is shown in the figure below. You have connected the switches to the routers with a crossover cable, and the computers to the switches with straight-through cables. Computer A cannot ping Computer B. What should you do?

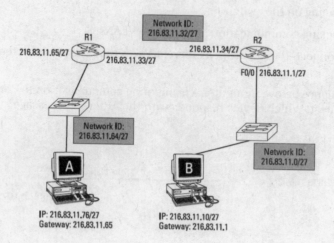

(A) Change the IP address of Computer A.

(B) Use crossover cables to connect computers to switches.

(C) Change the default gateway of Computer A.

(D) Use straight-through cables to connect switches to routers.

440. Having a green link light indicates that which of the following conditions have been met? (Select two.)

(A) A layer-3 protocol has been assigned at either end of the link.

(B) The network media is attached at both ends of the link.

(C) The IP address on the interface has been configured.

(D) A layer-2 protocol has been loaded and configured at either end of the link.

441. You are the network administrator for a company that has users located in different offices. The network configuration is shown in the figure below. You have connected the switches to the routers with a straight-through cable, and the computers to the switches with straight-through cables. Computer A cannot ping Computer B. What should you do?

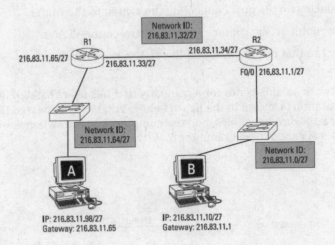

(A) Change the cable type connecting the switches to the routers.

(B) Change the cable type connecting the computers to the switches.

(C) Change the IP address on Computer A.

(D) Change the IP address of Computer B.

(E) Change the IP address on R1.

442. You use the following commands to create an access control list on the FastEthernet port of the router. Users are now reporting that they cannot communicate with the intranet site. What is the problem?

```
R1(config)# access-list 102 permit tcp any any eq 23
R1(config)# access-list 102 permit tcp any any eq 25
R1(config)# interface fastethernet0/1
R1(config-if)# ip access-group 102 in
```

(A) The first line should not be permit.

(B) The second line should not be permit.

(C) There is an implied deny all traffic at the end of the ACL.

(D) The `ip access group` command should not be used.

443. You have a switch using multiple VLANs that is connected to a router using a straight-through cable. You have configured the router as a router on the stick. You have configured the sub-interfaces on the router, but communication is not occurring between the VLANs. How do you fix the problem?

(A) Use a crossover cable to connect the switch to the router on a stick.

(B) Enable trunking on the port connecting the switch to the router.

(C) Add static routes so the router can route between the VLANs.

(D) Load RIPv2 so that routing between the VLANs can occur.

444. You are the network administrator for a company that has users located in different offices. The network configuration is shown in the figure below. You have connected the switches to the routers with straight-through cables, and the computers to the switches with straight-through cables. Computer A cannot ping Computer B. Why not?

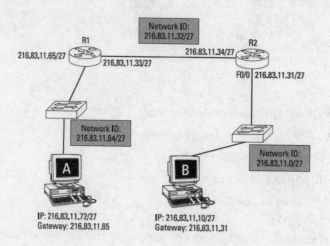

(A) Computer B's default gateway is invalid.

(B) Computer A's default gateway is invalid.

(C) A crossover was used to connect switches to routers.

(D) Computer B's IP address is incorrect.

Using Show Commands to Troubleshoot

445–462 Choose the best answer(s).

445. Looking at the output of the show interfaces command seen in the figure below, what is the MAC of the interface using the IP address 23.0.0.1?

```
NY-R1>show interfaces

FastEthernet0/0 is up, line protocol is up
  Hardware is Lance, address is 0010.11d9.d001 (bia 0010.11d9.d001)
  Internet address is 23.0.0.1/8
  MTU 1500 bytes, BW 100000 Kbit, DLY 100 usec, rely 255/255, load 1/255
  Encapsulation ARPA, loopback not set
  ARP type: ARPA, ARP Timeout 04:00:00,

(output cut for briefness)

FastEthernet0/1 is administratively down, line protocol is down
  Hardware is Lance, address is 0010.11d9.d002 (bia 0010.11d9.d002)
  MTU 1500 bytes, BW 100000 Kbit, DLY 100 usec, rely 255/255, load 1/255
  Encapsulation ARPA, loopback not set

(Output has been cut for briefness)

Serial0/2/0 is up, line protocol is up
  Hardware is HD64570
  Internet address is 24.0.0.1/8
  MTU 1500 bytes, BW 128 Kbit, DLY 20000 usec, rely 255/255, load 1/255
  Encapsulation HDLC, loopback not set, keepalive set (10 sec)
  (Output has been cut for briefness)
```

(A) HD64570

(B) ffff.ffff.ffff

(C) 0010.11d9.d002

(D) 0010.11d9.d001

446. What command was used to create the output shown in the figure below?

```
Address         Age (min)  Hardware Addr   Interface
23.0.0.1            -       0010.11D9.D001  FastEthernet0/0
23.0.0.10           4       0011.9520.8c27  FastEthernet0/0
23.0.0.100          10      0006.d6ab.a040  FastEthernet0/0

(Columns have been removed for briefness)
```

(A) show interfaces

(B) show ip arp

(C) show ip interface brief

(D) show controllers

447. Which of the following commands can you use to figure out the IP address of a neighboring router?

(A) `show cdp neighbors`

(B) `show cdp neighbors detail`

(C) `show cdp`

(D) `cdp run`

448. Looking at the output of the show interfaces command seen in the figure below, what is the encapsulation protocol being used by the serial port?

```
NY-R1>show interfaces

FastEthernet0/0 is up, line protocol is up
  Hardware is Lance, address is 0010.11d9.d001 (bia 0010.11d9.d001)
  Internet address is 23.0.0.1/8
  MTU 1500 bytes, BW 100000 Kbit, DLY 100 usec, rely 255/255, load 1/255
  Encapsulation ARPA, loopback not set
  ARP type: ARPA, ARP Timeout 04:00:00,

(output cut for briefness)

FastEthernet0/1 is administratively down, line protocol is down
  Hardware is Lance, address is 0010.11d9.d002 (bia 0010.11d9.d002)
  MTU 1500 bytes, BW 100000 Kbit, DLY 100 usec, rely 255/255, load 1/255
  Encapsulation ARPA, loopback not set

(Output has been cut for briefness)

Serial0/2/0 is up, line protocol is up
  Hardware is HD64570
  Internet address is 24.0.0.1/8
  MTU 1500 bytes, BW 128 Kbit, DLY 20000 usec, rely 255/255, load 1/255
  Encapsulation HDLC, loopback not set, keepalive set (10 sec)
  (Output has been cut for briefness)
```

(A) CDP

(B) PPP

(C) STP

(D) HDLC

449. Looking at the output in the figure below, what end of the point-to-point link is Serial0/2/0?

```
NY-R1#show controllers serial0/2/0
Interface Serial0/2/0
Hardware is PowerQUICC MPC860
DCE V.35, clock rate 64000

(output has been cut for briefness)
```

(A) DCE

(B) DTE

(C) MPC8600

(D) PowerQUICC

450. If an interface shows as administratively down, what command do you use to bring the interface up?

(A) `up`

(B) `enable`

(C) `no shutdown`

(D) `no down`

451. How do you view your ARP cache on a Cisco router? (Select two.)

(A) `show ip arp`

(B) `arp -a`

(C) `arp -show`

(D) `show arp`

452. Looking at the output in the figure below, what is the clock rate of serial0/2/0?

```
NY-R1#show controllers serial0/2/0
Interface Serial0/2/0
Hardware is PowerQUICC MPC860
DCE V.35, clock rate 64000

(output has been cut for briefness)
```

(A) 35 Kbps

(B) 64 Kbps

(C) 128 Kbps

(D) 860 Kbps

453. You receive the following output from the `show interfaces` command. What should you check?

```
Serial0/2/0 is up, line protocol is down
```

(A) Check the physical aspects of the link, such as the cable.

(B) Check that the IP address is set.

(C) Check that the data link protocol is configured.

(D) Verify that a route is defined to the remote network.

454. Looking at the output of the `show interfaces` command seen in the figure below, which of the following statements is true?

```
NY-R1>show interfaces

FastEthernet0/0 is up, line protocol is up
  Hardware is Lance, address is 0010.11d9.d001 (bia 0010.11d9.d001)
  Internet address is 23.0.0.1/8
  MTU 1500 bytes, BW 100000 Kbit, DLY 100 usec, rely 255/255, load 1/255
  Encapsulation ARPA, loopback not set
  ARP type: ARPA, ARP Timeout 04:00:00,

(output cut for briefness)

FastEthernet0/1 is administratively down, line protocol is down
  Hardware is Lance, address is 0010.11d9.d002 (bia 0010.11d9.d002)
  MTU 1500 bytes, BW 100000 Kbit, DLY 100 usec, rely 255/255, load 1/255
  Encapsulation ARPA, loopback not set

(Output has been cut for briefness)

Serial0/2/0 is up, line protocol is up
  Hardware is HD64570
  Internet address is 24.0.0.1/8
  MTU 1500 bytes, BW 128 Kbit, DLY 20000 usec, rely 255/255, load 1/255
  Encapsulation HDLC, loopback not set, keepalive set (10 sec)
  (Output has been cut for briefness)
```

(A) Serial port is using PPP.

(B) FastEthernet0/0 has no IP assigned.

(C) The bandwidth of FastEthernet0/0 is 1 Gbps.

(D) FastEthernet0/1 has not been configured.

455. You are having trouble communicating with a remote network. You have checked the status of the interfaces: Each interface is up, and the IP addresses look fine. What command do you use next?

(A) `show ip route`

(B) `show ip interface brief`

(C) `show controllers serial 0/0`

(D) `show cdp`

456. Which of the following commands would you use to troubleshoot issues at layer 3? (Select three.)

(A) `show ip interface brief`

(B) `show interfaces`

(C) `show protocols`

(D) `show controllers`

(E) `show ip route`

457. What command do you use to view whether your serial port is the DCE or DTE device?

(A) `show interface serial 0/0`

(B) `show controllers serial 0/0`

(C) `show ip protocols serial 0/0`

(D) `show serial 0/0`

458. Which of the following commands would you use to check for issues at layers 1 and 2? (Select two.)

(A) `show ip interface brief`

(B) `show interfaces`

(C) `show protocols`

(D) `show controllers`

(E) `show ip route`

459. Which of the following could be an indication of excessive collisions or bad packets submitted by a malfunctioning network card? (Select two.)

(A) Runt

(B) Bandwidth

(C) CRC

(D) MTU

460. Looking at the output in the figure below, how many packets have been received that were less than 64 bytes?

```
NY-R1>show interface fastethernet0/0
FastEthernet0/0 is up, line protocol is up (connected)
  Hardware is Lance, address is 0001.63c6.0d01 (bia 0001.63c6.0d01)
  Internet address is 10.0.0.1/8
  MTU 1500 bytes, BW 100000 Kbit, DLY 100 usec,
     reliability 255/255, txload 1/255, rxload 1/255
  Encapsulation ARPA, loopback not set
  ARP type: ARPA, ARP Timeout 04:00:00,
  Last input 00:00:08, output 00:00:05, output hang never
  Last clearing of "show interface" counters never
  Input queue: 0/75/0 (size/max/drops); Total output drops: 0
  Queueing strategy: fifo
  Output queue :0/40 (size/max)
  5 minute input rate 1150 bits/sec, 1 packets/sec
  5 minute output rate 1150 bits/sec, 1 packets/sec
     1689 packets input, 216192 bytes, 0 no buffer
     Received 4 broadcasts, 6 runts, 0 giants, 0 throttles
     0 input errors, 3 CRC, 0 frame, 0 overrun, 0 ignored, 0 abort
     0 input packets with dribble condition detected
     1693 packets output, 216308 bytes, 0 underruns
     0 output errors, 87 collisions, 1 interface resets
     0 babbles, 0 late collision, 0 deferred
     0 lost carrier, 0 no carrier
     0 output buffer failures, 0 output buffers swapped out
```

(A) 3

(B) 6

(C) 87

(D) 216,380

461. You would like to see the number of runt packets received. What command would you use?

(A) show cdp

(B) show cdp neighbors detail

(C) show ip interface brief

(D) show interfaces

462. You are troubleshooting performance issues on the network and suspect that a high number of packets are being retransmitted due to collisions. You use the show interface command to view the status on the interface. Looking at the output in the figure below, how many packets have been retransmitted due to collisions?

```
NY-R1>show interface fastethernet0/0
FastEthernet0/0 is up, line protocol is up (connected)
  Hardware is Lance, address is 0001.63c6.0d01 (bia 0001.63c6.0d01)
  Internet address is 10.0.0.1/8
  MTU 1500 bytes, BW 100000 Kbit, DLY 100 usec,
     reliability 255/255, txload 1/255, rxload 1/255
  Encapsulation ARPA, loopback not set
  ARP type: ARPA, ARP Timeout 04:00:00,
  Last input 00:00:08, output 00:00:05, output hang never
  Last clearing of "show interface" counters never
  Input queue: 0/75/0 (size/max/drops); Total output drops: 0
  Queueing strategy: fifo
  Output queue :0/40 (size/max)
  5 minute input rate 1150 bits/sec, 1 packets/sec
  5 minute output rate 1150 bits/sec, 1 packets/sec
     1689 packets input, 216192 bytes, 0 no buffer
     Received 4 broadcasts, 6 runts, 0 giants, 0 throttles
     0 input errors, 3 CRC, 0 frame, 0 overrun, 0 ignored, 0 abort
     0 input packets with dribble condition detected
     1693 packets output, 216308 bytes, 0 underruns
     0 output errors, 87 collisions, 1 interface resets
     0 babbles, 0 late collision, 0 deferred
     0 lost carrier, 0 no carrier
     0 output buffer failures, 0 output buffers swapped out
```

(A) 3

(B) 6

(C) 87

(D) 216,380

Using Debug Commands

463–465 Choose the best answer(s).

463. Which of the following commands is recommended to disable debugging?

(A) `no debug ip all`

(B) `no debug ip nat`

(C) `no debug ip rip`

(D) `no debug all`

464. You are troubleshooting problems with RIP and suspect that your router is no longer receiving RIP updates. What command would you use to help diagnose the problem?

(A) `debug ip rip`

(B) `debug all`

(C) `no debug all`

(D) `show interfaces`

465. You would like to view the details of all packets sent or received by the router. What command would you use?

(A) debug ip rip

(B) debug ip route

(C) debug ip ospf

(D) debug ip packet

Chapter 13

Cisco Device Security Best Practices

• •

*T*he CCNA certification expects IT professionals to have a working knowledge of how to configure a Cisco router and switch in a secure manner. CCNA certified professionals are expected to be able to configure proper banners, passwords, port security, and communication protocols. This chapter tests you on these issues and more.

The Problems You'll Work On

In this chapter, you'll review questions concerning the following topics:

- ✔ Using strong passwords and encrypting passwords in the configuration
- ✔ Configuring port security on your switches to limit which systems can connect to the port
- ✔ Using communication protocols that encrypt communication
- ✔ Creating usernames and passwords that are used to log in to the device

What to Watch Out For

Don't let common mistakes trip you up; watch for the following when working with these questions:

When answering questions for the CCNA exam(s), watch for choices involving security features that should be used. Here are a few key points to remember when answering security-related questions:

- ✔ Use strong passwords and encrypt passwords.
- ✔ Ensure that after the password is configured for a port, the login command is used to force the device to prompt for a password.
- ✔ If you have configured usernames and passwords for the device, ensure that you have used the login local command so that the device prompts for both a username and password.
- ✔ Always encrypt communication with SSH when possible.

Security Basics

466. What type of attack involves the hacker overloading a system and causing the system to crash or not perform its job role?

   (A)   Buffer overflow attack

   (B)   DoS attack

   (C)   Dictionary attack

   (D)   MiTM attack

467. You would like to control communication between the accounting and marketing groups. What feature of a Cisco switch will allow you to do this?

   (A)   CDP

   (B)   Port mirroring

   (C)   VLANs

   (D)   Port security

468. What network technology could be used to encrypt communication from point A to point B over an untrusted network?

   (A)   VPN

   (B)   VLAN

   (C)   NAP

   (D)   NAT

469. What type of firewall can filter traffic by analyzing the payload of a packet?

   (A)   Stateful packet inspection firewall

   (B)   Packet filtering firewall

   (C)   Application layer firewall

   (D)   Network address translation

470. What type of firewall filters traffic based on the context of the conversation and the layer-3 and layer-4 header?

   (A)   Packet filtering firewall

   (B)   Application layer firewall

   (C)   Proxy server

   (D)   Stateful packet inspection firewall

471. What type of attack involves the hacker altering the source IP address of a packet in order to bypass your packet filtering rules on the router?

(A) MiTM

(B) Spoofing

(C) DoS

(D) Buffer overflow

472. Your manager has asked you make sure that the Cisco router configuration files are protected from the intruders on the Internet. Which actions would you recommend? (Select two.)

(A) Only allow unrestricted access to the VTY ports.

(B) Use a firewall to control access to the device from the Internet.

(C) Use Telnet to remotely configure the device.

(D) Use SSH to remotely configure the device.

473. You are helping the security team create a network security plan for the business. Which of the following should you include in the plan?

(A) Disable antivirus automatic updates in order to reduce traffic.

(B) Lock network equipment in a secure location.

(C) Ensure that all Telnet ports use the password of telnet.

(D) Ensure to use the no service-password encryption command.

Security Configuration

474–479 Choose the best answer(s).

474. You have been asked to review the running-configuration of a customer's router and identify potential security issues related to the configuration. Review the output of the show running-config command, shown below. Which of the following are potential security issues with this configuration? (Select two.)

```
ROUTERB#show running-config

Building configuration...


(output omitted for briefness)

service timestamps log datetime msec

no service password-encryption

!

hostname ROUTERB

!

ip subnet-zero
```

```
!
interface FastEthernet0/1
  ip address 27.0.0.1 255.0.0.0
  no ip directed-broadcast
!
interface Serial0/0/0
  ip address 26.0.0.2 255.0.0.0
  no ip directed-broadcast
!
router rip
  network 26.0.0.0
  network 27.0.0.0
!
banner motd
Welcome to Glen's router! You have connected to 192.168.0.1!
!
line con 0
  password myc0nP@ss
  login

line aux 0
line vty 0 4
  password telnet
  login
end
```

(A)   The console password is not a complex password.

(B)   Passwords are not encrypted.

(C)   ip subnet zero is being used.

(D)   The banner is using inappropriate text.

475. The junior IT technician has configured the router for usernames and passwords, but the router is not prompting for usernames and passwords when connecting to the console port. You review the configuration, shown below. What is the problem?

```
ROUTERB#show running-config

Building configuration...

(output omitted for briefness)
no service password-encryption
!
hostname ROUTERB
!
ip subnet-zero
!
Username bob password P@ssw0rd
Username sue password Pa$$w0rd
!
interface FastEthernet0/1
  ip address 27.0.0.1 255.0.0.0
  no ip directed-broadcast
!
interface Serial0/0/0
  ip address 26.0.0.2 255.0.0.0
  no ip directed-broadcast
!
line con 0
  login

line aux 0
line vty 0 4
  password telnet
  login
end
```

    (A)   The console password is missing.

    (B)   Passwords are not encrypted.

    (C)   ip subnet zero is being used.

    (D)   The login local command should be used.

476. Sue has configured the console port with a password, but it does not seem to work. You review the configuration, shown below. What is causing the problem?

```
ROUTERB#show running-config

Building configuration...

(output omitted for briefness)
!
hostname ROUTERB
!
ip subnet-zero
!
interface FastEthernet0/1
  ip address 27.0.0.1 255.0.0.0
  no ip directed-broadcast
!
interface Serial0/0/0
  ip address 26.0.0.2 255.0.0.0
  no ip directed-broadcast
!
line con 0
  password Con$0le1

line aux 0
line vty 0 4
end
```

    (A)   The console password is not complex.

    (B)   Passwords are not encrypted.

    (C)   The `login` command is missing.

    (D)   The `login local` command is missing.

477. For security reasons, you have decided to disable the built-in web server on the Cisco device. Which command would you use?

    (A)   R1(config)#`no ip http server`

    (B)   R1(config)#`disable ip http server`

    (C)   R1(config)#`ip http server off`

    (D)   R1(config)#`ip http server disabled`

478. You would like to create a user named Bob that has privilege level 3. What command would you use?

    (A)   R1(config)#`username Bob password P@ssw0rd level 3`

    (B)   R1(config)#`username Bob privilege 3 password P@ssw0rd`

    (C)   R1#`username Bob privilege 3 password P@ssw0rd`

    (D)   R1#`username Bob password P@ssw0rd level 3`

479. How would you view your current privilege level on a Cisco device?

    (A)   `display privilege`

    (B)   `display level`

    (C)   `show level`

    (D)   `show privilege`

Switch Security

480–488 Choose the best answer(s).

480. What command is used to disable a port on the switch?

(A) switch(config)#shutdown port 5

(B) switch(config-if)#shutdown

(C) switch(config)#port 5 shutdown

(D) switch(config-if)#disable

481. You have been asked to configure port number 4 to only allow the system that is currently connected to the port access to the network via that port. What Cisco switch feature would you use?

(A) Maximum MAC addresses

(B) MAC address table

(C) STP

(D) Sticky

482. Which violation mode would you use to disable a port when an unauthorized device connects to the port, and have the port disabled until the administrator enables it?

(A) Restrict

(B) Shutdown

(C) Protect

(D) Disable

483. Which feature allows you to control which workstations can connect to a specific port on the switch?

(A) Port mirroring

(B) VLANs

(C) Port security

(D) MAC address table

484. You are trying to connect a system to a port on the switch, but having no luck. You use the `show interface f0/5` command to view the status of the port and receive the output shown below. What should you do to allow the system to connect via the port?

```
SW1#show interface f0/5
FastEthernet0/5 is administratively down, line protocol is down (disabled)
  Hardware is Lance, address is 0060.2fba.e405 (bia 0060.2fba.e405)
BW 100000 Kbit, DLY 1000 usec,
  reliability 255/255, txload 1/255, rxload 1/255
Encapsulation ARPA, loopback not set
Keepalive set (10 sec)
Half-duplex, 100Mb/s
```

    (A)   Change the MAC on the port.

    (B)   Change the IP on the port.

    (C)   Alter the MAC address table.

    (D)   Enable the port.

485. You wish to limit which device can connect to each port on the switch by configuring port security with the MAC address of each system currently connected to the switch. What command would you use?

    (A)   SW1(config-if)#`switchport port-security mac-address sticky`

    (B)   SW1(config-if)#`switchport port-security`

    (C)   SW1(config-if)#`mac-address sticky`

    (D)   SW1(config-if)#`port-security mac-address automatic`

486. Which of the following port modes supports the port security feature?

    (A)   secure

    (B)   trunk

    (C)   access

    (D)   workstation

487. You would like to configure port 5 on your switch to allow only one system to connect to the port that uses the MAC address of 1111.2222.3333. Which of the following configurations would you use?

(A) Use the following command:

```
SW1(config)#switchport mode access
SW1(config)#switchport port-security
SW1(config)#switchport port-security mac-address 1111.2222.3333
SW1(config)#switchport port-security maximum 1
SW1(config)#switchport port-security violation shutdown
```

(B) Use the following command:

```
SW1(config)#interface f0/5
SW1(config-if)#switchport mode access
SW1(config-if)#switchport port-security
SW1(config-if)#switchport port-security mac-address 1111.2222.3333
SW1(config-if)#switchport port-security maximum 1
SW1(config-if)#switchport port-security violation shutdown
```

(C) Use the following command:

```
SW1(config)#interface f0/5
SW1(config-if)#switchport mode access
SW1(config-if)#switchport port-security
SW1(config-if)#switchport port-security mac-address sticky
SW1(config-if)#switchport port-security maximum 1
SW1(config-if)#switchport port-security violation shutdown
```

(D) Use the following command:

```
SW1(config)#interface f0/5
SW1(config-if)#switchport mode trunk
SW1(config-if)#switchport port-security
SW1(config-if)#switchport port-security mac-address 1111.2222.3333
SW1(config-if)#switchport port-security maximum 1
SW1(config-if)#switchport port-security violation shutdown
```

488. Your manager would like to use a single system on the network for monitoring network traffic. You have connected the monitoring system to port 12 on the switch, but you are unable to monitor network traffic. What do you need to do? (Select two.)

(A) Connect the monitoring system to port 1 on the switch.

(B) Configure port security.

(C) Configure VLANs on the switch.

(D) Configure port mirroring on the switch.

Configuring Passwords

489–494 Choose the best answer(s).

489. You wish to have the Cisco device prompt you for a username and password. What command would you use?

(A) `router(config)#login local`

(B) `router(config-line)#login local`

(C) `router(config)#login`

(D) `router(config-line)#login`

490. Your manager would like all passwords encrypted in the configuration files on the Cisco routers and switches. What command is used to encrypt all passwords in the configuration files?

(A) `router#service password-encryption`

(B) `router(config)#enable service password-encryption`

(C) `router#enable service password-encryption`

(D) `router(config)#service password-encryption`

491. Which of the following commands are used to configure a password on your console port and ensure that the router prompts for a password anytime someone connects to that port?

(A) Use the following commands:

ROUTERA(config)#password con

ROUTERA(config)#login.

(B) Use the following commands:

ROUTERA(config)#line vty 0 4

ROUTERA(config-line)#password con

ROUTERA(config-line)#login.

(C) Use the following commands:

ROUTERA(config)#line con 0

ROUTERA(config-line)#password con

ROUTERA(config-line)#login.

(D) Use the following commands:

ROUTERA(config)#line con 0

ROUTERA(config-line)#password con.

492. You wish to create a username Rebecca with a password of mypass, what command would you use?

(A) router(config)#enable user rebecca password mypass

(B) router(config-if)#username rebecca password mypass

(C) router(config)#create user rebecca password mypass

(D) router(config)#username rebecca password mypass

493. You wish to configure a password for priv exec mode but have the password encrypted in the configuration file. What command would you use?

(A) enable secret P@ssw0rd

(B) enable password P@ssw0rd

(C) enable encrypted password P@ssw0rd

(D) enable secure password P@ssw0rd

494. What is the difference between the login command and the login local command?

(A) Login prompts for a username and password, whereas login local prompts for a password.

(B) Login is used for Telnet access, whereas login local is used for access using the local console port.

(C) Login is used for local console port access, whereas login local is used for Telnet access.

(D) Login prompts for a password, whereas login local prompts for a username and password.

Configuring Banners

495–497 Choose the best answer(s).

495. You are configuring banners on your Cisco router. Which of the following banners is displayed last?

(A) The exec banner

(B) The login banner

(C) The MOTD banner

(D) All banners are shown at the same time.

496. Which of the following commands configures a proper message of the day banner?

(A) Use the following commands:

```
R1(config)#banner motd #
R1(config)#This device is for authorized individuals only.
$
```

(B) Use the following commands:

```
R1#banner motd #
R1#This device is for authorized individuals only.
#
```

(C) Use the following commands:

```
R1(config)#banner motd #
R1(config)#This device is for authorized individuals only.
#
```

(D) Use the following commands:

```
R1(config)# motd banner
R1(config)#This device is for authorized individuals only.
```

497. Which of the following banner type displays before the user is asked to log in, but after the MOTD banner?

(A) Exec

(B) MOTD

(C) Logout

(D) Login

Remote Management

498–503 Choose the best answer(s).

498. Your manager would like to ensure that remote access to the router is only allowed using a secure communication protocol. Which command would you use?

(A) router(config)#transport input ssh

(B) router(config-line)#transport input ssh

(C) router(config-line)#transport input both

(D) router(config-line)#transport input telnet

499. You are responsible for configuring Telnet access to the router. Which of the following commands would you use to ensure a username and password are required for Telnet access?

(A) Use the following commands:

ROUTERA(config)#username bob password pass

ROUTERA(config)#line con 0

ROUTERA(config-line)#login local.

(B) Use the following commands:

ROUTERA(config)#username bob password pass

ROUTERA(config)#line vty 0 4

ROUTERA(config-line)#login.

(C) Use the following commands:

ROUTERA#username bob password pass

ROUTERA#config term

ROUTERA(config)#line vty 0 4

ROUTERA(config-line)#login.

(D) Use the following commands:

ROUTERA(config)#username bob password pass

ROUTERA(config)#line vty 0 4

ROUTERA(config-line)#login local.

500. You want to remotely manage your Cisco devices. What protocol should you use?

(A) Telnet

(B) SSH

(C) HTTP

(D) FTP

501. You are having trouble telnetting into a router from your client system. You can successfully ping the IP address of the router. What may be the problem?

(A)   The default gateway is incorrect.

(B)   There is no Telnet password.

(C)   The subnet mask on the client is incorrect.

(D)   The IP address on the client is on the wrong subnet.

502. Which of the following commands are used to configure the router to only support SSH for remote management?

(A)   Use the following commands:

R1(config)#crypto key generate rsa

R1(config)#line vty 0 4

R1(config-line)#login local

R1(config-line)#transport input ssh

(B)   Use the following commands:

R1(config)#crypto key generate rsa

R1(config)#line vty 0 4

R1(config-line)#login local

(C)   Use the following commands:

R1(config)#crypto key generate rsa

R1(config)#line vty 0 4

R1(config-line)#transport input telnet

(D)   Use the following commands:

R1(config)#crypto key generate rsa

R1(config)#line ssh 0 4

R1(config-line)#login local

R1(config-line)#transport input ssh

503. What command would you use to configure the Telnet ports to support both SSH and Telnet as protocols?

(A)   transport input ssh

(B)   transport input telnet

(C)   transport input ssh telnet

(D)   transport input http

Chapter 14

Introduction to Wireless Networking

· ·

A huge part of networking today is working with wireless networks. When preparing for your ICND1 exam, it is important to have the basics of wireless networking down, including wireless standards and security best practices. This chapter helps prepare you for any wireless networking questions you may get by testing you on wireless basics, standards, and protocols.

The Problems You'll Work On

In this chapter, you'll review questions concerning the following topics:

✔ Understanding wireless networking basics, such as the types of wireless networks

✔ Understanding wireless standards and their characteristics

✔ Getting familiar with wireless networking security best practices

✔ Handling wireless connectivity issues

What to Watch Out For

Don't let common mistakes trip you up; watch for the following when working with these questions:

✔ A number of different agencies deal with wireless as a standard. The Federal Communications Commission (FCC) is responsible for regulating the use of wireless devices and frequencies, whereas the Institute of Electrical and Electronics Engineers (IEEE) is responsible for defining the wireless standards. The Wi-Fi Alliance is responsible for ensuring compatibility and interoperability of wireless networking components.

✔ Some types of wireless networks, such as ad-hoc wireless networks, involve wireless clients connecting to one another without the use of an access point. This is also known as an *independent basic service set (IBSS)*. Using a wireless access point to connect all your wireless devices means you are running wireless in infrastructure mode, also known as a *basic service set (BSS)*. Using multiple access points to allow users to roam throughout the building is known as an *extended service set (ESS)*.

Wireless Basics

504–524 Choose the best answer(s).

504. What type of wireless network involves two wireless clients connecting to one another?

(A) FCC

(B) Infrastructure

(C) Domain-based

(D) Ad-hoc

505. Which of the following is considered the name of the wireless network?

(A) ESS

(B) SSID

(C) TKIP

(D) FCC

506. Which agency is responsible for defining the wireless standards?

(A) Wi-Fi Alliance

(B) FCC

(C) IETF

(D) IEEE

507. In the figure shown below, what type of wireless network exists?

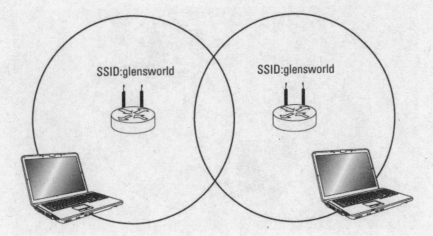

    (A)   ESS

    (B)   BSS

    (C)   TKIP

    (D)   FCC

508. Which of the following devices could cause interference with your wireless network? (Select two.)

    (A)   TV remote

    (B)   Cordless phone

    (C)   Microwave

    (D)   Toaster

509. You are installing a wireless network for a small office environment. The manager is worried that someone in the parking lot can connect to the wireless network. What could you do to help minimize the chances of that happening?

    (A)   Change the SSID.

    (B)   Change the ESSID.

    (C)   Enable SSID broadcasting.

    (D)   Change the power levels on the access point.

510. In the figure shown below what type of wireless network exists?

(A) ESS

(B) TKIP

(C) BSS

(D) FCC

511. You are experiencing intermittent problems with your wireless network and you suspect it is interference from other wireless devices. What can you do to solve the problem?

(A) Change the SSID.

(B) Enable MAC filtering.

(C) Disable SSID broadcasting.

(D) Change the channel on the wireless access point.

512. What type of wireless network involves the wireless clients connecting to a wireless access point to access the network?

(A) FCC

(B) Infrastructure

(C) Domain-based

(D) Ad-hoc

513. Which of the following facts are true of the WLAN diagram displayed below? (Select two.)

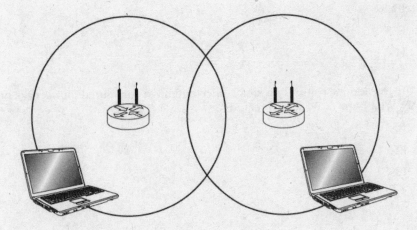

(A) The diagram represents an ESS network with each access point using a different SSID.

(B) The diagram represents an ESS network with both access points using the same SSID.

(C) The diagram represents a BSS network with both access points using the same SSID.

(D) Each access point is using a different channel.

(E) Each access point is using the same channel.

514. Which of the following are requirements for an ESS network? (Select three.)

(A) Use multiple access points with different SSIDs.

(B) Use multiple access points with the same SSIDs.

(C) Each access point uses a different frequency range.

(D) Each access point uses the same frequency range.

(E) Access points must overlap by 10 percent or greater.

(F) Access points must overlap by less than 10 percent.

515. Which agency is responsible for regulating the use of wireless and wireless frequencies?

(A) Wi-Fi Alliance

(B) IEEE

(C) IETF

(D) FCC

516. Which of the following is another term for an ad-hoc wireless network?

    (A) BSS

    (B) IBSS

    (C) ESS

    (D) FCC

517. You are the administrator for a small office and have configured four access points to create the WLAN. What type of WLAN is created?

    (A) BSS

    (B) ESS

    (C) IBSS

    (D) FCC

518. Which type of wireless network uses a single wireless access point with an SSID assigned?

    (A) BSS

    (B) ESS

    (C) TKIP

    (D) FCC

519. You have manufactured your own wireless network card and would like it tested and certified for Wi-Fi compliance. What organization would do this?

    (A) Wi-Fi Alliance

    (B) IEEE

    (C) IETF

    (D) FCC

520. You have installed a single access point to create a WLAN for a small office. What type of WLAN did you create?

    (A) BSS

    (B) ESS

    (C) TKIP

    (D) FCC

521. Which wireless LAN design ensures that a roaming user does not loose connectivity when moving from one wireless access point to another?

    (A) Ensure that all access points are using the same channel.

    (B) Ensure that each access point has a different SSID.

    (C) Ensure that the manufacturer of the access point and wireless network cards are the same.

    (D) Ensure that the area of coverage by both access points overlaps by at least 10%.

522. Which agency is responsible for ensuring compatibility with wireless networking components?

 (A) Wi-Fi Alliance

 (B) IEEE

 (C) IETF

 (D) FCC

523. Which three wireless channels do not overlap with one another?

 (A) 2, 4, 8

 (B) 1, 6, 11

 (C) 4, 8, 9

 (D) 3, 6, 9

524. Which type of wireless network supports roaming users by having multiple access points share the same SSID?

 (A) BSS

 (B) ESS

 (C) TKIP

 (D) FCC

Wireless Security

525–535 Choose the best answer(s).

525. Which of the following should be done with the SSID on a wireless network in order to follow good security practices? (Select two.)

 (A) Change the SSID.

 (B) Keep the default SSID.

 (C) Enable SSID broadcasting.

 (D) Disable SSID broadcasting.

526. Which of the following represent good security practices for wireless networks? (Select three.)

 (A) Disable WPA2.

 (B) Enable WPA2.

 (C) Disable MAC filtering.

 (D) Enable MAC filtering.

 (E) Enable SSID broadcasting.

 (F) Disable SSID broadcasting.

527. Which of the following wireless encryption protocols is an older protocol using RC4?

  (A) WEP

  (B) WAP

  (C) WPA

  (D) AES

528. Which of the following can be used to restrict which devices can connect to your wireless network?

  (A) Change the SSID

  (B) MAC Filtering

  (C) Enable SSID broadcasting

  (D) WPA2 encryption

529. You are installing a wireless access point for a small office. At a minimum, which wireless parameter must be configured in order for clients to connect to the wireless network?

  (A) MAC filtering

  (B) Port forwarding

  (C) SSID

  (D) WPA2 key

530. You are configuring a wireless network for a customer. What reason would you give the customer as to why WPA should be used instead of WEP for the encryption?

  (A) WPA rotates the key with each packet.

  (B) WPA forces the use of complex passwords.

  (C) WPA uses a 24-bit IV.

  (D) WPA keys stay the same the entire time the client is connected.

531. Which WPA2 mode involves using a pre-shared key as the method of security?

  (A) Personal

  (B) Enterprise

  (C) ESK

  (D) BSS

532. Which wireless encryption protocol uses the TKIP protocol?

  (A) WEP

  (B) WAP

  (C) WPA

  (D) AES

533. Which WPA mode uses a RADIUS server for authentication?

    (A)   Personal

    (B)   Enterprise

    (C)   WPA-PSK

    (D)   BSS

534. Which wireless encryption protocol uses AES for encryption?

    (A)   WEP

    (B)   WPA2

    (C)   WPA

    (D)   TKIP

535. What method of encryption does WPA2 use?

    (A)   RC4

    (B)   RC2

    (C)   AES-CCMP

    (D)   MD5

Wireless Standards

536–541 Choose the best answer(s).

536. Which wireless standard delivers data at 11 Mbps within the 2.4 GHz frequency range?

    (A)   802.11a

    (B)   802.11b

    (C)   802.11g

    (D)   802.11n

537. Which wireless standard is capable of transferring data over 150 Mbps and runs at both the 2.4 GHz and 5 GHz frequencies?

    (A)   802.11a

    (B)   802.11b

    (C)   802.11g

    (D)   802.11n

538. Which wireless standard runs at 54 Mbps and is compatible with 802.11b?

(A) 802.11a

(B) 802.11x

(C) 802.11g

(D) 802.11n

539. Which wireless network standard runs at 54 Mbps and uses the 5 GHz frequency?

(A) 802.11a

(B) 802.11b

(C) 802.11g

(D) 802.11n

540. Which IEEE standard defines wireless networking?

(A) 802.3

(B) 802.4

(C) 802.5

(D) 802.11

541. Which wireless standard is compatible with 802.11a?

(A) 802.13

(B) 802.11b

(C) 802.11g

(D) 802.11n

Chapter 15

Introduction to WANs

• •

In this chapter, you are tested on the basics of WAN technologies and configuring a serial interface to connect to the WAN environment. You can expect some serial port configuration questions on the Cisco ICND1 and ICND2 exams, along with some common troubleshooting scenarios administrators are faced with.

The Problems You'll Work On

In this chapter, you'll review questions concerning the following topics:

- ✔ Knowing WAN terminology
- ✔ Using different methods to connect to WANs
- ✔ Configuring serial links

What to Watch Out For

Don't let common mistakes trip you up; watch for the following when working with these questions:

- ✔ Know your different WAN technologies, such as circuit switched and packet switched. Circuit switch environments establish a pathway (a circuit) that is used for the duration of the communication. At the end of the conversation, the circuit is disconnected the next time communication occurs, a new circuit is established, and the pathway can be different. Know that the phone system and ISDN are examples of circuit switched environments.

- ✔ A dedicated leased line is a permanent point-to-point link that typically has more bandwidth than a circuit switched environment. T1 and T3 links are examples of leased lines.

- ✔ Packet switched environments deal with routing each packet a different way and then assembling them at the end. X.25 and frame relay are examples of packet switched networks.

- ✔ You can connect the serial port to an external CSU/DSU, which connects your network to a leased line such as that used by a T1 or T3 link. Routers may also have an internal, or integrated, CSU/DSU port, which connects directly to the leased line coming into your building from the service provider.

Introduction to WAN Terminology

542–552 Choose the best answer(s).

542. What is the bandwidth of a T1 WAN link?

(A) 1.544 Mbps

(B) 64 Kbps

(C) 256 Kbps

(D) 128 Kbps

543. Which of the following represents a dedicated WAN link that you pay a monthly subscription fee for?

(A) Leased line

(B) Fast Ethernet

(C) Circuit switched

(D) Ethernet

544. Which WAN technology needs to first establish a connection between two points before sending the data and has all the data travel the same pathway?

(A) Leased line

(B) Packet switched

(C) Circuit switched

(D) Ethernet

545. What is the bandwidth of a BRI subscription?

(A) 1.544 Mbps

(B) 64 Kbps

(C) 256 Kbps

(D) 128 Kbps

546. What is the bandwidth of a T3 link?

(A) 1.544 Mbps

(B) 44.736 Mbps

(C) 256 Kbps

(D) 128 Kbps

547. Which of the following technologies are dedicated leased lines?

    (A)   T1

    (B)   ISDN

    (C)   X.25

    (D)   Frame relay

548. What is the bandwidth of a PRI subscription?

    (A)   1.544 Mbps

    (B)   64 Kbps

    (C)   256 Kbps

    (D)   128 Kbps

549. Which type of WAN technology dedicates the bandwidth to the communication until the connection is terminated?

    (A)   Dedicated link

    (B)   Packet switch

    (C)   Circuit switch

    (D)   Leased line

550. Which of the following is considered a not-so-permanent WAN link?

    (A)   Leased line

    (B)   Fast Ethernet

    (C)   Circuit switched

    (D)   Ethernet

551. Which of the following is a circuit switching technology?

    (A)   T1

    (B)   ISDN

    (C)   X.25

    (D)   Frame relay

552. Which of the following WAN technologies are packet switching technologies? (Select all that apply.)

    (A)   T1

    (B)   ISDN

    (C)   X.25

    (D)   Frame relay

Methods of Connecting to WANs

553–558 Choose the best answer(s).

553. Which device on a point-to-point link needs to have the clock rate set?

    (A)   The DTE device

    (B)   The first device connected

    (C)   The DCE device

    (D)   Both devices

554. Which of the following ports would you use to connect to a T1 connection?

    (A)   AUI

    (B)   F0/1

    (C)   Serial 0/0

    (D)   Console

555. What is the name of the DTE/DCE cable that is used to connect two routers together via their serial ports?

    (A)   Console cable

    (B)   Serial cable

    (C)   Back-to-back serial cable

    (D)   Crossover cable

556. You are troubleshooting your WAN connection. What layers of the OSI model are you troubleshooting? (Select two.)

    (A)   Application layer

    (B)   Physical layer

    (C)   Network layer

    (D)   Presentation layer

    (E)   Data link layer

557. Which of the following devices would typically connect the serial port on your router to a T1 line?

    (A)   External CSU/DSU

    (B)   Internal CSU/DSU

    (C)   External modem

    (D)   Internal modem

558. Which of the following statements is true of a serial interface?

(A) The clock rate must be set on the DCE device.

(B) All Cisco routers are DCE devices.

(C) If the bandwidth is not set, you must set the clock rate.

(D) If the clock rate is not set, you must set the bandwidth.

Configuring Serial Links

559–579 Choose the best answer(s).

559. What is the default encapsulation protocol on a serial link for a Cisco router?

(A) PPP

(B) L2TP

(C) PPTP

(D) HDLC

560. You are connecting your Cisco router to a non-Cisco router over the serial link. Which of the following commands will you use?

(A) encapsulation hdlc

(B) encapsulation vpn

(C) encapsulation nat

(D) encapsulation ppp

561. You have disabled the serial 0/0 interface with the no shutdown command. How will the show interfaces command display the status of the interface?

(A) Serial 0/0 is administratively down, line protocol is down

(B) Serial 0/0 is down, line protocol is down

(C) Serial 0/0 is down, line protocol is up

(D) Serial 0/0 is up, line protocol is down

562. You have configured a test lab and you want to allow communication between two routers using PPP. Review the following code and identify any reasons why the two routers cannot communicate over the serial link.

```
MTL-R1(config)#interface s0/0
MTL-R1(config-if)#ip address 24.0.0.1 255.0.0.0
```

(A) The encapsulation protocol needs to be set.

(B) The IP address is incorrect.

(C) The subnet mask is incorrect.

(D) The name of the router needs to be changed.

563. You are configuring the DCE end of a point-to-point serial link. What command would you type that is not typed on the DTE device?

(A) `encapsulation hdlc`

(B) `clock rate 64000`

(C) `encapsulation ppp`

(D) `bandwidth 64000`

564. Looking at the output below, what is the protocol configured on the serial port?

```
Router>show interfaces
FastEthernet0/0 is up, line protocol is up (connected)
  Hardware is Lance, address is 0009.7c82.4401 (bia 0009.7c82.4401)
  Internet address is 10.0.0.1/24
  MTU 1500 bytes, BW 100000 Kbit, DLY 100 usec,
     reliability 255/255, txload 1/255, rxload 1/255
  Encapsulation ARPA, loopback not set
  ARP type: ARPA, ARP Timeout 04:00:00,
  Last input 00:00:08, output 00:00:05, output hang never
  Last clearing of "show interface" counters never

  <remaining output omitted>

Serial1/0 is up, line protocol is up (connected)
  Hardware is HD64570
  Internet address is 10.1.0.1/24
  MTU 120 bytes, BW 128 Kbit, DLY 20000 usec,
     reliability 255/255, txload 1/255, rxload 1/255
  Encapsulation HDLC, loopback not set, keepalive set (10 sec)
  Last input never, output never, output hang never
  Last clearing of "show interface" counters never
  Input queue: 0/75/0 (size/max/drops); Total output drops: 0
  Queueing strategy: weighted fair

  <remaining output omitted>
```

(A) ARPA

(B) PPTP

(C) HDLC

(D) PPP

565. Looking at the output shown below, what type of device is router R1?

```
R1>show controllers s1/0
Interface Serial1/0
Hardware is PowerQUICC MPC860
DCE V.35, clock rate 64000
idb at 0x81081AC4, driver data structure at 0x81084AC0
SCC Registers:
General [GSMR]=0x2:0x00000000, Protocol-specific [PSMR]=0x8
Events [SCCE]=0x0000, Mask [SCCM]=0x0000, Status [SCCS]=0x00
Transmit on Demand [TODR]=0x0, Data Sync [DSR]=0x7E7E
Interrupt Registers:
Config [CICR]=0x00367F80, Pending [CIPR]=0x0000C000
Mask   [CIMR]=0x00200000, In-srv  [CISR]=0x00000000
Command register [CR]=0x580
```

(A) DTE

(B) SIS

(C) ABR

(D) DCE

566. Which of the following encapsulation protocols will allow communication with non-Cisco devices?

(A) PPP

(B) HDLC

(C) Frame relay

(D) IPX

567. Which packet switched technology uses a fixed length packet size known as a cell?

(A) ATM

(B) X.25

(C) Frame relay

(D) ISDN

568. If you want to load a Cisco proprietary encapsulation protocol over the serial link, what command do you use?

(A) `encapsulation ppp`

(B) `encapsulation hdlc`

(C) `serial link ppp`

(D) `serial link hdlc`

569. Your router is unable to communicate over the WAN link that is connected to serial 0/0. What commands would you use to verify the status of the port? (Select two.)

(A) `show ip route`

(B) `show interfaces`

(C) `show ppp`

(D) `show hdlc`

(E) `show ip interface brief`

570. What are the requirements to configure PPP authentication between NY-R1 and TOR-R1? (Choose three.)

(A) Set the hostname on each router to the same name.

(B) Set the hostname on each router to a unique name.

(C) Create a username on each router named PPP.

(D) Create a username on each router that matches the hostname of the other router.

(E) Enable PPP authentication on both routers and specify either PAP or CHAP as the authentication protocol.

(F) Enable PPP authentication on the first router configured and specify either PAP or CHAP as the authentication protocol.

571. What command would you use to verify if a serial port is a DCE or DTE device?

(A) `show interface serial 0/0`

(B) `show ip interface`

(C) `show ip interface brief`

(D) `show controllers serial 0/0`

572. Your manager has asked you about the HDLC protocol on Cisco devices. Which of the following statements are true? (Select two.)

(A) It is used to connect routers from different vendors.

(B) It is the default encapsulation protocol for serial links on Cisco routers.

(C) It is the default layer-2 protocol for Ethernet connections.

(D) It is the default layer-2 protocol for Fast Ethernet connections.

(E) It is a Cisco proprietary implementation.

573. You have a branch office connected to your head office using a WAN link over the serial ports. You have recently upgraded the router and are unable to communicate across the WAN link. Using the output below, what should you do to get the link up and running?

```
Router#show interface s1/0
Serial1/0 is up, line protocol is down (disabled)
   Hardware is HD64570
   Internet address is 10.1.0.1/24
   MTU 120 bytes, BW 128 Kbit, DLY 20000 usec,
      reliability 255/255, txload 1/255, rxload 1/255
   Encapsulation PPP, loopback not set, keepalive set (10 sec)
   LCP Closed
```

(A) Connect the cable to the serial port properly.

(B) Change the encapsulation protocol.

(C) Change the IP address to 10.1.0.1/8.

(D) Set the bandwidth to 256 Kbps.

574. What encapsulation protocol would you use on the serial port in order to support authentication?

(A) PPTP

(B) HDLC

(C) SSTP

(D) PPP

575. The router administrator is troubleshooting the WAN link and wondering what the meaning of line protocol up means. (Select two.)

(A) The link is up.

(B) The IP address information is correct.

(C) Communication over the layer-2 protocol is working.

(D) Routing table has been updated.

576. You are the network administrator who manages a router in the Toronto office named TOR-R1 and the New York office name NY-R1. You would like to configure PPP as the encapsulation protocol over the WAN link with PPP authentication between the two routers. Which of the following commands represent the configuration on the Toronto router?

(A) Use the following commands:

TOR-R1(config)#username TOR-R1 password mypass

TOR-R1(config)#interface serial 0/0

TOR-R1(config-if)#encapsulation hdlc

TOR-R1(config-if)#ppp authentication chap

(B) Use the following commands:

TOR-R1(config)#username NY-R1 password mypass

TOR-R1(config)#interface serial 0/0

TOR-R1(config-if)#encapsulation ppp

TOR-R1(config-if)#ppp authentication chap

(C) Use the following commands:

TOR-R1(config)#interface serial 0/0

TOR-R1(config-if)#encapsulation ppp

TOR-R1(config-if)#ppp authentication pap

(D) Use the following commands:

TOR-R1(config)#username NY-R1 password mypass

TOR-R1(config)#interface serial 0/0

TOR-R1(config-if)#ppp authentication chap

577. Which authentication protocol with PPP is considered the most secure?

(A) HDLC

(B) PPP

(C) PAP

(D) CHAP

578. Which of the following authentication protocols supported by PPP should be used?

    (A) PAP

    (B) PPTP

    (C) PPP

    (D) CHAP

579. Which of the following commands would you use on the serial interface to configure CHAP authentication?

    (A) `ppp authentication chap`

    (B) `chap authentication`

    (C) `set serial chap`

    (D) `authentication chap`

Part II
ICND 2 – Exam 200-101

1,001
Questions

In this part...

The only way to become proficient in networking is through a lot of practice. By having access to 1001 CCNA questions with different levels of difficulty you will be well on your way to achieving some level of proficiency. Every basic networking concept is included, and you will see a large variety of the types of questions that you can expect to encounter. By mastering these types of questions you will be well on your way to having a very solid CCNA foundation!

In Part II, you are presented with a number of questions, organized by topic, that prepare you for the ICND2 exam (exam 200-101). The topics covered here include

- Switching technologies such as STP
- Etherchannel
- VLANs
- VTP
- IOS boot process and file management
- Router essentials and route summarization
- RIP and OSPF
- EIGRP
- IP services
- Frame Relay
- WAN technologies

Chapter 16

ICND1 Review

● ●

This chapter reviews some of the key points you should be familiar with from ICND1. Your familiarity with that background information will help you pass the ICND2 exam. This chapter covers core concepts not tested directly on the ICND2 exam, but which are required knowledge to understand some of the troubleshooting scenarios in ICND2. Good luck with ICND2!

The Problems You'll Work On

In this chapter, you'll review questions concerning the following topics:

✔ Reviewing networking basics

✔ Remembering IP addressing, subnetting, and VLSM

✔ Configuring routers and IP routing

✔ Configuring switches

✔ Focusing on troubleshooting and security

✔ Reviewing wireless and WANs

What to Watch Out For

Don't let common mistakes trip you up; watch for the following when working with these questions:

✔ Be sure to review networking basics, such as OSI cable types, and the flow of information in the communication process.

✔ Review the basics of IP addressing and know your subnetting and variable length subnet mask. When working on subnetting situations, remember issues regarding illegal addresses and ensure that your subnet mask can handle the size network needed.

✔ Know the basics of router configuration, including configuring interfaces, banners, and ports, such as the console port and telnet ports. Review how to create usernames and passwords on the router, and how to encrypt all passwords on the device.

✔ For switches, review basic switch configuration, such as assigning an IP address to the switch and a default gateway. Know how to configure VLANs and port security on the switch.

✔ Ensure you review all the show commands from ICND1 and practice them; they will help you troubleshoot for your ICND2 exam.

Networking Basics

580–593 Choose the best answer(s).

580. Which of the following statements are true when discussing routers and switches? (Select two.)

(A) Routers decrease the number collision domains.

(B) Routers increase the number of broadcast domains. —

(C) Switches increase the number of collision domains. —

(D) Switches decrease the number of broadcast domains.

581. What is the effect of the command copy tftp flash?

(A) Initiate a copy of a file from a TFTP server to flash memory. —

(B) Initiate a copy of a file from flash memory to a TFTP server.

(C) Copy files between two TFTP servers using the faster flash protocol.

(D) This is an invalid command.

582. Which OSI model header contains the source and destination fields of the packet?

(A) Data link

(B) Physical

(C) Network —

(D) Transport

583. You have connected the switches to the routers using crossover cables, and the client systems to the straight-through cables. You have configured Network A with the 192.168.3.0/24 IP range, and Network B with the 192.168.4.0/24 range. The systems cannot communicate off the network. What should you do?

(A) Change the straight-through to crossover

(B) Change the IP range of Network A to 192.168.4.0/24

(C) Change the IP range of Network B to 192.168.3.0/24

(D) Change the crossover to straight-through —

584. Which of the following devices are considered layer-2 devices? (Select two.)

(A) Hub

(B) Bridge —

(C) Switch —

(D) Router

(E) Repeater

585. Which of the following scenarios require a crossover cable? (Select three.)

    (A) Computer to router

    (B) Switch to switch

    (C) Switch to router

    (D) Computer to computer

    (E) Computer to switch

586. Which layer of the OSI model handles logical addressing and routing?

    (A) Data Link

    (B) Transport

    (C) Network

    (D) Physical

587. What organization is responsible for defining standards for Ethernet networking?

    (A) ISO

    (B) IEC

    (C) CSA

    (D) IEEE

588. Which of the following is a layer-2 device found on a network? (Select two.)

    (A) Firewall

    (B) Router

    (C) Switch

    (D) Repeater

    (E) Bridge

    (F) Gateway

589. Refer to the figure below. Each cable used has been assigned a letter and the cables that have been used are listed in your choices. Select the letter choices which specify the locations in which the correct cables have been used. (Select two.)

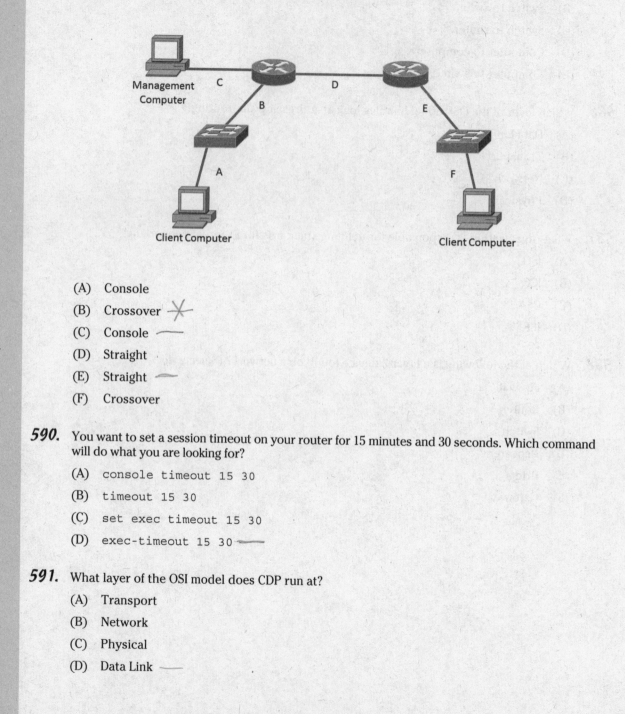

(A)   Console

(B)   Crossover

(C)   Console

(D)   Straight

(E)   Straight

(F)   Crossover

590. You want to set a session timeout on your router for 15 minutes and 30 seconds. Which command will do what you are looking for?

(A)   `console timeout 15 30`

(B)   `timeout 15 30`

(C)   `set exec timeout 15 30`

(D)   `exec-timeout 15 30`

591. What layer of the OSI model does CDP run at?

(A)   Transport

(B)   Network

(C)   Physical

(D)   Data Link

592. MAC addresses are composed of two main components. What are they? (Select two.)

 (A) OUI

 (B) Hexadecimal

 (C) Datalink values

 (D) Vendor assigned values

593. Which of the IEEE standards defines Gigabit Ethernet over copper wires?

 (A) 802.3ab

 (B) 802.5

 (C) 802.11

 (D) 802.3u

IP Addressing, Subnetting and VLSM

594–613 Choose the best answer(s).

594. Which TCP/IP protocol is responsible for reliable delivery?

 (A) UDP

 (B) TCP

 (C) IP

 (D) ICMP

595. Which of the following IPv6 addresses is the equivalent to the 127.0.0.1 IPv4 address? (Select two.)

 (A) ::1

 (B) 2001::1

 (C) fe80::0

 (D) 0000:0000:0000:0000:0000:0000:0000:0001

596. Which of the following application layer protocols use TCP as the transport layer protocol? (Select two.)

 (A) SNMP

 (B) SMTP

 (C) TFTP

 (D) FTP

 (E) DNS Query

597. Which of the following is a valid IPv6 address?

(A) fec0:3d16:xyz5:92c4:ed36:317e:410e:3f28

(B) fe80:d351:3f16:dc41:ed36:317e:410e:3f28 ——

(C) 2001:d351::dc41:ed36::3f28

(D) 2002:dc41:ed36:317e:410e:3f28

598. Which of the following are considered private IP addresses? (Select two.)

(A) 12.45.28.10

(B) 172.25.56.10 ——

(C) 127.0.0.1

(D) 192.148.44.5 ——

(E) 10.45.3.20

599. You are designing an IP scheme for a network that will contain up to 8 subnets with no more than 26 hosts on each. Which of the following subnet masks will be used?

(A) 255.255.255.224 ——

(B) 255.255.255.192

(C) 255.255.255.240

(D) 255.255.255.248

600. Which of the following statements are true about the UDP protocol? (Select two.)

(A) All packets are sent individually. ——

(B) All packets will arrive in order.

(C) Packet delivery is guaranteed.

(D) Packet delivery is not guaranteed. ——

(E) Lost or damaged packets will be resent.

601. How many bits are in an IPv6 address?

(A) 32

(B) 64

(C) 128 ——

(D) 256

602. Given the network shown in the figure below, which network ID would be the smallest that can be used for segment A?

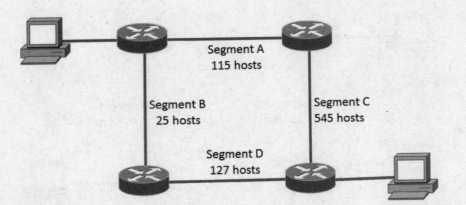

    (A)   192.168.15.0/25 —

    (B)   172.18.0.0/22

    (C)   10.222.0.0/10

    (D)   192.168.7.0/24

603. When working with the TCP/IP protocol suite, what protocol makes use of windowing?

    (A)   IP

    (B)   TCP —

    (C)   UDP

    (D)   ARP

604. Given the network shown in the figure below, which network ID would be the smallest that can be used for segment C?

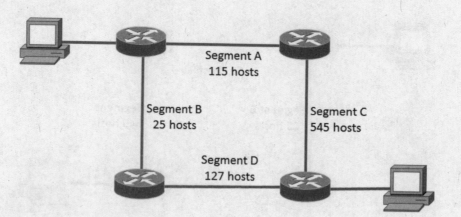

Segment A
115 hosts

Segment B
25 hosts

Segment C
545 hosts

Segment D
127 hosts

    (A)   192.168.15.0/25

    (B)   172.18.0.0/22 ——

    (C)   10.222.0.0/10

    (D)   192.168.7.0/24

605. What are the three steps and order of the TCP three-way handshake process?

    (A)   ACK, SYN, SYN/ACK

    (B)   SYN/ACK, ACK, SYN

    (C)   SYN, SYN/ACK, ACK ——

    (D)   SYN/ACK, SYN, ACK

606. When working with a mask that is 22 bits long, which subnet mask is an alternate representation of 22 bits?

    (A)   255.255.240.0

    (B)   255.255.248.0

    (C)   255.255.252.0 ——

    (D)   255.255.254.0

607. Given the network shown in the figure below, which network ID would be the smallest that can be used for segment B?

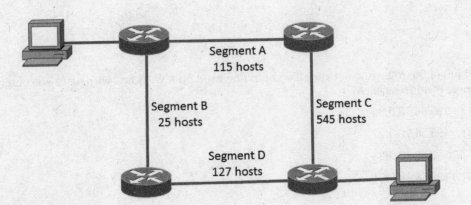

Segment A
115 hosts

Segment B
25 hosts

Segment C
545 hosts

Segment D
127 hosts

(A)   192.168.15.0/25

(B)   172.18.0.0/26 ———

(C)   10.222.0.0/29

(D)   192.168.7.0/24

608. Which of the following is the broadcast address of 216.83.25.87/26?

(A)   216.83.25.128

(B)   216.83.25.63

(C)   216.83.25.64

(D)   216.83.25.127 ———

609. Which of the following is the third valid address of the network containing 220.19.36.112/27?

(A)   220.19.36.131

(B)   220.19.36.99 ———

(C)   220.19.36.67

(D)   220.19.36.115

610. Your manager has asked about the new IPv6 address format. He asks which of the following addresses is a link-local address. What is your answer?

(A)   2001:d4b1:c526:e929:cd14:2d1e:3b14:92ef

(B)   ::1

(C)   fe80:d351:3f16:dc41:ed36:317e:410e:3f28 ———

(D)   2005::2

611. The first 24 bits of the MAC address is known as the _____.

    (A) CDP

    (B) ACL

    (C) NAP

    (D) OUI ——

612. Which of the following network IDs should be used on a WAN link with just two routers using a single IP address each?

    (A) 195.56.78.0/30 ——

    (B) 195.56.78.0/27

    (C) 195.56.78.0/28

    (D) 195.56.78.0/31

613. Which of the following IPv6 communication methods is best known as "1-to-nearest"?

    (A) Multicast

    (B) Broadcast

    (C) Unicast

    (D) Anycast ——

Configuring Routers and IP Routing

614–650 Choose the best answer(s).

614. You need to back up your router configuration to a TFTP server. Which of the following commands would you use?

    (A) `R1#copy tftp running-config` ——

    (B) `R1#copy running-config tftp`

    (C) `R1#backup running-config tftp`

    (D) `R1#restore running-config tftp`

615. You are troubleshooting a routing problem and need to view your routing table. What command would you use?

    (A) `show route`

    (B) `route show`

    (C) `show ip route` ——

    (D) `enable show route`

616. You have shelled out of your telnet session and wish to view the telnet sessions that are currently running in the background. What command would you use?

(A) R1>show telnet ——

(B) R1>show telnet sessions

(C) R1>show sessions

(D) R1>show background sessions

617. You are the administrator for router R1 shown in the figure below. You need to add a static route for the 13.0.0.0 network. What command would you use?

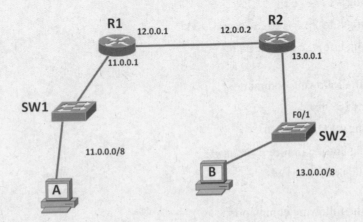

(A) R1(config)#ip route 13.0.0.0 255.0.0.0 12.0.0.1 ——

(B) R1(config)#ip route 13.0.0.0 255.0.0.0 12.0.0.2

(C) R1#ip route 13.0.0.0 255.0.0.0 12.0.0.2

(D) R1(config)#ip route 13.0.0.0 255.0.0.0 13.0.0.1

618. Which of the following configures a console password on your Cisco device?

(A)   Use of the following commands:

```
R1#config term
R1(config)#line con 0
R1(config-line)#password P@ssw0rd
R1(config-line)#login
```

(B)   Use of the following commands: ———

```
R1#config term
R1(config)#line con 0
R1(config-line)#password P@ssw0rd
R1(config-line)#login local
```

(C)   Use of the following commands:

```
R1#config term
R1(config)#line aux 0
R1(config-line)#password P@ssw0rd
R1(config-line)#login
```

(D)   Use of the following commands:

```
R1#config term
R1(config)#line con 0
R1(config-line)#login
```

619. You wish to delete a route from the routing table, what command would you use?

(A)   `delete route`

(B)   `no route`

(C)   `no ip route` ———

(D)   `route delete`

620. You have routing tables specifying gateways for the networks of 10.0.0.0/8, 10.10.0.0/16, 10.10.10.0/24, and 10.10.10.10/32. You have attempted ping a device with an address of 10.10.10.11. Which entry in the routing table will direct your traffic to a gateway or router?

(A)   10.0.0.0/8

(B)   10.10.0.0/16

(C)   10.10.10.0/24

(D)   10.10.10.10/32 ———

(E)   The first matching entry in the routing table

(F)   The last matching entry in the routing table

621. Which devices added to your network will reduce the size of a broadcast domain?

(A)   Switch

(B)   Router ——

(C)   Bridge

(D)   Repeater

622. You need to configure your Fast Ethernet port 0/0 for the IP address of 14.0.0.1 and ensure that the card is enabled. What commands would you use?

(A)   Use of the following commands:

```
R1#config term
R1(config)#interface f0/0
R1(config-if)#ip address 14.0.0.1 255.0.0.0
R1(config-if)#shutdown
```

(B)   Use of the following commands:

```
R1#config term
R1(config)#ip address 14.0.0.1 255.0.0.0
R1(config)#no shutdown
```

(C)   Use of the following commands:

```
R1#config term
R1(config)#interface f0/0
R1(config-if)#ip address 14.0.0.1 255.0.0.0
R1(config-if)#encapsulation ppp
```

(D)   Use of the following commands: ——

```
R1#config term
R1(config)#interface f0/0
R1(config-if)#ip address 14.0.0.1 255.0.0.0
R1(config-if)#no shutdown
```

623. You wish to configure your serial 0/0 interface as the DCE end of a point-to-point link. Which of the follow represents the commands you would use?

   (A) Use of the following commands:

```
R1#config term
R1(config)#interface f0/0
R1(config-if)#ip address 14.0.0.1 255.0.0.0
R1(config-if)#encapsulation ppp
R1(config-if)#clock rate 64000
R1(config-if)#shutdown
```

   (B) Use of the following commands:

```
R1#config term
R1(config)#interface S0/0
R1(config-if)#ip address 14.0.0.1 255.0.0.0
R1(config-if)#encapsulation ppp
R1(config-if)#clock rate 64000
R1(config-if)#no shutdown
```

   (C) Use of the following commands: ⸺

```
R1#config term
R1(config)#interface S0/0
R1(config-if)#ip address 14.0.0.1 255.0.0.0
R1(config-if)#encapsulation ppp
R1(config-if)#no shutdown
```

   (D) Use of the following commands:

```
R1#config term
R1(config)#interface S0/0
R1(config-if)#ip address 14.0.0.1 255.0.0.0
R1(config-if)#no shutdown
```

624. You need to ensure that CDP is enabled on your Cisco device. What command would you type?

   (A) R1#cdp run

   (B) R1(config)#enable cdp

   (C) R1#cdp enable

   (D) R1(config)#cdp run ⸺

625. You have configured RIP routing on your routers. You have configured a static route to the same destination that your router learns of through RIP. Which entry is placed in the routing table?

(A) RIP route

(B) Static route

(C) Neither

(D) Both

626. You wish to configure a username bob and ensure telnet requires a username and password before allowing access to the device. Which of the following configuration allows this?

(A) Use of the following commands:

```
R1#config term
R1(config)#username bob password P@ssw0rd
R1(config)#line vty 0 4
R1(config-line)#login local
```

(B) Use of the following commands:

```
R1#config term
R1(config)#username bob password P@ssw0rd
R1(config)#line vty 0 4
R1(config-line)#login
```

(C) Use of the following commands:

```
R1#config term
R1(config)#username bob password P@ssw0rd
R1(config)#line vty 0 4
```

(D) Use of the following commands:

```
R1#config term
R1(config)#line vty 0 4
R1(config-line)#password P@ssw0rd
R1(config-line)#login
```

627. You have created access list I to include all IP address that can use NAT. How would you configure NAT on the router to have all internal IP assress use the public IP assigned to the serial 0/0 interface?

(A) `ip nat interface serial 0/0 overload 1`

(B) `ip nat list 1 interface serial 0/0 overload`

(C) `nat interface serial 0/0 overload`

(D) `ip nat inside source list 1 interface serial 0/0 overload`

628. You wish to recover a forgotten password on your router. What value would you set the configuration register to?

(A) 2102 ——

(B) 2100

(C) 2122

(D) 2142

629. Which of the following does OSPF use to calculate the cost of a link?

(A) Hop count ——

(B) Delay

(C) Load

(D) Bandwidth

630. You are configuring a serial port on the router. What command would set the clock rate to 32 Kb/s?

(A) clock rate 32

(B) clock speed 32

(C) clock rate 32000

(D) clock speed 32000 ——

631. You are looking to implement a routing protocol with the following features:

- ✔ Scalable
- ✔ Support for VLSM
- ✔ Vendor compatibility
- ✔ Low overhead

Which protocol should you choose?

(A) OSPF ——

(B) RIP v1

(C) EIGRP

(D) IGRP

632. There are many reasons for network congestion that can affect data movement and delivery. Which of the following are leading causes of congestion? (Select three.)

(A) Multicasting

(B) An excessive number of hosts in a broadcast domain ——

(C) Full duplex interfaces

(D) Broadcast storms ——

(E) Half-duplex interfaces ——

633. Which of the following are link-state routing protocols? (Select two.)

    (A) RIP

    (B) IGRP

    (C) OSPF

    (D) IS-IS

634. You have configured a switch port for trunk mode. What type of device is typically connected to this type of port?

    (A) Computer

    (B) Router

    (C) Printer

    (D) Switch

635. What are three metrics that are used by routing protocols to determine an optimal network path? (Select three.)

    (A) hop count

    (B) bandwidth

    (C) delay

    (D) packet length

    (E) distance

    (F) quantity

636. Which dynamic routing protocols support both route summarization and VLSM? (Select three.)

    (A) EIGRP

    (B) RIP v1

    (C) RIP v2

    (D) OSPF

    (E) IGRP

    (F) VTP

637. You have configured your router for NAT as per the figure below, but most of your network users are not able to connect to external resources. What command will fix the problem? (Select two.)

```
Router1>enable
Router1#configure terminal
Router1(config)#access-list 1 permit 10.0.0.0 0.255.255.255
Router1(config)#ip nat inside source list 1 interface FastEthernet 0/0
Router1(config)#interface FastEthernet0/0
Router1(config-if)#ip address 192.168.1.1 255.255.255.0
Router1(config-if)#ip nat outside
Router1(config-if)#interface FastEthernet0/1
Router1(config-if)#ip address 10.0.0.1 255.0.0.0
Router1(config-if)#ip nat inside
```

——(A) `ip nat inside source list 1 interface FastEthernet 0/0 overload`

   (B) `ip nat pool no-overload 10.0.0.2 10.0.0.63 prefix 8`

       `ip nat inside source list 1 pool no-overload`

   (C) `ip nat pool no-overload 192.168.1.2 192.168.1.63 prefix 24`

       `ip nat inside source list 2 pool no-overload`

   (D) `ip nat pool no-overload 192.168.1.2 192.168.1.63 prefix 24`

       `ip nat inside source list 1 pool no-overload`

638. What is the purpose of the overload option when working with NAT?

   (A) It changes the function of PAT to NAT.

   (B) It reverses the role of the inside and outside interfaces.

——(C) It changes the function of NAT to PAT.

   (D) It serves no purpose for NAT.

639. What is the Administrative Distance of a static route?

   (A) 0

—— (B) 1

   (C) 5

   (D) 20

640. Which of these dynamic routing protocols do not support VLSM? (Select two.)

—— (A) RIP v1

   (B) RIP v2

   (C) EIGRP

   (D) OSPF

——(E) IGRP

641. Which of the following commands would configure your router as a DHCP server, give out the address 192.168.1.1 as the default gateway value to clients, and lease the address to clients for 7 days?

(A) Use of the following commands:

```
R1(config)#ip dhcp pool NY_Network
R1(dhcp-config)#network 192.168.1.0 255.255.255.0
R1(dhcp-config)#default-router 192.168.1.1
R1(dhcp-config)#lease 7 0 0
```

(B) Use of the following commands:

```
R1(config)#ip dhcp pool NY_Network
R1(dhcp-config)#network 192.168.1.0 255.255.255.0
R1(dhcp-config)#default-router 192.168.1.1
R1(dhcp-config)#lease 0 0 7
```

(C) Use of the following commands:

```
R1(config)#ip pool NY_Network
R1(dhcp-config)#network 192.168.1.0 0.0.0.255
R1(dhcp-config)#default-router 192.168.1.1
R1(dhcp-config)#lease 7 0 0
```

(D) Use of the following commands:

```
R1(config)#ip dhcp pool NY_Network
R1(dhcp-config)#network 192.168.1.0 255.255.255.0
R1(dhcp-config)#default-gateway 192.168.1.1
R1(dhcp-config)#lease 7 0 0
```

642. You are the network administrator for a network that is already running OSPF. You configure OSPF on your router with the following commands, but your router is not sharing routing information with other OSPF routers. What is wrong?

```
Enable
Config term
Router ospf 1
Network 12.0.0.0 255.0.0.0 area 0
```

(A) You have configured the wrong subnet mask.

(B) You have configured the wrong wildcard mask.

(C) You have configured the wrong process ID.

(D) You have configured the wrong network ID.

643. Which of the following is one of the things you need to do to configure a router to route between VLANs using only a single connection to the switch?

    (A) Install RIPv1.

    (B) Install RIPv2.

    (C) Install OSPF.

    —— (D) Configure sub-interfaces on the router.

644. You are configuring NAT on your router and need to create an access list that includes all IP addresses in the 192.168.3.0 network so that they can use NAT services. Which of the following would you use as the access list?

    —— (A) `R1(config)#access-list 1 permit 192.168.3.0 0.0.0.255`

    (B) `R1#access-list 1 permit 192.168.3.0 0.0.0.255`

    (C) `R1(config)#access-list 1 permit 192.168.3.0 255.255.255.0`

    (D) `R1(config)#access-list 1 deny 192.168.3.0 0.0.0.255`

645. You need to configure OSPF on your router for network 192.168.2.0. What two commands would you use? (Select two.)

    —— (A) `router ospf`

    (B) `router ospf 3`

    (C) `network 192.168.2.0 255.255.255.0 area 0`

    (D) `network 192.168.2.0 0.0.0.255`

    —— (E) `network 192.168.2.0 0.0.0.255 area 0`

646. You have a router with the following configuration. What is the OSPF router ID of the router?

```
Loopback 0: 1.1.1.1
Loopback 1: 2.2.2.2
FastEthernet 0/0: 12.0.0.1
FastEthernet 0/1: 13.0.0.1
Serial 0/0: 14.0.0.1
```

    (A) 1.1.1.1

    (B) 13.0.0.1

    —— (C) 14.0.0.1

    (D) 2.2.2.2

    (E) 12.0.0.1

647. What keystroke is used to suspend a telnet session?

   (A) CTRL-S

   (B) CTRL-SHIFT-6, then X

   (C) CTRL-SHIFT-DEL, then X

——(D) CTRL-X

648. You have client computers on your network that are having issues establishing sessions with a remote website. The router is performing NAT. You would like to reset their dynamic NAT addresses through the router. What command will erase their NAT entries in the router?

   (A) `clear ip nat translations`

   (B) `clear ip nat translations *`

   (C) `no ip nat translations`

——(D) `no ip nat translations *`

649. Which routing protocol supports transport protocols of IP, IPX, and Appletalk?

   (A) IGRP

   (B) RIP v2

——(C) OSPF

   (D) EIGRP

650. You have configured multiple routing protocols on your network. There is a path discovered to a remote network segment by each routing protocol. Which protocol's path will be chosen by your router?

——(A) OSPF

   (B) IGRP

   (C) EIGRP

   (D) RIP

Configuring Switches

651–668 Choose the best answer(s).

651. Which of the following commands is used to assign a default gateway to a Cisco switch?

   (A) R1(config)#`default-router 23.0.0.1`

   (B) R1(config)#`ip default-router 23.0.0.1`

   (C) R1(config)#`default-gateway 23.0.0.1`

——(D) R1(config)#`ip default-gateway 23.0.0.1`

652. You issue the command show mac-address-table on your switch. There are several MAC addresses listed for many of the ports. What is the significance of multiple addresses being listed on a port?

    (A)   Identifies an internal problem on the switch.

    ——(B)   Multiple addresses are normal if STP is in use on the switch.

    (C)   Multiple addresses let you know that the port is connected to another switch or hub.

    (D)   There is no significance because this cannot happen.

653. Which of the selections will reduce the size of a collision domain? (Select two.)

    ——(A)   Upgrading a hub to a switch

    (B)   Implementing VLANs

    ——(C)   Adding a bridge between two hubs

    (D)   Adding a router between two switches

654. You have one switch on which you have created three VLANs. You have decided that you need to have devices on these VLANs communicate with each other. You need to add which device to your network to allow the communication?

    (A)   Repeater

    (B)   Switch

    (C)   Bridge

    ——(D)   Router

655. Which of the following commands would you use if you wanted the port security feature to learn the MAC addresses of connected systems?

    ——(A)   R1(config-if)#switchport port-security mac-address sticky

    (B)   R1(config-if)#switchport port-security mac-address learnmac

    (C)   R1(config-if)#switchport sticky

    (D)   R1(config-if)#switchport mac-address 00-00-00-00-00-00

656. Which Cisco command was used to create the output in the figure below?

```
Capability Codes: R - Router, T - Trans Bridge, B - Source Route Bridge
                  S - Switch, H - Host, I - IGMP, r - Repeater, P - Phone
Device ID    Local Intrfce   Holdtme   Capability   Platform   Port ID
Switch       Fas 0/0         174           S        2960       Fas 0/1
R2           Ser 0/3/0       175           R        C2800      Ser 0/3/0
R3           Ser 0/3/1       175           R        C2800      Ser 0/3/0
R1#
```

(A) show ip route

(B) show ip interface brief

—— (C) show cdp neighbors

(D) show controllers

657. You wish to view the list of VLANs and the ports associated with each VLAN. What command would you use?

—— (A) show vlan

(B) show ip vlan

(C) show net vlan

(D) show ip interface brief

658. You wish to configure all the ports on the switch for access mode. What command should you use?

(A) SW1(config-if)#switchport mode access

(B) SW1(config-if)#switchport mode access all_ports

(C) SW1(config-if)#switchport all mode access

—— (D) SW1(config-if-range)#switchport mode access

659. You wish to configure an interface on the switch for full duplex mode. What command would you use?

(A) SW1(config-if)#full duplex

—— (B) SW1(config-if)#duplex full

(C) SW1(config)#duplex full

(D) SW1#full duplex

660. VLAN information is propagated to all switches on a network through which protocol?

(A) RIP

(B) STP

—— (C) VTP

(D) CDP

661. When a switch is participating in a STP network, how is the root bridge determined on the network? (Select two.)

    (A) Highest priority

    (B) Lowest priority

    (C) Highest MAC address

    (D) Lowest MAC address

662. What are possible port states for a switch port that is participating in Spanning Tree Protocol (STP)? (Select three.)

    (A) Passing

    (B) Blocking

    (C) Learning

    (D) Negotiating

    (E) Participating

    (F) Forwarding

663. Which port security violation mode disables the interface on the switch if an invalid system connects to the port until the administrator enables the interface?

    (A) Disable

    (B) Protect

    (C) Shutdown

    (D) Restrict

664. Which of the following commands creates a VLAN named MKT?

    (A) 3524XL#no vlan 2 name MKT

    (B) 3524XL(vlan)#vlan 2 name MKT

    (C) 3524XL(vlan)#create vlan 2 name MKT

    (D) 3524XL(vlan)#set vlan 2 name MKT

665. In order to configure port security on a Cisco switch, what mode does the port need to be running in?

    (A) Trunk

    (B) Link

    (C) Access

    (D) Network

666. You wish to verify that port security was configured on port 6 of the switch. What command would you use?

—— (A) `show port-security interface f0/6`

(B) `show port-security 6`

(C) `show interface port-security`

(D) `show interface f0/6 port-security`

667. Given the network shown in the figure below, what switch will be the root bridge and what port will be the blocking port? (Select one switch and one port.)

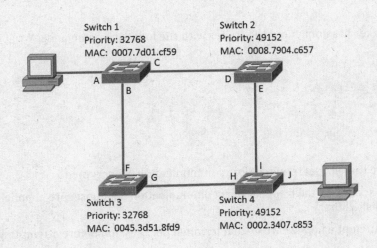

(A) Switch 1 will be root bridge

(B) Switch 2 will be root bridge

(C) Switch 3 will be root bridge

—— (D) Switch 4 will be root bridge

(E) Port B will be blocking

—— (F) Port E will be blocking

(G) Port I will be blocking

(H) Port H will be blocking

668. You are using Catalyst 2950 24 port switch. You have pressed the mode button to enable UTIL mode. All the port LEDs turn green except for the last GBIC port. What is the bandwidth utilization on the switch?

(A) Less than 12.5%

(B) Between 12.5% and 25%

(C) Between 25% and 50%

—— (D) Between 50% and 100%

Troubleshooting and Security

669–688 Choose the best answer(s).

669. You wish to verify that you can communicate with a host on the network. What command would you use?

(A) `ip arp`

(B) `ip rarp`

(C) `ping <ip_address>`

(D) `cdp run`

670. Your coworker has configured the router with the following commands. What do they do?

```
line vty 0 4
password telnetP@ss
login
transport input ssh
```

(A) Ensure that virtual terminal port communication is encrypted

(B) Allow secure virtual terminal port communication if a nonsecure channel cannot be established first

(C) First attempt a non-secure virtual terminal port session before attempting a secure session

(D) Attempt a secure session before attempting an unsecure session if the secure session fails

671. You have used both enable secret and enable password commands to set passwords for your router. How do you get to the # prompt?

(A) Use the secret password.

(B) Use the enable password.

(C) Use either the secret or enable passwords.

(D) Use both the secret and enable passwords.

672. The output of the `show interface` command is shown in the figure below. How many CRC errors have been encountered on this switch port?

```
Router1# show interface Ethernet 0/0
Interface Ethernet0/0 "", is up, line protocol is up
  Hardware is 88E6095, BW 100 Mbps, DLY 100 usec
      Auto-Duplex(Full-duplex), Auto-Speed(100 Mbps)
      Input flow control is unsupported, output flow control is unsupported
      Available but not configured via nameif
      MAC address 0007.7d01.cf51, MTU not set
      IP address unassigned
      629 packets input, 106946 bytes, 0 no buffer
      Received 290 broadcasts, 0 runts, 0 giants
      5 input errors, 5 CRC, 0 frame, 0 overrun, 0 ignored, 0 abort
      0 pause input, 0 resume input
      0 L2 decode drops
      329 switch ingress policy drops
      11 packets output, 6892 bytes, 0 underruns
      0 pause output, 0 resume output
      0 output errors, 0 collisions, 0 interface resets
      0 late collisions, 0 deferred
      0 rate limit drops
      0 switch egress policy drops
      0 input reset drops, 0 output reset drops
```

(A) 5

(B) 11

(C) 329

(D) 629

673. What are effects of using a half-duplex setting on a switch port? (Select two.)

(A) Data can be sent only in one direction at a time.

(B) Data can be sent in both directions at any time.

(C) There will be an increase in the number of collisions.

(D) There will be an increase in throughput.

(E) There will be a decrease in the number of collisions.

674. What information is displayed by the `show version` command?

(A) Current date and time

(B) Number of configured VLANs

(C) Current configuration version

(D) How the system was last restarted

675. A standard ACL is able to filter traffic based only on which of these items?

    (A)   Destination IP address

    (B)   Source IP address

— (C)   Source MAC address

    (D)   Protocol

    (E)   VLAN

    (F)   TCP and UDP ports

676. What is a valid purpose for implementing ACLs?

    (A)   Virus detection

    (B)   Monitoring bytes and packets

— (C)   IP route filtering

    (D)   Traffic classification

677. You wish to encrypt all passwords on the Cisco device. What command would you use?

    (A)   `password encrypt`

— (B)   `service password-encryption`

    (C)   `set password-encryption`

    (D)   `enable password-encryption`

678. Which of the following commands would you use to troubleshoot layer 3 issues? (Select two.)

— (A)   `show interfaces`

— (B)   `show ip route`

    (C)   `show controllers`

    (D)   `show ip protocols`

679. You wish to view the IP addresses of Cisco devices closest to you. Which command would you use?

— (A)   `show cdp neighbors detail`

    (B)   `show ip route`

    (C)   `show ip interface brief`

    (D)   `show cdp neighbors`

680. You have configured a banner using the following command. What is wrong with the configuration?

```
R1(config)#banner motd #

Enter TEXT message. End with the character '#'.

Welcome to Glen's network!

If you require assistance call the help desk at 555-5555.
```

    (A)   The # should be $.

    (B)   The # should be @.

    (C)   The phone number is wrong.

    (D)   Banners should not welcome someone.

681. Which command was used to create the output displayed in the figure below?

```
Interface          IP-Address      OK? Method Status                    Protocol
FastEthernet0/0    11.0.0.1        YES manual up                        up
FastEthernet0/1    unassigned      YES unset  administratively down     down
Serial0/3/0        12.0.0.1        YES manual up                        up
Serial0/3/1        14.0.0.2        YES manual up                        up
Vlan1              unassigned      YES unset  administratively down     down
R1#
```

    (A)   `show ip route`

    (B)   `show interface`

    (C)   `show ip interface brief`

    (D)   `show controllers`

682. You have configured a router with an ACL and placed it on the inbound direction of an interface. When are packets processed against this ACL?

    (A)   Before and after routing packets to an outbound interface

    (B)   After routing packets to an outbound interface

    (C)   Before routing packets to an outbound interface

    (D)   None of the above

683. You rely on CDP for network administration within your network, but you would like to prevent CDP information from being accessed from external devices. Which set of commands should you execute on your router?

    (A)   `no cdp run`

    (B)   `no cdp enable`

    (C)   `interface serial0/0`

              `no cdp enable`

    (D)   `interface serial0/0`

              `no cdp run`

684. You have used SSH to connect to your switch, which is experiencing performance issues. You have enabled several debug options, but you do not see the output of the commands on your screen. What must you do to enable this functionality?

———(A)   Type `terminal monitor`.

(B)   Switch to a telnet connection.

(C)   Type `debug all`.

(D)   You can only see this output on a direct console connection.

685. You have lost the password for a network switch. What is the first step in the switch Cisco IOS password recovery process?

(A)   Enter configuration mode

(B)   Enter rommon

(C)   Flash with the latest IOS

———(D)   Run the EXEC mode command reload rommon

686. You have configured your switch for SSH access using the commands shown in the figure below. When you attempt to connect to the switch you are not able to connect with ssh, but you are still able to connect to the switch with telnet. What is the likely cause the problem?

```
Switch1#config terminal
Switch1(config)#username cisco password cisco
Switch1(config)#ip domain-name madeupname.org
Switch1(config)#crytpo key generate rsa
Switch1(config)#ip ssh version 2
Switch1(config)#line vty 0 4
Switch1(config-line)#login local
```

(A)   You failed to generate a key pair.

(B)   You did not enable ssh.

(C)   You did not configure the vty.

———(D)   You need to assign a user to use ssh.

687. You have configured messages for banner exec, banner incoming, banner login, and banner motd. When you connect to a console interface, what is the first message you will see?

(A)   banner exec

(B)   banner incoming

(C)   banner login

———(D)   banner motd

688. Your router does not have a boot directive in the current configuration. What is the order that the router will use to locate a valid IOS to load?

   (A)   Flash, NVRAM, ROM

—— (B)   NVRAM, TFTP server, ROM

   (C)   Flash, TFTP server, ROM

   (D)   TFTP server, Flash, ROM

Wireless and WANs

689–699 Choose the best answer(s).

689. What is the transmission rate of 802.11g?

   (A)   11 Mbps

   (B)   120 Mbps

—— (C)   54 Mbps

   (D)   300 Mbps

690. When a wireless network contains access points, it is referred to as which type of network?

   (A)   802.11b

   (B)   Ad-hoc

   (C)   Secured

—— (D)   Infrastructure

691. You have just implemented a new 802.11b access point. What is the maximum speed of devices connected to this access point?

   (A)   1 Mbps

   (B)   10 Mbps

—— (C)   11 Mbps

   (D)   54 Mbps

692. What is the speed of an ISDN BRI link?

——(A)   1.544 Mbps

   (B)   64 Kbps

   (C)   128 Kbps

   (D)   512 Kbps

693. Which of the following represents the term used for a wireless network made up of multiple access points using the same SSID?

(A)   BSS

(B)   WEP

(C)   WPA2

(D)   ESS

694. What are three impacts that occur when objects are in the path of wireless or RF signals? (Select three.)

(A)   Disruption

(B)   Reflection

(C)   Crosstalk

(D)   Scattering

(E)   Repetition

(F)   Absorption

695. You have a serial port on your router and when you run show interface serial, you are told, Serial1 is up, line protocol is down. What are two possible causes of this error? (Select two.)

(A)   You have not set a clock rate.

(B)   No cable is connected to the serial port.

(C)   There are no keepalives on the link.

(D)   You have set the incorrect encapsulation type.

696. You are implementing a new 802.11n network using the 2.4GHz channels. How many non-overlapping channels are available for use in the United States?

(A)   1

(B)   3

(C)   11

(D)   15

697. Which selection is an authentication protocol that can be used on WAN connections that have used PPP encapsulation?

(A)   VTP

(B)   CDP

(C)   CHAP

(D)   POP

698. What component does your router use to connect to a T1 leased line?

____(A)   CSU/DSU

(B)   PAD

(C)   Modem

(D)   Cell

699. Which of the commands are valid on a WAN interface, but would not be used on a LAN interface? (Select two.)

(A)   no shutdown

(B)   duplex

____(C)   encapsulation ppp

(D)   speed

____(E)   authentication chap

Chapter 17

Switching Technologies

∙∙

*T*he ICND2 exam expects you to be comfortable with switching technologies such as VLANs, Spanning Tree Protocol (STP), VLAN Trunking Protocol (VTP), Etherchannel, and port security. Some of these concepts were introduced in the ICND1 exam. The ICND2 exam expects you to know not only the purpose of each of these protocols and technologies, but also how to configure and troubleshoot them! Spend some time practicing the configuration of these technologies, and then answer the following questions.

The Problems You'll Work On

In this chapter, you'll review questions concerning the following topics:

  ✔ Understanding Spanning Tree Protocol (STP)

  ✔ Configuring VLANs

  ✔ Configuring VLAN Trunking Protocol (VTP)

  ✔ Implementing Etherchannel

  ✔ Managing port security

What to Watch Out For

Don't let common mistakes trip you up; watch for the following when working with these questions:

  ✔ Spanning Tree Protocol is a layer 2 protocol designed to prevent layer 2 loops on the network. It does this by deciding which link should be placed in a blocking state. STP takes time to converge as each port on a switch goes through many states, such as blocking, listening, learning, and forwarding.

  ✔ Rapid Spanning Tree Protocol (RSTP) converges quickly by selecting alternate and potential backup ports. When a link goes down, RSTP doesn't reconverge; it simply activates one of the alternate or backup ports. This saves a lot of time!

  ✔ Know how to configure VLANs and port security on a Cisco switch. Virtual LANs are communication boundaries that allow you to separate your network even on a single switch. Know that trunk links are special ports that can carry traffic for all VLANs.

  ✔ VLAN Trunking Protocol (VTP) is a protocol that is used to simplify the management of VLANs across switches in the enterprise. With VTP, you create the list of VLANs on the VTP server and then that list is sent to any VTP clients configured for the same VTP domain. A VTP domain is a group of switches that will share VLAN information.

Understanding Spanning Tree Protocol (STP)

700–716 Choose the best answer(s).

700. In regards to STP, what is the default priority on a Cisco switch?

(A) 32,768

(B) 16,384

(C) 8,192

(D) 4,096

701. Which layer of the OSI model does RSTP run at?

(A) Physical

(B) Data Link

(C) Network

(D) Transport

702. Which of the following is a benefit of RSTP over STP?

(A) RSTP transitions to a forwarding state faster than STP does.

(B) RSTP has more port states than STP.

(C) RSTP uses the same port roles that STP uses.

(D) RSTP can route between VLANs.

703. Which of the following terms describes a spanning tree network where all switch ports are in either forwarding or blocking state?

(A) Redundant

(B) Converged

(C) Fault tolerant

(D) Treed

704. Which of the following is selected by STP as the root bridge?

(A) The switch with the highest priority

(B) The switch with the highest bridge ID

(C) The switch with the lowest IP address configured

(D) The switch with the lowest bridge ID

705. PVST+ introduced which of the following port states?

(A) Forwarding

(B) Learning

(C) Discarding

(D) Listening

706. Which of the following represent STP port states? (Select three.)

(A) Blocking

(B) Listening

(C) Disabled

(D) Forwarding

707. Looking at the output of the show spanning-tree command displayed in the figure below, is SW1 the root bridge?

```
SW1#show spanning-tree
VLAN0001
  Spanning tree enabled protocol rstp
  Root ID    Priority    4097
             Address     00E0.F72C.AEC0
             This bridge is the root
             Hello Time  2 sec  Max Age 20 sec  Forward Delay 15 sec

  Bridge ID  Priority    4097  (priority 4096 sys-id-ext 1)
             Address     00E0.F72C.AEC0
             Hello Time  2 sec  Max Age 20 sec  Forward Delay 15 sec
             Aging Time  20

Interface        Role Sts Cost      Prio.Nbr Type
---------------- ---- --- --------- -------- --------------------------------
Fa0/1            Desg FWD 19        128.1    P2p
Fa0/24           Desg FWD 19        128.24   P2p
```

(A) Yes

(B) No

708. Looking at the following switch information, how can you configure SwitchC as the root bridge?

Name: SwitchA

Priority: 32768

MAC: 00-00-0c-00-b0-01

Name: SwitchB

Priority: 32768

MAC: 00-50-0d-10-00-00

Name: SwitchC

Priority: 32768

MAC: 0b-3f-27-00-93-3a

(A) Increase the priority.

(B) Lower the priority.

(C) Change the MAC address.

(D) Change the name.

709. Once the root switch has been selected, each switch must then determine its root port. Which port is selected as the root port?

(A)   The port with the lowest MAC address

(B)   The port with the highest MAC address

(C)   The port with the lowest cost

(D)   The port with the highest cost

710. Which of the following are true regarding RSTP? (Select three.)

(A)   RSTP uses the same port roles as STP

(B)   Reduces converging time after a link failure

(C)   STP transitions quicker to a forwarding state than RSTP

(D)   Uses additional port roles over STP

(E)   Transitions to a forwarding state faster than STP

711. You would like to verify if your switch is the root bridge. What command would you use?

(A)   `show stp`

(B)   `show spanning-tree`

(C)   `show tree`

(D)   `show root bridge`

712. You have three switches connected in a loop with the configuration of each switch shown below. Which switch will be selected as the root bridge?

Name: SwitchA

Priority: 32768

MAC: 00-00-0c-00-b0-01

Name: SwitchB

Priority: 32768

MAC: 00-50-0d-10-00-00

Name: SwitchC

Priority: 32768

MAC: 0b-3f-27-00-93-3a

(A)   SwitchA

(B)   SwitchB

(C)   SwitchC

(D)   All of them

713. Which of the follow commands was used to create the output in the figure below?

```
Name: Fa0/1
Switchport: Enabled
Administrative Mode: dynamic auto
Operational Mode: static access
Administrative Trunking Encapsulation: dot1q
Operational Trunking Encapsulation: native
Negotiation of Trunking: On
Access Mode VLAN: 1 (default)
Trunking Native Mode VLAN: 1 (default)
Voice VLAN: none
Administrative private-vlan host-association: none
Administrative private-vlan mapping: none
Administrative private-vlan trunk native VLAN: none
Administrative private-vlan trunk encapsulation: dot1q
Administrative private-vlan trunk normal VLANs: none
Administrative private-vlan trunk private VLANs: none
Operational private-vlan: none
Trunking VLANs Enabled: ALL
Pruning VLANs Enabled: 2-1001
Capture Mode Disabled
Capture VLANs Allowed: ALL
Protected: false
Appliance trust: none
```

(A) show stp

(B) show spanning-tree

(C) Show interface fastethernet 0/1

(D) show interface fastethernet 0/1 switchport

714. Which of the following identifies additional port roles used by RSTP?

(A) Designated

(B) Root

(C) Blocking

(D) Alternate

715. You would like to ensure that when a system connects to a switch that it receives connectivity right away with little wait time. Which of the following commands would you use?

(A) (config-if)#spanning-tree portfast

(B) (config-if)#spanning-tree lowwait

(C) (config)#spanning-tree portfast

(D) (config-if)# portfast

716. Using the figure below, what do you need to do on switch SW2 in order to ensure it is the root bridge?

```
SW2#show spanning-tree vlan 1
VLAN0001
  Spanning tree enabled protocol ieee
    Root ID    Priority    4097
               Address     00E0.F72C.AEC0
               Cost        19
               Port        1(FastEthernet0/1)
               Hello Time  2 sec  Max Age 20 sec  Forward Delay 15 sec

    Bridge ID  Priority    32769  (priority 32768 sys-id-ext 1)
               Address     000D.BD54.01EE
               Hello Time  2 sec  Max Age 20 sec  Forward Delay 15 sec
               Aging Time  20

Interface        Role Sts Cost      Prio.Nbr Type
---------------- ---- --- --------- -------- ------------------------------
Fa0/1            Root FWD 19        128.1    P2p
Fa0/24           Altn BLK 19        128.24   P2p
```

(A) Add an additional interface.

(B) Increase the aging time.

(C) Increase the priority above 4096.

(D) Decrease the priority below 4096.

Configuring VLANs

717–726 Choose the best answer(s).

717. Which of the following statements are true of VLANs and their usage? (Select two.)

(A) Communication between VLAN requires a router.

(B) You cannot use VLANs across switches.

(C) A VLAN that spans across switches requires a router.

(D) Each VLAN requires its own IP subnet.

(E) Multiple VLANs can use the same IP subnet if sub-interfaces are used on the router.

718. Which of the following are VLAN tagging protocols?

(A) ISL

(B) 802.1d

(C) 802.1q

(D) 802.11

719. You would like to create a VLAN called MKT on your switch. Which command(s) would you use?

(A) Use the following commands:

```
vlan 10
name MKT
```

(B) Use the following command:

```
vlan MKT
```

(C) Use the following command:

```
vlan name MKT
```

(D) Use the following command:

```
vlan name MKT num 10
```

720. Which of the following statements is true of the native VLAN?

(A) Both sides of the trunk link should use the same native VLAN.

(B) Both sides of the trunk link should use different native VLANs.

(C) Native VLAN is only used when the frame is tagged VLAN 1.

(D) Native VLANs are only used to tag voice traffic.

721. You want to ensure that only VLAN 10 and VLAN 20 traffic can pass over a trunk link. Which command would you use?

(A) SW1(config-if)#trunk allowed vlan 10,20

(B) SW1(config)#switchport trunk allowed vlan 10,20

(C) SW1(config-if)#switchport trunk allowed vlan 10,20

(D) SW1(config)#trunk allowed vlan 10,20

722. Looking at the figure below, which of the following statements are true about the interVLAN routing?

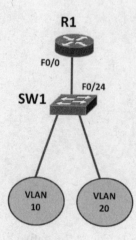

R1

F0/0

F0/24

SW1

VLAN 10

VLAN 20

(A) VTP must be enabled on R1

(B) F0/0 must be configured with sub-interfaces

(C) RIP must be enabled on SW1

(D) F0/0 on R1 and F0/24 on the switch must use the same encapsulation protocol

(E) F0/24 on the switch must be configured with sub-interfaces

723. Two switches are connected together by a crossover cable. The ports connecting the two switches have been configured for access mode. You have systems on each switch that are part of VLAN 20 and VLAN 30. What is your assessment of this configuration?

(A) Systems will not be able to communicate between the two switches.

(B) Systems in VLAN 20 can communicate across the switches.

(C) Systems in VLAN 30 can communicate across the switch.

(D) Change the cable from a crossover cable to a straight-through in order to allow systems to communicate between the two switches.

724. Using the figure below, which of the following statements are true of router R1?

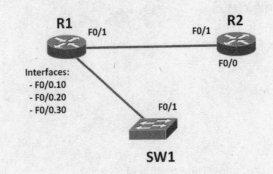

(A) There are too many sub-interfaces on f0/0.

(B) Interface f0/0 should be configured as an access port.

(C) Interface f0/0 should be configured as a trunk port.

(D) Interface F0/1 should be configured as a trunk port.

725. You have created VLAN 10 and would like to place Fast Ethernet port 0/8 in VLAN 10. Which command(s) would you use?

(A) Use the following command:

```
sw(config)#switchport access vlan 10
```

(B) Use the following commands:

```
sw(config)#interface f0/8
sw(config-if)# access vlan 10
```

(C) Use the following commands:

```
sw(config)#interface f0/8
sw(config-if)#switchport access vlan 10
```

(D) Use the following commands:

```
sw(config)#interface f0/8
sw(config-if)#switchport vlan 10
```

726. Which of the following port types cannot be ISL trunk ports?

(A) 1 Gbps

(B) 100 Mbps Fast Ethernet

(C) 10 Mbps Ethernet

(D) 10 Gbps

Configuring VLAN Trunking Protocol (VTP)

727–734 Choose the best answer(s).

727. Which protocol is used to facilitate the management of VLANs?

(A) STP

(B) 802.1q

(C) ISL

(D) VTP

728. Which VTP mode does not allow the creating of VLANs?

(A) Client mode

(B) Server mode

(C) Transparent mode

(D) Parent mode

729. You wish to prevent the sending of VLAN traffic to other switches if the destination switch does not have any ports in a specific VLAN. What VTP feature would you enable?

(A) VTP domain

(B) VTP pruning

(C) VTP password

(D) VTP passphrase

730. You would like to configure switch SW2 to receive VLAN information for the glensworld VTP domain. Which command(s) would allow you to do this?

(A) Use the following commands:

```
vtp domain P@ssw0rd
vtp password glensworld
vtp mode server
```

(B) Use the following commands:

```
vtp domain glensworld
vtp password P@ssw0rd
vtp mode transparent
```

(C)   Use the following commands:

```
vtp domain glensworld
vtp password P@ssw0rd
vtp mode client
```

(D)   Use the following command:

```
vtp mode client
```

731.   Which VTP mode allows the creation of VLANs but does not accept changes from other VTP systems and does forward VTP messages on to other devices?

(A)   Server mode

(B)   Client mode

(C)   Transparent mode

(D)   Parent mode

732.   Which of the following commands configures a port on the Cisco switch for trunking using 802.1q protocol?

(A)   Use the following commands:

```
sw(config-if)#switchport mode trunk
sw(config-if)#encapsulation dot1q
```

(B)   Use the following commands:

```
sw(config-if)#switchport mode trunk
sw(config-if)#encapsulation isl
```

(C)   Use the following commands:

```
sw(config-if)#switchport mode trunk
sw(config-if)#switchport trunk encapsulation isl
```

(D)   Use the following commands:

```
sw(config-if)#switchport mode trunk
sw(config-if)#switchport trunk encapsulation dot1q
```

733. You have configured SW1 as a VTP server for the GlensWorld VTP domain and a password of P@ssw0rd. You use the following commands to configure SW2 as a VTP client, but are unsuccessful. What is the problem?

```
vtp domain glensworld
vtp password P@ssw0rd
vtp mode client
```

(A)   The password needs changing.

(B)   The VTP mode should be set to transparent.

(C)   The VTP domain should be unique.

(D)   The VTP domain name is case sensitive.

734. You have typed the following command on switch SW1. Using the figure below, what effect will the commands have on the network?

```
Interface f0/24
Switchport mode access
```

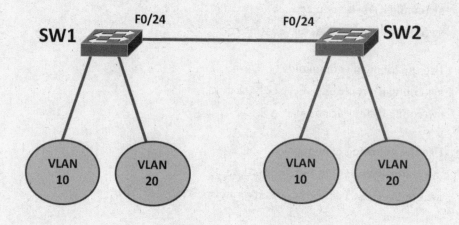

(A)   All systems in VLAN 10 can communicate with one another.

(B)   Systems will not be able to communicate between the two switches.

(C)   All systems in VLAN 20 can communicate with one another.

(D)   Systems can communicate between the two switches.

Implementing Etherchannel and Port Security

735–737 Choose the best answer(s).

735. You wish to configure an Etherchannel link made up of two Fast Ethernet trunk ports without any negotiations. What command would you use when configuring the interfaces?

   (A) `channel-group 1 mode active`

   (B) `channel-group 1 mode passive`

   (C) `channel-group 1 mode off`

   (D) `channel-group 1 mode on`

736. Which of the following is true in regards to the following commands?

```
Interface fa0/8
Switchport mode access
Switchport port-security
Switchport port-security maximum 3
Switchport port-security mac-address 1111.2222.3333
```

   (A) The switch will learn three MAC addresses and associate them with port 8.

   (B) The switch will learn eight MAC addresses and associate them with port 3.

   (C) The system with the MAC address of 1111.2222.3333 can connect to port 8 along with three other systems.

   (D) The system with the MAC address of 1111.2222.3333 can connect to port 8 along with two other systems.

737. You have configured three trunk ports in an Etherchannel group. What will happen when one port in the grouping fails?

   (A) The channel cost is increased.

   (B) The channel cost is decreased.

   (C) STP places the grouping in a blocking state.

   (D) STP places the grouping in a forwarding state.

Chapter 18

Cisco IOS Fundamentals

•••

*I*n this chapter, you are exposed to questions that relate to fundamental operation of your Cisco device, such as understanding the boot process, understanding IOS images, managing files with IFS commands, and basic licensing operations.

The Problems You'll Work On

In this chapter, you'll review questions concerning the following topics:

- ✔ Understanding the Cisco IOS boot process
- ✔ Working with IOS images
- ✔ Managing Cisco IOS files
- ✔ Working with licenses

What to Watch Out For

Don't let common mistakes trip you up; watch for the following when working with these questions:

- ✔ Your Cisco device has different types of memory: ROM memory stores the POST routines, bootstrap program, and the mini-IOSes, while flash memory stores the IOS images. RAM (or VRAM) stores temporary information such as your current configuration, MAC table, and routing table. Non-volatile RAM (or NVRAM) stores your startup configuration.

- ✔ Ensure you understand the boot process of a Cisco device. On startup, the POST routines are performed, then the bootstrap program locates an IOS in flash memory and extracts it to RAM. The system then checks for a startup configuration file; if one does not exist it will check for a TFTP server. If a TFTP server does not exist with the startup configuration then the device will prompt for the initial configuration dialog.

- ✔ Know that you can view the current IOS information with the show version command. If you wish to view all of the IOS images you have in flash memory you can use the show flash command. Be sure to understand how to read the show version output and identify information from the IOS details displayed with that command.

Understanding the Cisco IOS Boot Process

738–750 Choose the best answer(s).

738. Where is the POST routines stored on a Cisco device?

(A) NVRAM

(B) RAM

(C) ROM

(D) Flash memory

739. Which of the following describes the benefit of booting from a TFTP server?

(A) If the server is unavailable then the backup IOS is used.

(B) A central place to upgrade the IOS

(C) Faster than loading from flash

(D) Slower than loading from flash

740. What happens after the bootstrap program locates the IOS in flash memory?

(A) It formats the IOS.

(B) It copies it to ROM.

(C) The IOS is loaded into RAM.

(D) It copies it to NVRAM.

741. You wish to disrupt the boot process on the Cisco device. What keystroke would you press?

(A) Ctrl-Alt-Break

(B) Ctrl–Break

(C) Ctrl-Alt-Ins

(D) Alt-Break

742. Which type of memory is used to store the bootstrap program?

(A) NVRAM

(B) RAM

(C) ROM

(D) Flash memory

743. The startup configuration is stored in which type of memory?

(A) ROM

(B) NVRAM

(C) RAM

(D) FLASH

744. What happens if a startup config does not exist on boot-up?

(A) The device will try to connect to a TFTP server for the configuration.

(B) The device fails to boot.

(C) The device loads a default config from ROM.

(D) The device loads a default config from flash.

745. What command would you use to configure the router to not load the startup configuration?

(A) `config-register 2102`

(B) `config-register 1200`

(C) `config-register 2100`

(D) `config-register 2142`

746. Which component is responsible for locating an operating system to load in memory?

(A) Bootstrap

(B) ROM

(C) Flash

(D) IOS

747. Looking at the figure below, what is the command to configure the Cisco device to boot from the IOS stored in flash memory?

```
R1#show flash

System flash directory:
File  Length    Name/status
  3   50938004  c2800nm-advipservicesk9-mz.124-15.T1.bin
  2   28282     sigdef-category.xml
  1   227537    sigdef-default.xml
[51193823 bytes used, 12822561 available, 64016384 total]
63488K bytes of processor board System flash (Read/Write)

R1#
```

(A) `boot system tftp c2800nm-advipservicesk9-mz.124-15.T1.bin`

(B) `boot system flash c2800nm-advipservicesk9-mz.124-15.T1.bin`

(C) `boot system flash sigdef-category.xml`

(D) `boot system flash sigdef-default.xml`

748. What command would you use to change the configuration file that is applied on startup?

    (A)   `boot config <file>`

    (B)   `set startup-file`

    (C)   `boot system config <file>`

    (D)   `boot private-config <file>`

749. You are troubleshooting the startup of your Cisco switch. What command was used in the figure below to display the following output?

```
BOOT path-list       :
Config file          : flash:/config.text
Private Config file  : flash:/private-config.text
Enable Break         : no
Manual Boot          : no
HELPER path-list     :
Auto upgrade         : yes
NVRAM/Config file
       buffer size:    65536
Switch#
```

    (A)   `show config`

    (B)   `show IOS`

    (C)   `show flash`

    (D)   `show boot`

750. The bootstrap program is stored in what type of memory on the Cisco router?

    (A)   NVRAM

    (B)   RAM

    (C)   ROM

    (D)   Flash memory

Working with IOS Images

751–760 Choose the best answer(s).

751. Looking at the figure below, what is the name of the image file that contains the Cisco IOS?

```
R1#show flash

System flash directory:
File  Length   Name/status
  3   50938004 c2800nm-advipservicesk9-mz.124-15.T1.bin
  2   28282    sigdef-category.xml
  1   227537   sigdef-default.xml
[51193823 bytes used, 12822561 available, 64016384 total]
63488K bytes of processor board System flash (Read/Write)

R1#
```

(A) sigdef-default.xml

(B) sigdef-category.xml

(C) name/status

(D) c2800nm-advipservicesk9-mz.124-15.T1.bin

752. You wish to back up your IOS image to a TFTP server. What command would you use?

(A) `copy flash tftp`

(B) `copy boot tftp`

(C) `copy image tftp`

(D) `copy <filename> tftp`

753. Which of the following would be a downfall of loading the IOS image from a TFTP server?

(A) If the server is unavailable devices cannot boot up.

(B) Faster than flash

(C) A central place to upgrade the IOS

(D) Fault tolerance available

754. You have a copy of your IOS image located on a TFTP server. What command would you use to restore the IOS to your device?

(A) `restore flash tftp`

(B) `restore tftp flash`

(C) `copy tftp rom`

(D) `copy tftp flash`

755. You wish to find out what version of the Cisco IOS you are running. What command would you run?

   (A)   `show mem`

   (B)   `show memory`

   (C)   `show ios`

   (D)   `show version`

756. What command would you use to configure the Cisco device to boot from an IOS image located on a TFTP server?

   (A)   `boot tftp <filename.bin>`

   (B)   `boot system <filename.bin>`

   (C)   `boot system tftp <filename.bin>`

   (D)   `boot system flash <filename.bin>`

757. By default, the Cisco bootstrap program loads which IOS image if one is not specified?

   (A)   The first image on a TFTP server

   (B)   The last image on a TFTP server

   (C)   The last image stored in flash

   (D)   The first image stored in flash

758. What command would you use to specify a secondary bootstrap image?

   (A)   `boot config`

   (B)   `boot system`

   (C)   `boot bootstrap`

   (D)   `boot`

759. You need to find out what IOS image file was used to boot the router. What command would you use?

   (A)   `show ios`

   (B)   `show version`

   (C)   `show boot`

   (D)   `show image`

760. What command would you use to configure your router to load the IOS image from a TFTP server?

(A) `boot system flash <filename>`

(B) `boot system <filename>`

(C) `boot system tftp <filename>`

(D) `boot system flash-tftp <filename>`

Managing Cisco IOS Files

761–772 Choose the best answer(s).

761. You wish to delete a file from flash memory. What command would you use?

(A) `delete flash:<filename>`

(B) `kill flash:<filename>`

(C) `delete <filename>`

(D) `kill <filename>`

762. You wish to invoke the initial configuration dialog. What command would you use?

(A) `init`

(B) `show init`

(C) `init dialog`

(D) `setup`

763. What file extension do Cisco IOS images use?

(A) .jpg

(B) .image

(C) .exe

(D) .bin

764. You are customizing the boot preferences and would like to change the size of the NVRAM buffer used for the IFS. What command would you use?

(A) `boot buffersize`

(B) `boot config-file`

(C) `buffersize-boot`

(D) `config-file boot`

765. You would like to know how much memory exists on the Cisco device. What command would you use?

(A) `show memory`

(B) `show version`

(C) `show ram`

(D) `show ios`

766. Looking at the output of the figure below, what command was used?

```
Directory of flash:/
    1  -rw-     4414921          <no date>  c2960-lanbase-mz.122-25.FX.bin
    2  -rw-         676          <no date>  vlan.dat
64016384 bytes total (59600787 bytes free)
Switch#
```

(A) `show system:`

(B) `show flash:`

(C) `show version`

(D) `show nvram`

767. What command can you use on your Cisco router to display the available flash memory?

(A) `show version`

(B) `show memory`

(C) `show flash`

(D) `show mem`

768. You wish to display the contents of NVRAM. What command would you use?

(A) `dir nvram:`

(B) `dir`

(C) `dir flash:`

(D) `show nvram`

769. Looking at the figure below, what is the platform for the device?

```
R1#show version
Cisco IOS Software, 2800 Software (C2800NM-ADVIPSERVICESK9-M), Version 12.4(15)T1,
RELEASE SOFTWARE (fc2)
Technical Support: http://www.cisco.com/techsupport
Copyright (c) 1986-2007 by Cisco Systems, Inc.
Compiled Wed 18-Jul-07 06:21 by pt_rel_team

ROM: System Bootstrap, Version 12.1(3r)T2, RELEASE SOFTWARE (fc1)
Copyright (c) 2000 by cisco Systems, Inc.

System returned to ROM by power-on
System image file is "c2800nm-advipservicesk9-mz.124-15.T1.bin"

cisco 2811 (MPC860) processor (revision 0x200) with 60416K/5120K bytes of memory
Processor board ID JAD05190MTZ (4292891495)
M860 processor: part number 0, mask 49
2 FastEthernet/IEEE 802.3 interface(s)
2 Low-speed serial(sync/async) network interface(s)
239K bytes of NVRAM.
62720K bytes of processor board System flash (Read/Write)

Configuration register is 0x2102

R1#
```

(A)   2800

(B)   12.4

(C)   2 FastEthernet

(D)   2102

770. Which file contained in flash memory on a Cisco switch is used to store secured configuration data such as cryptography keys?

(A)   config.text

(B)   secured.text

(C)   keys.text

(D)   private-config.text

771. You wish to display the contents of flash memory using IFS commands. What command would you use?

(A)   `dir nvram`

(B)   `dir flash:`

(C)   `display flash`

(D)   `get flash:`

772. Looking at the figure below, how much flash memory exists in the device?

```
R1#show version
Cisco IOS Software, 2800 Software (C2800NM-ADVIPSERVICESK9-M), Version 12.4(15)T1,
RELEASE SOFTWARE (fc2)
Technical Support: http://www.cisco.com/techsupport
Copyright (c) 1986-2007 by Cisco Systems, Inc.
Compiled Wed 18-Jul-07 06:21 by pt_rel_team

ROM: System Bootstrap, Version 12.1(3r)T2, RELEASE SOFTWARE (fc1)
Copyright (c) 2000 by cisco Systems, Inc.

System returned to ROM by power-on
System image file is "c2800nm-advipservicesk9-mz.124-15.T1.bin"

cisco 2811 (MPC860) processor (revision 0x200) with 60416K/5120K bytes of memory
Processor board ID JAD05190MTZ (4292891495)
M860 processor: part number 0, mask 49
2 FastEthernet/IEEE 802.3 interface(s)
2 Low-speed serial(sync/async) network interface(s)
239K bytes of NVRAM.
62720K bytes of processor board System flash (Read/Write)

Configuration register is 0x2102

R1#
```

(A) 62720 K

(B) 2800 K

(C) 239 K

(D) 5120 K

Working with Licenses

773–775 Choose the best answer(s).

773. You wish to remove a license from your Cisco device. What command would you use?

(A) `remove license ipservices`

(B) `delete ipservices`

(C) `license clear ipservices`

(D) `delete license ipservices`

774. You have copied a new Cisco license file called r1fs-ips from the TFTP server to flash memory. How do you install this new license on your Cisco switch?

(A) `license install tftp: r1fs-ips`

(B) `license install flash: r1fs-ips`

(C) `license r1fs-ips`

(D) `license flash: r1fs-ips`

775. You wish to display the current license information. What command would you use?

(A) `display license file`

(B) `show license file`

(C) `license show file`

(D) `show all`

Chapter 19

Router Essentials and Route Summarization

• •

In this chapter, you are presented with questions that test you on essential routing concepts in order to prepare you for the ICND2 exam. This chapter reviews basic information regarding routing protocols and also tests your knowledge of calculating summary routes, given detail route information.

The Problems You'll Work On

In this chapter, you'll review questions concerning the following topics:

- ✔ Understanding static and dynamic routing
- ✔ Recognizing routing terminology
- ✔ Working with route summarization
- ✔ Knowing about inter-VLAN routing

What to Watch Out For

Don't let common mistakes trip you up; watch for the following when working with these questions:

- ✔ For the ICND2 exam, be sure to know the benefits and drawbacks of both static routing and dynamic routing.
- ✔ Know the basics of routing protocols such as distance vector versus link state routing protocols.
- ✔ Know the administrative distances associated with each of the routing protocols.
- ✔ Know that route summarization is designed to keep a small routing table and how to calculate a summary route, given the actual routes.
- ✔ You will be tested heavily on routing between VLANs and how to configure a router on a stick. Know that on the router, you need to configure sub-interfaces and set the encapsulation protocol for each sub-interface.

Understanding Static and Dynamic Routing

776–797 Choose the best answer(s).

776. Which of the following are true of RIPv1? (Select two.)

(A)   Administrative distance of 90

(B)   Is classful

(C)   Administrative distance of 120

(D)   Is classless

(E)   Vendor specific

777. You have configured a network as shown in the figure below. From router R1, you can ping the S0/0 interface on router R2, but you cannot ping the F0/0 interface on router R2. What is the cause of the problem?

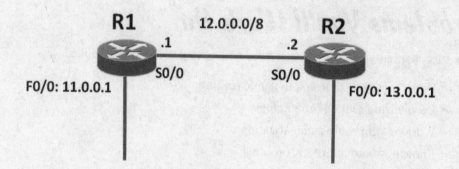

(A)   The default gateway of router R2 is incorrect.

(B)   There is no route for the 13.0.0.0 network on router R1.

(C)   You need to load RIP on router R2.

(D)   The default gateway on router R1 is incorrect.

778. Which of the following is true of classful routing protocols?

(A)   They send subnet mask info with the routing update.

(B)   They use wildcard masks.

(C)   They use the route with the highest cost pathway.

(D)   They do not send the subnet mask info with the routing update.

779. Which of the following is true of RIPv2? (Select two.)

    (A)   Administrative distance of 90

    (B)   Is classful

    (C)   Administrative distance of 120

    (D)   Is classless

    (E)   Vendor specific

780. Distance vector routing protocols use which of the following as their metric?

    (A)   Bandwidth

    (B)   Link speed

    (C)   Hop count

    (D)   Available bandwidth

781. What is the administrative distance of RIP?

    (A)   90

    (B)   100

    (C)   110

    (D)   120

    (E)   1

782. Which of the following is true of EIGRP? (Select two.)

    (A)   Uses cost as its metric

    (B)   Is vendor-specific

    (C)   Is an open standard

    (D)   Administrative distance of 110

    (E)   Administrative distance of 90

783. Which of the following identifies the benefit of static routing over dynamic routing? (Select two.)

    (A)   More secure because the administrator must add the routes.

    (B)   Less secure because the administrator must add the routes.

    (C)   Bandwidth is being used to update the routing tables.

    (D)   No bandwidth is being used to update the routing tables.

784. What is the default administrative distance of a static route?

(A) 90

(B) 100

(C) 110

(D) 120

(E) 1

785. Which of the following is true of OSPF? (Select two.)

(A) Elects a DR

(B) Is vendor-specific

(C) Administrative distance of 90

(D) Uses cost as its metric

(E) Administrative distance of 110

786. What is the administrative distance of OSPF?

(A) 90

(B) 100

(C) 110

(D) 120

(E) 1

787. You are the network administrator for a small network that has two routers (R1 and R2, as shown in the figure below) that are connected via serial interfaces. You have used the command `Ip route 13.0.0.0 255.0.0.0 12.0.0.2` on R1 to finalize configuration. What happens if the serial interface on R2 shuts down?

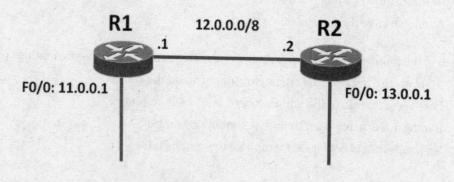

(A) A triggered update is sent from R2 to R1.

(B) A triggered update is sent from R1 to R2.

(C) The route of 13.0.0.0 remains on router R1.

(D) A poison reverse packet is sent from R2 to R1.

788. You have no static routes configured on the router. A router learns about a route to the same network from OSPF, EIGRP, and RIP. Which route is added to the routing table?

(A) The RIP route

(B) The EIGRP route

(C) The OSPF route

(D) All the routes

789. Which of the following is a benefit of triggered updates?

(A) It decreases convergence time by sending out an update as soon as there is a change to the network topology.

(B) They are more accurate than scheduled updates.

(C) They are supported by all routing protocols.

(D) It increases convergence time by sending out an update as soon as there is a change to the network topology.

790. You are troubleshooting communication on router R1. You use the show ip route command to display the routing table. Using the output of the figure below, how will information be sent from R1 to a system with the IP address of 15.0.0.25?

```
R1(config)#do show ip route
Codes: C - connected, S - static, I - IGRP, R - RIP, M - mobile, B - BGP
       D - EIGRP, EX - EIGRP external, O - OSPF, IA - OSPF inter area
       N1 - OSPF NSSA external type 1, N2 - OSPF NSSA external type 2
       E1 - OSPF external type 1, E2 - OSPF external type 2, E - EGP
       i - IS-IS, L1 - IS-IS level-1, L2 - IS-IS level-2, ia - IS-IS inter area
       * - candidate default, U - per-user static route, o - ODR
       P - periodic downloaded static route

Gateway of last resort is not set

C    11.0.0.0/8 is directly connected, FastEthernet0/0
C    12.0.0.0/8 is directly connected, Serial0/3/0
D    13.0.0.0/8 [90/2172416] via 12.0.0.2, 00:00:56, Serial0/3/0
C    14.0.0.0/8 is directly connected, Serial0/3/1
D    15.0.0.0/8 [90/2681856] via 12.0.0.2, 00:00:56, Serial0/3/0
                [90/2681856] via 14.0.0.2, 00:00:45, Serial0/3/1
```

(A) Directly through FastEthernet 0/0

(B) Always through 13.0.0.2

(C) Always through 12.0.0.2

(D) Through 12.0.0.2, and through 14.0.0.2

(E) Always through 14.0.0.2

791. Which of the following is true of link state routing protocols? (Select two.)

(A) Choose the route with the lowest hop count

(B) They use more resources as they store multiple tables in memory

(C) Use a single table to share routing information

(D) Use triggered updates to reduce the time to converge

792. You would like to ensure that a static route is used as a backup over a route using the same pathway discovered by a dynamic routing protocol. What parameter would you change?

    (A) Cost

    (B) Bandwidth

    (C) Administrative distance

    (D) Clock rate

793. What are the three tables that a link state routing protocol typically uses? (Select three.)

    (A) Topology table

    (B) MAC table

    (C) Neighbor table

    (D) STP table

    (E) Routing table

794. Which of the following routing protocols does not auto summarize routes?

    (A) RIP

    (B) OSPF

    (C) EIGRP

    (D) IGRP

795. Looking at the figure below, when router R1 sends data to router R4, what pathway will be used?

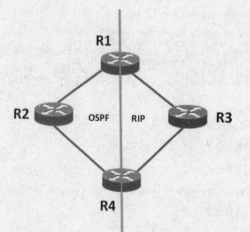

    (A) R1 cannot reach R4.

    (B) Through R3.

    (C) Through R2.

    (D) R1 will drop all packets for R4.

796. Which of the following commands alters the administrative distance on the static route from the default value?

    (A)   `ip route 21.0.0.0 255.0.0.0 20.0.0.2`

    (B)   `ip route 21.0.0.0 255.0.0.0 20.0.0.2 admin-distance 110`

    (C)   `admin-distance static route 21.0.0.0 255.0.0.0 20.0.0.2 110`

    (D)   `ip route 21.0.0.0 255.0.0.0 20.0.0.2 110`

797. You would like to enable IPv6 routing on your Cisco router. What command would you use?

    (A)   `ip route ipv6`

    (B)   `ip route local ipv6`

    (C)   `ipv6 forwarding`

    (D)   `ipv6 unicast-routing`

Recognizing Routing Terminology

798–803 Choose the best answer(s).

798. Which of the following does a link state routing protocol use to build the topology database? (Select two.)

    (A)   Hop count

    (B)   Hello messages

    (C)   Static routes

    (D)   BPDU from other devices

    (E)   LSA from other routers

799. Which of the following is the term for packets that are flooded when a topology change occurs?

    (A)   Holddown timer

    (B)   Poison reverse

    (C)   Count to infinity

    (D)   LSA

    (E)   Split horizon

800. Which of the following causes a router to ignore updates from lower metric paths for a period of time?

    (A)   Holddown timer

    (B)   Poison reverse

    (C)   Count to infinity

    (D)   LSA

    (E)   Split horizon

801. Which of the following is the term for preventing a router from sending updates on a route through the interface on which it received the knowledge of the route?

(A) Holddown timer

(B) Poison reverse

(C) Count to infinity

(D) LSA

(E) Split horizon

802. Which of the following involves a router learning that a route is down from its neighbor, and then sending an update back to the neighbor on the route with an infinite metric?

(A) Holddown timer

(B) Poison reverse

(C) Count to infinity

(D) LSA

(E) Split horizon

803. Which of the following routing protocols are vendor specific?

(A) RIP

(B) EIGRP

(C) OSPF

(D) ARP

Working with Route Summarization

804–808 Choose the best answer(s).

804. What is the goal of route summarization?

(A) To support different size subnets

(B) To share routing table information other routers

(C) To prevent loops on the network

(D) To reduce the size of the routing table

805. You are configuring OSPF and need to determine the summary route for networks 131.107.16.0 up to 131.107.19.0. Which of the following identifies the summary route?

(A) 131.107.0.0/22

(B) 131.107.16.0/24

(C) 131.107.16.0/21

(D) 131.107.16.0/22

806. You are configuring OSPF and need to determine the summary route for networks 172.16.0.0 up to 172.16.7.0. Which of the following identifies the summary route?

    (A) 172.16.0.0/20

    (B) 172.16.0.0/21

    (C) 172.16.0.0/22

    (D) 172.16.0.0/23

807. Which of the following identifies the summary route for networks 10.4.0.0 up to 10.7.0.0?

    (A) 10.0.0.0/14

    (B) 10.0.0.0/15

    (C) 10.4.0.0/14

    (D) 10.4.0.0/13

808. Which of the following identifies the summary route for networks 120.12.0.0 to 12.15.0.0?

    (A) 120.12.0.0/16

    (B) 120.12.0.0/14

    (C) 120.12.0.0/23

    (D) 120.12.0.0/13

Knowing about Inter-VLAN Routing

809–813 Choose the best answer(s).

809. You have a router connected to a switch that has three VLANs. You would like to configure the router so that it can be used to route traffic between the three VLANs. What do you need to do?

    (A) Add two more routers to the network — one for each VLAN

    (B) Enable RIP

    (C) Configure router on a stick

    (D) Configure OSPF

810. Which of the following switch commands would you use on the port that is connected to a router on a stick?

    (A) SW1(config-if)#switchport mode trunk

    (B) SW1(config-if)#switchport mode access

    (C) SW1(config-if)#switchport mode sub-interface

    (D) SW1(config-if)#switchport port-security

811. Router R1 is connected to a switch that has three VLANs. You are configuring the router to route traffic between the three VLANs. What do you need to do? (Select two.)

(A) Configure the interface that is connected to the switch as a trunk port using the same encapsulation protocol.

(B) Enable RIP on the router.

(C) Configure the interface that is connected to the switch as an access port.

(D) Configure the interface that is connected to the switch with three sub-interfaces.

(E) Use different encapsulation protocols on the switch and router.

812. Looking at the figure below, how would you configure the router and switch to route between the VLANs? (Select two.)

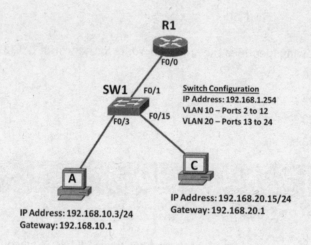

Switch Configuration
IP Address: 192.168.1.254
VLAN 10 – Ports 2 to 12
VLAN 20 – Ports 13 to 24

IP Address: 192.168.10.3/24
Gateway: 192.168.10.1

IP Address: 192.168.20.15/24
Gateway: 192.168.20.1

(A) On R1 perform the following commands:

R1(config)#interface f0/0

R1(config-if)#no shutdown

R1(config)#interface f0/0.10

```
R1(config-subif)#encapsulation trunk 10
R1(config-subif)#ip address 192.168.10.1 255.255.255.0
R1(config)#interface f0/0.20
R1(config-subif)#encapsulation trunk 20
R1(config-subif)#ip address 192.168.20.1 255.255.255.0
```

(B) On R1 perform the following commands:

```
R1(config)#interface f0/0
R1(config-if)#no shutdown
R1(config)#interface f0/0.10
R1(config-subif)#encapsulation dot1q 10
R1(config-subif)#ip address 192.168.10.1 255.255.255.0
R1(config)#interface f0/0.20
R1(config-subif)#encapsulation dot1q 20
R1(config-subif)#ip address 192.168.20.1 255.255.255.0
```

(C) On SW1 perform the following commands:

```
SW1(config)#interface f0/1
SW1(config-if)#switchport mode access
```

(D) On SW1 perform the following commands:

```
SW1(config)#interface f0/1
SW1(config-if)#switchport mode trunk
```

813. Sue has been assigned the task of creating a router-on-a-stick network. She has configured what is shown in the figure below. Assuming all interfaces have been properly configured, what else needs to be done?

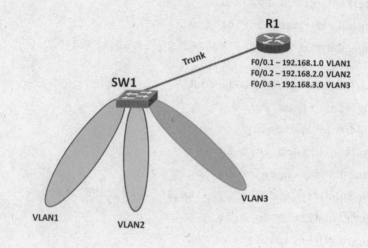

F0/0.1 – 192.168.1.0 VLAN1
F0/0.2 – 192.168.2.0 VLAN2
F0/0.3 – 192.168.3.0 VLAN3

(A) Nothing

(B) Perform the following commands on the router:
```
Router rip
Network 192.168.1.0
Network 192.168.2.0
Network 192.168.3.0
```

(C) Change the trunk port to an access port

(D) Perform the following commands on the router:
```
router eigrp 1
Network 192.168.1.0
Network 192.168.2.0
Network 192.168.3.0
```

Chapter 20

RIP and OSPF

• •

In this chapter, you are presented with questions related to two industry standard routing protocols: the Routing Information Protocol (RIP) and the Open Shortest Path First (OSPF). The ICND2 exam tests you heavily on OSPF, and you may come across some RIP questions, too, so be sure to know both protocols well!

The Problems You'll Work On

In this chapter, you'll review questions concerning the following topics:

- ✔ Understanding RIP
- ✔ Configuring RIP
- ✔ Understanding OSPF
- ✔ Configuring OSPF

What to Watch Out For

Don't let common mistakes trip you up; watch for the following when working with these questions:

- ✔ RIP is a distance vector routing protocol that has two versions: RIPv1 and RIPv2. RIP has an administrative distance of 120 by default that sends routing updates every 30 seconds.

- ✔ RIPv2 is a classless routing protocol that supports VLSM and authentication.

- ✔ OSPF is a link state routing protocol that has a default administrative distance of 110. OSPF identifies neighboring routers by sending Hello messages every ten seconds.

- ✔ OSPF does not auto summarize routes by default: You must configure summarization. OSPF uses a metric know as cost, which is calculated based on the bandwidth of the link.

- ✔ OSPF minimizes bandwidth usage by electing a Designated Router (DR) that all routers will exchange information with. The DR will then send routing information to all other routers. The DR is elected by the router with the highest OSPF priority. If there are multiple routers with the same priority, then the router with the highest router ID is used. If the router ID has not been set, then a router ID is chosen by (a) the highest IP address on a loopback interface, or (b) if there are no loopback addresses, then the highest IP on a physical interface.

Understanding RIP

814–821 Choose the best answer(s).

814. What is the administrative distance of RIP?

(A) 90

(B) 120

(C) 110

(D) 1

815. After configuring RIP, you are not receiving any RIP entries in your routing table. What command could you use to verify you are receiving RIP updates?

(A) `show rip messages`

(B) `show rip`

(C) `debug ip rip`

(D) `ip rip debug`

816. Which RIP version supports VLSM?

(A) Version 1

(B) Version 2

(C) Version 3

(D) Version 4

817. Which of the following identifies differences between RIPv1 and RIPv2? (Select two.)

(A) RIPv2 sends updates every 60 seconds.

(B) RIPv2 is classful.

(C) RIPv2 sends updates using multicast communication.

(D) RIPv2 sends updates using broadcast communication.

(E) RIPv2 supports authentication.

818. You have configured RIPv2 and you do not want it to auto summarize routes. What command would you use?

(A) `delete auto-summary`

(B) `no auto-summary`

(C) `negate summary`

(D) `auto-summary stop`

819. Looking at the figure below, what version of RIP has been enabled?

```
R1#debug ip rip
RIP protocol debugging is on
R1#RIP: received v1 update from 12.0.0.2 on Serial0/3/0
        13.0.0.0 in 1 hops
RIP: sending  v1 update to 255.255.255.255 via FastEthernet0/0 (11.0.0.1)
RIP: build update entries
        network 12.0.0.0 metric 1
        network 13.0.0.0 metric 2
RIP: sending  v1 update to 255.255.255.255 via Serial0/3/0 (12.0.0.1)
RIP: build update entries
        network 11.0.0.0 metric 1
```

(A) Version 2

(B) Version 1

(C) Version 4

(D) Version 3

820. How frequently does RIPv2 send out routing table updates?

(A) Every 30 seconds

(B) Every 60 seconds

(C) Every 90 seconds

(D) Every 120 seconds

821. You want to change the administrative distance of RIP to a value other than its default. What command would you use?

(A) R1(config-router)#distance 80

(B) R1(config-router)#distance 120

(C) R1(config)#distance 80

(D) R1(config)#distance 120

Configuring RIP

822–829 Choose the best answer(s).

822. You have already configured RIPv1, but have recently learned of the benefits of RIPv2. What additional command(s) would you use to enable RIPv2?

(A) R1(config-router)#version 2

(B) R1(config-router)#enable version 2

(C) R1(config)#version 2

(D) R1(config-router)#no version 1

823. Looking at the figure below, what is the administrative distance?

```
R1#show ip protocols
Routing Protocol is "rip"
Sending updates every 30 seconds, next due in 11 seconds
Invalid after 180 seconds, hold down 180, flushed after 240
Outgoing update filter list for all interfaces is not set
Incoming update filter list for all interfaces is not set
Redistributing: rip
Default version control: send version 1, receive any version
  Interface            Send  Recv  Triggered RIP  Key-chain
  FastEthernet0/0       1     2 1
  Serial0/3/0           1     2 1
Automatic network summarization is in effect
Maximum path: 4
Routing for Networks:
        11.0.0.0
        12.0.0.0
Passive Interface(s):
Routing Information Sources:
        Gateway         Distance       Last Update
        12.0.0.2             25        00:00:16
Distance: 25 (default is 120)
```

(A) 25

(B) 30

(C) 180

(D) 120

824. You have configured RIP on your router and want to view the entries in the routing table. What command would you use?

(A) `show rip`

(B) `show rip entries`

(C) `show ip route`

(D) `show ip rip`

825. You have a router with two networks you wish to advertise through RIP – the 192.168.3.0 and the 192.168.4.0 networks. Which of the following identifies the commands you would use?

(A) Use the following commands:

R1(config)#`router rip`

R1(config-router)#`network 192.168.3.0`

R1(config-router)#`network 192.168.4.0`

(B) Use the following commands:

R1(config)#`network 192.168.3.0`

R1(config)#`network 192.168.4.0`

(C) Use the following commands:

R1(config)#`router rip`

R1(config-router)#`network 192.168.3.0 0.0.0.255`

R1(config-router)#`network 192.168.4.0 0.0.0.255`

(D) Use the following commands:

R1(config)#`router rip`

R1(config-router)#`network 192.168.3.0 area 1`

R1(config-router)#`network 192.168.4.0 area 1`

826. Looking at the figure below, how many hops away is the 14.56.7.8 system?

```
R2#show ip route
Codes: C - connected, S - static, I - IGRP, R - RIP, M - mobile, B - BGP
       D - EIGRP, EX - EIGRP external, O - OSPF, IA - OSPF inter area
       N1 - OSPF NSSA external type 1, N2 - OSPF NSSA external type 2
       E1 - OSPF external type 1, E2 - OSPF external type 2, E - EGP
       i - IS-IS, L1 - IS-IS level-1, L2 - IS-IS level-2, ia - IS-IS inter area
       * - candidate default, U - per-user static route, o - ODR
       P - periodic downloaded static route

Gateway of last resort is not set

R    11.0.0.0/8 [120/1] via 12.0.0.1, 00:00:05, Serial0/3/0
R    14.0.0.0/8 [120/3] via 12.0.0.5, 00:00:05, Serial0/3/0
C    12.0.0.0/8 is directly connected, Serial0/3/0
C    13.0.0.0/8 is directly connected, FastEthernet0/0
R2#
```

(A) 1

(B) 120

(C) 5

(D) 3

827. You want to view how frequently RIP is sending updates. What command would you use?

(A) `show rip`

(B) `show protocols`

(C) `show rip config`

(D) `show ip protocols`

828. Looking at the figure below, what command was used to create the output?

```
Routing Protocol is "rip"
Sending updates every 30 seconds, next due in 16 seconds
Invalid after 180 seconds, hold down 180, flushed after 240
Outgoing update filter list for all interfaces is not set
Incoming update filter list for all interfaces is not set
Redistributing: rip
Default version control: send version 1, receive any version
  Interface              Send  Recv  Triggered RIP  Key-chain
  Serial0/3/0            1     2 1
  FastEthernet0/0        1     2 1
Automatic network summarization is in effect
Maximum path: 4
Routing for Networks:
      12.0.0.0
      13.0.0.0
Passive Interface(s):
Routing Information Sources:
      Gateway          Distance       Last Update
      12.0.0.1              120       00:00:20
Distance: (default is 120)
R2#
```

(A) show ip route

(B) show ip protocols

(C) show rip

(D) show ospf

829. Which of the following commands would you use to change the administrative distance with RIP?

(A) Use the following commands:

R1(config)#router rip

R1(config-router)#distance 44

(B) Use the following commands:

R1(config)#router eigrp

R1(config-router)#distance 44

(C) Use the following commands:

R1#router rip

R1#distance 44

(D) Use the following command:

R1(config)#distance 44

Understanding OSPF

830–842 Choose the best answer(s).

830. What is the maximum number of equal cost routes that can exist in the routing table with OSPF?

(A) 1

(B) 2

(C) 4

(D) 8

831. What is the default administrative distance of routes learned with OSPF?

(A) 90

(B) 120

(C) 110

(D) 1

832. Which of the following does OSPF use as a metric value?

(A) Bandwidth

(B) Hop count

(C) Cost

(D) Distance

833. When the OSPF priorities on all the routers are the same, how is the DR selected?

(A) The router with the lowest router ID

(B) The router with the highest router ID

(C) The router with the priority set to 0

(D) One is randomly selected.

834. How frequently are hello messages sent with OSPF?

(A) Every 90 seconds

(B) Every 60 seconds

(C) Every 30 seconds

(D) Every 10 seconds

835. Which of the following areas is considered the "backbone" area with OSPF?

(A) Area 1

(B) Area 0

(C) Area 2

(D) Area 10

836. How frequently does RIPv1 send out routing table updates?

(A) Every 30 seconds

(B) Every 60 seconds

(C) Every 90 seconds

(D) Every 120 seconds

837. What is the purpose of a Designated Router (DR) with OSPF?

(A) It acts as a backup if the BDR fails.

(B) It assigns IP addresses to clients on the network.

(C) It converts private addresses to public addresses.

(D) All other routers exchange info with the DR to cut down on bandwidth usage.

838. You wish to ensure that router R1 never becomes the DR. What should you do?

(A) Set the priority to 0.

(B) Set the priority to 1.

(C) Set the priority to 99.

(D) Set the priority to 255.

839. How often are hello messages sent with OSPF?

(A) Every 12 seconds

(B) Every 20 seconds

(C) Every 10 seconds

(D) Every 30 seconds

840. What happens when the DR fails?

(A) The BDR becomes the DR and an election for a new BDR occurs.

(B) A new DR is elected.

(C) The router ID is changed.

(D) The priority of the OSPF router is set to 0.

841. What are two reasons why two OSPF routers would not be able to create neighbor relationships? (Select two.)

    (A)   The router IDs are different.

    (B)   Hello and Dead Interval timers are not configured the same on both routers.

    (C)   The routers are in the same area.

    (D)   The routers are in different areas.

    (E)   There is no loopback interface configured on each router.

842. What is the purpose of the BDR with OSPF?

    (A)   The BDR informs routers of priorities.

    (B)   The BDR contains fault tolerant links to head office.

    (C)   The BDR contains fault tolerant links to a central network.

    (D)   The BDR is used when the DR fails.

Configuring OSPF

843–851 Choose the best answer(s).

843. Looking at the commands below, what is the purpose of the "1"?

```
Router ospf 1
Network 192.168.2.0 0.0.0.255 area 0
```

    (A)   It is the OSPF priority.

    (B)   It is the router ID.

    (C)   It is the process ID for OSPF.

    (D)   It is a bit flag setting OSPF to "on."

844. Looking at the figure below, what does the /65 indicate in the third route of the routing table?

```
R1>show ip route
Codes: C - connected, S - static, I - IGRP, R - RIP, M - mobile, B - BGP
       D - EIGRP, EX - EIGRP external, O - OSPF, IA - OSPF inter area
       N1 - OSPF NSSA external type 1, N2 - OSPF NSSA external type 2
       E1 - OSPF external type 1, E2 - OSPF external type 2, E - EGP
       i - IS-IS, L1 - IS-IS level-1, L2 - IS-IS level-2, ia - IS-IS inter area
       * - candidate default, U - per-user static route, o - ODR
       P - periodic downloaded static route

Gateway of last resort is not set

C    11.0.0.0/8 is directly connected, FastEthernet0/0
C    12.0.0.0/8 is directly connected, Serial0/3/0
O    13.0.0.0/8 [110/65] via 12.0.0.2, 00:42:33, Serial0/3/0
R1>
```

(A)   The administrative distance

(B)   The bandwidth

(C)   The hop count

(D)   The cost

845. Your router has the interface configuration shown below. What is the router ID of the router?

Loopback0: 12.0.0.1

Loopback1: 14.0.0.1

F0/1: 24.0.0.1

F0/2: 96.0.0.1

(A)   14.0.0.1

(B)   12.0.0.1

(C)   24.0.0.1

(D)   96.0.0.1

846. Looking at the figure below, what would the router-ID of the router be?

```
R2#show ip interface brief
Interface        IP-Address    OK? Method Status                Protocol
FastEthernet0/0  13.0.0.1      YES manual up                    up
FastEthernet0/1  unassigned    YES unset  administratively down down
Serial0/3/0      12.0.0.2      YES manual up                    up
Serial0/3/1      unassigned    YES unset  administratively down down
Vlan1            unassigned    YES unset  administratively down down
R2#
```

(A)   12.0.0.1

(B)   R1

(C)   R2

(D)   13.0.0.1

847. What commands would you use to configure OSPF and add network 192.168.5.0/24 to area 0? (Select two.)

    (A) `router ospf area 0`

    (B) `router ospf 1`

    (C) `network 192.168.5.0 0.0.0.255 area 0`

    (D) `network 192.168.5.0 255.255.255.0`

    (E) `network 192.168.5.0 0.0.0.255`

848. You want to change the OSPF priority of router R1. What command would you use?

    (A) `ospf priority 20`

    (B) `ip priority ospf 20`

    (C) `priority ospf 20`

    (D) `ip ospf priority 20`

849. Which of the following is used to calculate OSPF cost?

    (A) Bandwidth

    (B) Delay

    (C) Hop count

    (D) Latency

850. You want to change the router ID of a Cisco router running OSPF. What command would you use?

    (A) R1(config-router)#`router-id 105`

    (B) R1(config-router)#`router-id 13.0.0.1`

    (C) R1(config)#`router-id 13.0.0.1`

    (D) R1#`router-id 105`

851. Hello messages are sent to which of the following addresses?

    (A) 255.255.255.255

    (B) 224.0.0.5

    (C) 239.0.0.5

    (D) 255.0.0.0

Chapter 21

Routing with EIGRP

• •

*T*he ICND2 exam tests your knowledge of different routing protocols, and one of the protocols you will receive questions on is the EIGRP routing protocol. Study the details of EIGRP, and then try the questions in this chapter to test your knowledge level of Cisco's hybrid routing protocol!

The Problems You'll Work On

In this chapter, you'll review questions concerning the following topics:

- ✓ Understanding EIGRP
- ✓ Configuring EIGRP
- ✓ Troubleshooting EIGRP

What to Watch Out For

Don't let common mistakes trip you up; watch for the following when working with these questions:

- ✓ Know the details of EIGRP, such as the fact that it is a hybrid routing protocol that uses some distance vector features and link state routing protocol features. EIGRP has an administrative distance and is a Cisco proprietary protocol.

- ✓ Know the difference between a successor route and a feasible successor route. EIGRP stores the best route to a destination, known as a successor route, in the routing table. All routes are stored in the topology table as well, including backup routes to the successor route. These backup routes are known as feasible successor routes.

- ✓ When the successor route fails, the feasible successor route immediately becomes the successor and a new feasible successor route is elected. Having the backup (feasible successor) stored in the topology table reduces convergence time because it is available immediately.

- ✓ Know the commands to configure EIGRP. You use the router eigrp <AS #> command to enable EIGRP. You then use the network command with the network ID and the wildcard mask to enable EIGRP routing on that network. Know how to calculate the wildcard mask. The quickest method is to take the subnet mask away from 255.255.255.255. For example, if a subnet mask is 255.255.255.192, then the wildcard mask for that network is 0.0.0.63.

- ✓ Know your commands to troubleshoot EIGRP. Some commands you should be familiar with are show ip route, show ip eigrp neighbors, show ip eigrptopology, and show ip protocols. Know which commands display what information: That can help you troubleshoot in scenario-based questions.

Understanding EIGRP

852–872 Choose the best answer(s).

852. Which of the following is used when the successor route fails?

(A) Alternate route

(B) Feasible successor route

(C) BDR

(D) DR

853. What is the purpose of the feasible successor route?

(A) It is a backup route located in the routing table.

(B) It is the primary route located in the routing table.

(C) It is the primary route located in the topology table.

(D) It is a backup route located in the topology table.

854. Which of the following is true in regards to the autonomous system (AS) number with EIGRP?

(A) It should be unique on each router.

(B) It must match on all routers that you want to share routing information.

(C) It must match the value of the last octet in the IP address of the WAN interface.

(D) It represents the hop count to the next network.

855. What happens when EIGRP has two paths with equal metrics to the same destination?

(A) It uses the first path.

(B) It uses the shortest path.

(C) It load balances between the two paths.

(D) It uses the last path.

856. In regards to the commands shown below, what does the 10 represent?

```
NY-R1(config)#router eigrp 10
NY-R1(config-router)#network 11.0.0.0
```

(A) The maximum hop count

(B) The maximum equal paths

(C) The autonomous system

(D) The administrative distance

857. The EIGRP algorithm looks at all the routes in the topology table and chooses the best route to a destination. The best route is known as the _____.

(A) Feasible successor route

(B) Successor route

(C) Designated route

(D) Backup designated route

858. Which table does the successor route exist in? (select two)

(A) Topology table

(B) Neighbors table

(C) Routing table

(D) MAC table

859. EIGRP is considered which of the following?

(A) A hybrid protocol

(B) A link state protocol

(C) A distance vector protocol

(D) A layer-2 protocol

860. What is the administrative distance of EIGRP?

(A) 150

(B) 120

(C) 110

(D) 90

861. Which table does the feasible successor route exist in?

(A) Neighbors table

(B) Routing table

(C) Topology table

(D) MAC table

862. A router has learned of three routes to the same destination. The first is from RIPv2 with a metric of 6, the second route is from OSPF with a metric of 10, and the third route is from EIGRP with a metric of 2172416. Which route will be used?

(A) The RIPv2 route

(B) The OSPF route

(C) All of them

(D) The EIGRP route

863. What is the benefit of having a feasible successor route with EIGRP?

(A) Load balancing

(B) Quicker convergence

(C) Less hops

(D) More hops

864. With EIGRP, which of the following is also known as the routing domain ID?

(A) Router-ID

(B) BDR ID

(C) Metric value

(D) Autonomous system number

865. Which of the following describes a feasible successor?

(A) Backup route stored in topology table

(B) Primary route stored in topology table

(C) Backup route stored in routing table

(D) Primary route stored in routing table

866. Which of the following are true in regards to EIGRP? (Select two.)

(A) Is vendor specific

(B) Uses cost as the metric

(C) Has a default administrative distance of 90

(D) Elects a DR and BDR

867. Which of the following is true of the EIGRP successor route? (Select two.)

(A) Successor routes are backup routes to feasible successor routes.

(B) Successor routes forward traffic.

(C) May have a backup in a feasible successor route.

(D) Successor routes are used when a feasible successor route fails.

868. Which of the following describes a successor route?

(A) Backup route stored in topology table

(B) Primary route stored in neighbors table

(C) Backup route stored in routing table

(D) Primary route stored in routing table

869. Which of the following does EIGRP use as its metrics by default? (Select two.)

    (A)   Hop count

    (B)   Cost

    (C)   Load

    (D)   Bandwidth

    (E)   Delay

870. Which of the following are true regarding successor routes? (Select three.)

    (A)   They are the backup to a feasible successor route.

    (B)   They are backed by feasible successor routes.

    (C)   They are stored in the neighbors table.

    (D)   They are used to forward traffic to the destination.

    (E)   They are stored in the routing table.

871. What does an EIGRP router do if its successor route is active but there is no feasible successor route?

    (A)   Elects a DR

    (B)   The router sends a multicast message to all adjacent neighbors.

    (C)   Elects a BDR

    (D)   Broadcast a message looking for a feasible successor

872. When looking at the EIGRP topology, what code is used to indicate that there are no changes in the EIGRP topology?

    (A)   Active

    (B)   Passive

    (C)   Reply status

    (D)   Query

Configuring EIGRP

873–879 Choose the best answer(s).

873. What command is used to start EIGRP on your router?

    (A)   R1(config)# `start eigrp 5`

    (B)   R1(config)# `start router eigrp`

    (C)   R1(config)# `router eigrp 5`

    (D)   R1(config)# `router eigrp`

874. You wish to disable auto summarization with EIGRP. What command would you use?

(A) R1(config)# `no auto-summary`

(B) R1# `no auto-summary`

(C) R1(config-router)# `no auto-summary`

(D) R1(config-router)# `disable auto-summary`

875. You are configuring router R1 and wish to enable EIGRP on all interfaces for the 11.0.0.0 network and 12.0.0.0 network. What command would you use?

(A) Use the following commands:

R1(config)#`router eigrp`

R1(config-router)#`network 11.0.0.0`

R1(config-router)#`network 12.0.0.0`

(B) Use the following commands:

R1(config)#`router eigrp 10`

R1(config-router)#`network 11.0.0.0 255.0.0.0`

R1(config-router)#`network 12.0.0.0 255.0.0.0`

(C) Use the following commands:

R1(config)#`router eigrp 10`

R1(config-router)#`network 11.0.0.0 0.255.255.255`

R1(config-router)#`network 12.0.0.0 0.255.255.255`

(D) Use the following command:

R1(config)#`router eigrp 11.0.0.0,12.0.0.0`

876. You wish to change the administrative distance of EIGRP. What command would you use?

(A) R1(config)#`distance 35 35`

(B) R1(config-router)#`admin-distance 35 35`

(C) R1(config-router)#`distance 35 35`

(D) R1(config-router)#`distance eigrp 35 35`

877. You have configured three routers with the configuration shown below. The routers are not exchanging routing updates. What should you do?

> NY-R1(config)#router eigrp 10
>
> NY-R1(config-router)#network 11.0.0.0
>
> BOS-R1(config)#router eigrp 20
>
> BOS-R1(config-router)#network 12.0.0.0
>
> TOR-R1(config)#router eigrp 30
>
> TOR-R1(config-router)#network 13.0.0.0

  (A) Configure different AS on all routers.

  (B) Configure the same AS on all routers.

  (C) Promote the feasible successor.

  (D) Force election of a new DR.

878. You have started the EIGRP process. What command would you use to enable EIGRP for network 192.168.3.64/27?

  (A) network 192.168.3.64 255.255.255.0

  (B) network 192.168.3.64 0.0.0.255

  (C) network 192.168.3.64 0.0.0.31

  (D) network 192.168.3.64 0.0.0.0

879. You have started the EIGRP process. What command would you use to enable EIGRP for network 172.16.16.0/20?

  (A) network 172.16.0.0 0.0.255.255

  (B) network 172.16.16.0 0.0.255.255

  (C) network 172.16.16.0 255.255.240.0

  (D) network 172.16.16.0 0.0.15.255

Troubleshooting EIGRP

880–889 Choose the best answer(s).

880. Looking at the figure below, how many packets are waiting to be delivered to the EIGRP neighbor?

```
R1#show ip eigrp neighbors
IP-EIGRP neighbors for process 10
H   Address          Interface      Hold Uptime      SRTT   RTO   Q    Seq
                                    (sec)            (ms)         Cnt  Num
0   12.0.0.2         Se0/3/0        10   00:03:11    40     1000  0    4
```

(A) 40

(B) 0

(C) 10

(D) 4

881. You have configured EIGRP on router R1 and would like to configure router R2 for the same AS. Looking at the figure below, what AS is R1 using?

```
R1#show ip protocols

Routing Protocol is "eigrp  10 "
  Outgoing update filter list for all interfaces is not set
  Incoming update filter list for all interfaces is not set
  Default networks flagged in outgoing updates
  Default networks accepted from incoming updates
  EIGRP metric weight K1=1, K2=0, K3=1, K4=0, K5=0
  EIGRP maximum hopcount 100
  EIGRP maximum metric variance 1
Redistributing: eigrp 10
  Automatic network summarization is in effect
  Automatic address summarization:
  Maximum path: 4
  Routing for Networks:
     11.0.0.0
     12.0.0.0
  Routing Information Sources:
    Gateway        Distance       Last Update
    12.0.0.2       90             99622
  Distance: internal 90 external 170
```

(A) 10

(B) 4

(C) 90

(D) 100

882. What command was used in the figure below to display the output?

```
IP-EIGRP neighbors for process 10
H   Address            Interface      Hold Uptime    SRTT   RTO   Q    Seq
                                      (sec)          (ms)         Cnt  Num
0   12.0.0.2           Se0/3/0        10   00:03:11  40     1000  0    4
```

(A) `show ip eigrp neighbors`

(B) `show ip eigrp topology`

(C) `show ip route`

(D) `show ip eigrp route`

883. You would like to view the IP addresses of neighboring devices with EIGRP. What command should you use?

(A) `show ip eigrp interfaces`

(B) `show ip eigrp topology`

(C) `show ip eigrp traffic`

(D) `show ip eigrp neighbors`

884. Looking at the figure below, which pathway would be used to reach the system with the IP address of 15.22.34.10?

```
R1#show ip route
Codes: C - connected, S - static, I - IGRP, R - RIP, M - mobile, B - BGP
       D - EIGRP, EX - EIGRP external, O - OSPF, IA - OSPF inter area
       N1 - OSPF NSSA external type 1, N2 - OSPF NSSA external type 2
       E1 - OSPF external type 1, E2 - OSPF external type 2, E - EGP
       i - IS-IS, L1 - IS-IS level-1, L2 - IS-IS level-2, ia - IS-IS inter area
       * - candidate default, U - per-user static route, o - ODR
       P - periodic downloaded static route

Gateway of last resort is not set

C    11.0.0.0/8 is directly connected, FastEthernet0/0
C    12.0.0.0/8 is directly connected, Serial0/3/0
D    13.0.0.0/8 [90/2172416] via 12.0.0.2, 08:19:07, Serial0/3/0
C    14.0.0.0/8 is directly connected, Serial0/3/1
D    15.0.0.0/8 [90/2681856] via 14.0.0.1, 08:19:07, Serial0/3/1
                [90/2681856] via 12.0.0.2, 08:19:07, Serial0/3/0
D    16.0.0.0/8 [90/2172416] via 14.0.0.1, 08:19:07, Serial0/3/1
R1#
```

(A) R1 would always send to 14.0.0.1 unless it fails.

(B) R1 would alternate between 14.0.0.1 and 12.0.0.2.

(C) R1 would always send to 12.0.0.2 unless it fails.

(D) R1 would send to 13.0.0.1 unless it fails.

885. You have configured EIGRP and wish to check the queue count and retransmit interval for established adjacency. What command would you use?

(A) show ip eigrp neighbors

(B) show ip eigrp topology

(C) show ip eigrp traffic

(D) show ip eigrp interfaces

886. Looking at the figure below, how many paths can EIGRP use to the same destination?

```
R1#show ip protocols

Routing Protocol is "eigrp  10 "
  Outgoing update filter list for all interfaces is not set
  Incoming update filter list for all interfaces is not set
  Default networks flagged in outgoing updates
  Default networks accepted from incoming updates
  EIGRP metric weight K1=1, K2=0, K3=1, K4=0, K5=0
  EIGRP maximum hopcount 100
  EIGRP maximum metric variance 1
Redistributing: eigrp 10
  Automatic network summarization is in effect
  Automatic address summarization:
  Maximum path: 4
  Routing for Networks:
      11.0.0.0
      12.0.0.0
  Routing Information Sources:
    Gateway          Distance       Last Update
    12.0.0.2           90             99622
  Distance: internal 90 external 170
```

(A) 4

(B) 10

(C) 90

(D) 170

887. You are troubleshooting EIGRP. What commands could you use to view the autonomous system number? (Select two.)

(A) show ip protocols

(B) show ip route

(C) show ip eigrp as_num

(D) show ip eigrp topology

888. Looking at the figure below, how long does it take router R1 to send an EIGRP packet to its neighbor and receive a reply?

```
R1#show ip eigrp neighbors
IP-EIGRP neighbors for process 10
H    Address              Interface      Hold Uptime      SRTT   RTO   Q    Seq
                                         (sec)            (ms)         Cnt  Num
0    12.0.0.2             Se0/3/0        10   00:03:11    40     1000  0    4
```

(A) 10 seconds

(B) 0 seconds

(C) 4 ms

(D) 40 ms

889. What command was used in the figure below to display the output?

```
Routing Protocol is "eigrp  10 "
   Outgoing update filter list for all interfaces is not set
   Incoming update filter list for all interfaces is not set
   Default networks flagged in outgoing updates
   Default networks accepted from incoming updates
   EIGRP metric weight K1=1, K2=0, K3=1, K4=0, K5=0
   EIGRP maximum hopcount 100
   EIGRP maximum metric variance 1
Redistributing: eigrp 10
   Automatic network summarization is in effect
   Automatic address summarization:
   Maximum path: 4
   Routing for Networks:
      11.0.0.0
      12.0.0.0
   Routing Information Sources:
    Gateway          Distance        Last Update
    12.0.0.2            90            99622
   Distance: internal 90 external 170
```

(A) `show ip protocols`

(B) `show ip route`

(C) `show ip eigrp neighbors`

(D) `show ip eigrp topology`

Chapter 22

Configuring IP Services

• •

Previous chapters have reviewed various dynamic routing protocols and how to perform basic switch and router configuration. This chapter delves deeper into options available for maintaining network routing connections, as well as how to work with some of the monitoring and diagnostic tools that are built into the Cisco IOS.

The Problems You'll Work On

In this chapter, you'll review questions concerning the following topics:

- ✔ Reviewing various High Availability (HA) options for reliable routing
- ✔ Managing and using Syslog servers and information
- ✔ Understanding SNMP v2 and v3
- ✔ Accessing performance and usage statistics using NetFlow

What to Watch Out For

Don't let common mistakes trip you up; watch for the following when working with these questions:

- ✔ Cisco does not provide its own Syslog server, so questions related to Syslog will focus on device configuration rather than server configuration. Many free and commercial servers are available to you, such as SolarWind's Kiwi Syslog Server and the open source syslog-ng.

- ✔ Both HA and dynamic routing protocols allow for recovery when routers become unavailable, but all HA solutions allow for recovery times in seconds rather than minutes. Both protocols can play a role in an effective enterprise network.

- ✔ Know the differences between SNMP v2 and v3, the latter of which is primarily support for authentication and encryption, and is more complex in setup.

- ✔ Understand the concepts of the NetFlow process, and be aware that the data sent to the NetFlow collectors includes statistics about all data that passes the router, and who the endpoints were on either side of the conversation. So you will see information such as "IP x.x.x.x had 5 conversations with IP y.y.y.y, and each conversation took x bytes and x packets to conclude." This is valuable information when attempting to diagnose network performance issues.

- ✔ Be aware that the server that collects, gathers, and analyzes NetFlow data is called a collector, and although Cisco has products that will perform the NetFlow collector function, many third-party products do so as well.

Reviewing Various High Availability (HA) Options

890–906 Choose the best answer(s).

890. What configuration change is needed at the desktop workstation when activating a second router that has been configured using VRRP?

(A) A secondary router must be defined.

(B) The default gateway needs to be updated.

(C) No changes are required if the timer is set to 1 or above.

(D) No changes are required.

891. Which of the following are Cisco HA options for routing? (Select two.)

(A) DHCP

(B) GLBP

(C) RIP

(D) VRRP

892. What are requirements for VRRP to be used on a network? (Select two.)

(A) One router

(B) Two routers

(C) Additional virtual IP address

(D) Additional virtual MAC address

893. When using GLBP, if the AVG router fails, what router becomes the next AVG? (Select two.)

(A) The router with the highest IP address

(B) The first router that was configured for GLBP

(C) The router with the highest priority

(D) The router with the lowest IP address

894. What is the advertisement timer for VRRP?

(A) 1 second

(B) 2 seconds

(C) 5 seconds

(D) 10 seconds

895. What is the major difference between GLBP and either VRRP or HSRP?

    (A)   VRRP supports faster failovers.

    (B)   GLBP is designed as an Active/Passive solution.

    (C)   GLBP performs Active/Active load balancing.

    (D)   HSRP supports faster failovers.

896. What statements are true about GLBP? (Select two.)

    (A)   Routers share a common virtual IP address.

    (B)   Routers have unique virtual IP addresses.

    (C)   Routers share a common virtual MAC address.

    (D)   Routers have unique virtual MAC addresses.

897. Which HA option for routers will have the lowest level of impact to users on the network during a failover?

    (A)   VRRP

    (B)   GLBP

    (C)   SSO

    (D)   HSRP

898. When working with GLBP, what is the role of the AVG?

    (A)   Is the active router processing all data

    (B)   Is the standby router waiting to assume the active role

    (C)   Manages which data will be processed by which router

    (D)   Send status messages to network management and syslog servers

899. What is the benefit offered by the SSO addition to HSRP?

    (A)   Preserves forwarding path

    (B)   Enables load balancing

    (C)   Enables a redundant path

    (D)   Sets the failover order

900. When using GLBP, two routers are configured with the commands shown in the figure below.

```
Router1(config)#interface fastethernet 0/0
Router1(config-if)#ip address 10.1.8.11 255.255.255.0
Router1(config-if)#glbp 10 ip 10.1.8.10

Router2(config)#interface fastethernet 0/0
Router2(config-if)#ip address 10.1.8.12 255.255.255.0
Router2(config-if)#glbp 10 ip 10.1.8.10
```

The AVG role is running on Router1 with the highest priority. Router1 is rebooted and the AVG role is transferred to Router2. When will the AVG role move back to Router1?

(A) When Router1 comes back on line

(B) 5 minutes after Router1 comes back on line

(C) Never.

(D) When Router2 is loses network connectivity

901. You are configuring VRRP and have used the commands shown in the figure below. It is not working. What changes would you make to the configuration to make it work?

```
Router1# configure terminal
Router1(config)# interface GigabitEthernet 0/0/0
Router1(config-if)# ip address 172.16.6.5 255.255.255.0
Router1(config-if)# vrrp 10 ip 172.16.6.1
Router1(config-if)# end

Router2# configure terminal
Router2(config)# interface GigabitEthernet 0/0/0
Router2(config-if)# ip address 172.16.6.6 255.255.255.0
Router2(config-if)# vrrp 10 ip 172.16.6.1 secondary
Router2(config-if)# end
```

(A) Change the interface IP address to match on both routers.

(B) Issue shutdown and no shutdown on the interfaces.

(C) VRRP may not be supported on these routers.

(D) Three routers are required for VRRP.

(E) All routers require matching VRRP primary and secondary IP addresses.

902. Which of the following are valid GLBP debug commands? (Select two.)

(A) debug glbp

(B) debug glbp errors

(C) debug glbp data

(D) debug glbp packets

903. You have configured HSRP but want to add SSO. What changes do you need to make to Router2 to complete this configuration?

(A) Use the following commands:

Router1(config)#redundancy

Router1(config)#mode sso

Router1(config)#exit

(B) Use the following commands:

Router1(config)#redundancy

Router1(config)#mode sso

Router1(config)#exit

Router1(config)#no standby sso

Router1(config)#standby sso

(C) Use the following commands:

Router1(config)#mode sso

Router1(config)#no standby sso

Router1(config)#standby sso

(D) Use the following commands:

Router1(config)#redundancy

Router1(config-red)#mode sso

Router1(config-red)#exit

Router1(config)#no standby sso

Router1(config)#standby sso

904. Members of a GLBP group communicate with hello messages using the IP address of _____ on ____ port _____.

(A) 224.0.0.100, TCP, 3222

(B) 225.0.0.55, UDP, 3222

(C) 224.0.0.102, UDP, 3222

(D) 225.0.0.55, TCP, 3222

905. The output shown in the figure below is from the show glbp command. You are having problems creating the router group to support HA routing. What options should you examine on the two devices? (Select two.)

```
Router# show glbp 10

FastEthernet0/0 - Group 10
  State is Active
    2 state changes, last state change 23:50:33
  Virtual IP address is 10.21.8.10
  Hello time 5 sec, hold time 18 sec
    Next hello sent in 4.300 secs
  Redirect time 1800 sec, forwarder time-out 28800 sec
  Authentication text "stringabc"
  Preemption enabled, min delay 60 sec
  Active is local
  Standby is unknown
  Priority 254 (configured)
  Weighting 105 (configured 110), thresholds: lower 95, upper 105
    Track object 2 state Down decrement 5
  Load balancing: host-dependent
  There is 1 forwarder (1 active)
  Forwarder 1
    State is Active
      1 state change, last state change 23:50:15
    MAC address is 0007.b400.0101 (default)
    Owner ID is 0005.0050.6c08
    Redirection enabled
    Preemption enabled, min delay 60 sec
    Active is local, weighting 105
```

(A)   Group numbers match

(B)   Priorities match

(C)   Preemption settings match

(D)   Hello times match

(E)   Virtual IP addresses match

906. How many standby groups can be assigned to a router when using HSRP?

(A)   1

(B)   16

(C)   256

(D)   512

Managing and Using Syslog Servers

907–914 Choose the best answer(s).

907. How does a syslog server separate incoming log information?

(A) By client MAC address

(B) By client IP address

(C) It does not separate information.

(D) It depends on the server.

908. What command will display the settings of logging on your switch or router?

(A) `display logging`

(B) `show logging`

(C) `show log options`

(D) `show log settings`

909. When logging messages to a syslog server, what severity levels are you able to send to the syslog server?

(A) Only level 0

(B) Below level 2

(C) Below level 5

(D) All severity levels

910. You have received the information shown in the figure below on your syslog server. What does this information tell you about your devices on the network?

```
*Mar  6 22:48:34.452 UTC: %LINEPROTO-5-UPDOWN: Line protocol on Interface Loopback0,
    changed state to up
```

(A) There was a change in the state of the gigabit 0/0 interface.

(B) Something happened March 5.

(C) There was a message sent by the device kernel.

(D) There was a change in the state of the loopback0 interface.

911. You have configured your router using the commands shown in the figure below, but your Syslog server is not showing any data. Why not?

```
Router1#configure terminal
Router1(config)#service timestamps log datetime
Router1(config)#logging host 10.1.8.50
Router1(config)#logging trap warnings
```

(A) Your traffic is being blocked by NAT translation.

(B) You need to copy the running-configuration startup-configuration.

(C) The syslog server is configured for a non-standard port.

(D) The router needs to be restarted for the configuration to take effect.

912. What is the default port on which a syslog server operates?

(A) UDP 110

(B) UDP 514

(C) TCP 514

(D) TCP 110

913. What elements make up a basic syslog message? (Select two.)

(A) Time

(B) Link speed

(C) Severity

(D) IOS Version

914. You have been having issues with your router, which becomes unresponsive and will not respond to any of the administrative interfaces. Your only option is to reboot the router with a power reset. What tool can help you to identify the issue that is affecting the router?

(A) SNMP

(B) TFTP

(C) Syslog

(D) SMTP

Understanding SNMP v2 and v3

915–924 Choose the best answer(s).

915. What is the name given to an alert generated by an SNMP agent?

(A) Capture

(B) Log

(C) Syslog

(D) Trap

916. Which of these are examples of SNMP Trap receivers? (Select two.)

(A) HP Openview

(B) Oracle SQL

(C) Nagios

(D) Java

917. What is the name given to a piece of data that can be retrieved via SNMP?

(A) MIB

(B) DATA

(C) RFC

(D) OID

918. What is the default port used by SNMP?

(A) UDP 125

(B) TCP 161

(C) TCP 125

(D) UDP 161

919. What is name of the documented list of OID for a product?

(A) RFC

(B) MIB

(C) IETF

(D) SSH

920. What is the purpose of a community name in SNMP?

(A)   Host selection

(B)   Security grouping

(C)   OID selection

(D)   Security password

921. What is the major advantage of SNMP v3 over SNMP v2? (Select two.)

(A)   User authentication

(B)   64-bit community names

(C)   Bi-directional handshaking

(D)   Data encryption

(E)   Customizable ports

922. What are the two standard permission types used by SNMP? (Select two.)

(A)   Query

(B)   Read

(C)   Write

(D)   Set

923. What security step can be used to secure SNMP?

(A)   Enable NAT on the device

(B)   Implement case-sensitive community names

(C)   Implement access lists

(D)   RSA-encode community names

924. What are options for securing SNMP traffic on your network? (Select three.)

(A)   Using secure community names

(B)   Restricting access to read-only

(C)   Using IOS version 12.5.1

(D)   Implementing access lists

(E)   Enabling password encryption

Accessing Statistics Using NetFlow

925–927 Choose the best answer(s).

925. What information is required to send NetFlow data to a collector? (Select two.)

(A) The IP address of the collector

(B) The DNS hostname of the client

(C) The port the collector is using

(D) The NetFlow proxy address

926. Which of the following are components in NetFlow data analysis? (Select two.)

(A) Firewall

(B) Syslog server

(C) NetFlow-enabled device

(D) NetFlow collector

927. You have configured NetFlow to send data to your collector using the four lines shown in the figure below.

```
Router1(config)#interface gigabit 0/0
Router1(config-if)#ip route-cache flow
Router1(config-if)#exit
Router1(config)#ip flow-export 10.1.1.25
```

The collector is not showing any data. What is the likely cause of the problem? (Select two.)

(A) The collector is configured for a non-default port.

(B) The router does not support sending NetFlow data.

(C) The collector is using a different version.

(D) The router must be using a dynamic routing protocol.

Chapter 23

Frame Relay

● ●

F rame Relay was once the de facto standard for Wide Area Network connections. While it is still in use in many places, it is often being replaced with faster technologies. This chapter reviews your knowledge of these technologies, which you will likely find entrenched on many networks that you encounter.

The Problems You'll Work On

In this chapter, you'll review questions concerning the following topics:

- ✔ Identifying the hardware components that are used in a Frame Relay networking implementation
- ✔ Diagnosing issues with Frame Relay configurations
- ✔ Managing multisite Frame Relay configurations
- ✔ Reviewing configurations and monitoring the status of Frame Relay connections

What to Watch Out For

Don't let common mistakes trip you up; watch for the following when working with these questions:

- ✔ Two main hardware components are used in Frame Relay networks: DTE (Data Terminal Equipment), which is a customer device, such as a router; and DCE (Data Communication Equipment), which is typically a service provider's interface to a Frame Relay switched network. You need to know how to classify these hardware devices.
- ✔ Your connection between your local and remote office networks is virtual, and it can be either permanent (PVC) or temporary (SVC). Know the key differences between these two circuit types.
- ✔ Addressing on a Frame Relay network is based upon virtual addresses assigned to clients in the form of a DLCI (Data Link Connection Identifier). Know how to work this key piece of information.
- ✔ Be aware of the communication intervals for the different components of the Frame Relay network, such as LMI and keepalives. These will be important when trying to diagnose networking issues.

Understanding Frame Relay Basics

928–934 Choose the best answer(s).

928. What two devices are used on a Frame Relay connection? (Select two.)

(A) Modulator/Demodulator

(B) DTE

(C) Modem

(D) DCE

929. There are two types of virtual circuits (VC) used on Frame Relay networks. What are they? (Select two.)

(A) PVC

(B) DTE

(C) DCE

(D) SVC

930. What type of virtual circuit (VC) destroys call sessions upon completion of transmission?

(A) DTE

(B) SVC

(C) DCE

(D) PVC

931. Frame Relay supports which topologies? (Select all that apply.)

(A) Full Mesh

(B) Bus

(C) Partial Mesh

(D) Star

(E) Polyhedron

932. The DLCI (data-link connection identifier) is a 10-bit number which is used for what purpose?

(A) A wide area identifier used to pair the connection with the device at the other end of the circuit

(B) A local identifier between the local router and local frame relay switch

(C) A local identifier used by the client device and the frame relay device

(D) A remote identifier used by the client device to select a wide area device

933. What is the purpose of the LMI (Local Management Interface)?

(A)   A management console on the DCE

(B)   Signaling standard between the router (DTE) and Frame Relay switch (DCE)

(C)   A management console on the DTE

(D)   A set of standards for multiplexing data over the Frame Relay network

934. When dealing with a Full Mesh network with 5 sites, how many links will be required to create the full mesh?

(A)   5

(B)   10

(C)   20

(D)   25

Configuring Frame Relay

935–942 Choose the best answer(s).

935. Which item references the bandwidth that will be available to a Frame Relay service subscriber?

(A)   LMI

(B)   CIR

(C)   DLCI

(D)   BECN

936. Which protocol allows the router to automatically discover the network address of the remote DCE device on the virtual circuit (VC)?

(A)   Address Resolution Protocol

(B)   Local Management Interface

(C)   Routing Information Protocol

(D)   Inverse Address Resolution Protocol

937. What Frame Relay component is the clock speed of the connection to the Frame Relay cloud?

(A)   Clock rate

(B)   DTE

(C)   Local Access Rate

(D)   DCE

938. Rather than using Inverse ARP, DLCIs may be associated with network layer addresses by using which of the following?

(A) ARP

(B) Static ARP

(C) static map commands

(D) LAR

939. What is the result when traffic on the PVC exceeds the CIR?

(A) All TCP traffic is marked as discard eligible.

(B) All excess traffic is marked as discard eligible.

(C) All excess traffic is discarded.

(D) All excess traffic is marked and the CIR flag is set to enabled.

940. Which devices need to be configured with matching encapsulation types?

(A) Matching DTEs

(B) Matching DTE and DCE

(C) All DCEs

(D) None of the above

941. How often does a router send in Inverse ARP to all active DLCIs?

(A) 10 seconds

(B) 30 seconds

(C) 60 seconds

(D) 120 seconds

942. How often do routers exchange LMI information with a switch?

(A) 1 second

(B) 10 seconds

(C) 30 seconds

(D) 60 seconds

Implementing Frame Relay

943–951 Choose the best answer(s).

943. What is the purpose of a CSU/DSU?

(A) It translates protocol addresses to and from IP.

(B) It connects a router to a Frame Relay switch.

(C) It maintains open connections for PVCs.

(D) It is responsible for updating routing protocols over the Frame Relay network.

944. Which topology for Frame Relay has many, but not all sites connected to all other sites?

    (A)   Partial Mesh

    (B)   Full Mesh

    (C)   Star

    (D)   Super Star

945. What Frame Relay component represents the highest average data rate?

    (A)   CIR

    (B)   LMI

    (C)   LAR

    (D)   DLCI

946. What are valid LMI types used by Cisco routers? (Select two.)

    (A)   ANSI

    (B)   ARP

    (C)   Inverse ARP

    (D)   Q.993A

947. What defines the connection or logical circuit between the local router and the local Frame Relay switch?

    (A)   CIR

    (B)   LMI packet

    (C)   DLCI

    (D)   BECON Frame

948. You have issued the command frame-relay map ip 192.168.155.2 155 broadcast. What does this command do?

    (A)   All broadcast traffic for on DLCI 155 will be sent to 192.168.155.2.

    (B)   Sets the source IP address that will send data to DLCI 155

    (C)   Identifies the DCLI to be used for traffic being sent to 192.168.155.2

    (D)   Defines that DLCI 155 will be used when receiving data from IP 192.168.155.2

949. When entering the command frame-relay interface-dlci 155, what action are you performing?

    (A)   Specifying the remote DLCI that will be used

    (B)   Assigning a remote sub-interface to a DLCI

    (C)   Assigning a main interface DLCI

    (D)   Assigning a DCLI to a local serial sub-interface

950. You would like to implement connections to 5 branch offices over a single physical serial connection. How will you do this?

(A) This is not possible.

(B) Clone the serial interface using the virtual interface command.

(C) You will only be able to implement 4 connections per serial interface.

(D) Implement your configuration on sub-interfaces on the serial connection.

951. You are connecting 5 sites together with a Frame Relay network. You have had VCs created between each pair of routers that you will be using. If you are using point-to-point sub-interfaces, how may IP subnets will you need to use?

(A) 1

(B) 5

(C) 10

(D) 15

Troubleshooting Frame Relay

952–965 Choose the best answer(s).

952. You have run the command shown in the figure below. Does the output identify an error, and if so, what is the likely issue?

```
Router#debug frame-relay lmi
*Mar 15 11:16:16.063: Serial1/2(out): StEnq, myseq 23, yourseen 22, DTE up
*Mar 1 11:16:16.063: datagramstart = 0x7B00E94, datagramsize = 13
*Mar 15 11:16:16.063: FR encap = 0xFCF10309
*Mar 15 11:16:16.063: 00 75 01 01 00 03 02 2B 2A
*Mar 15 11:16:16.063:
*Mar 15 11:16:16.071: Serial1/2(in): Status, myseq 23
*Mar 1 11:16:16.071: RT IE 1, length 1, type 0
*Mar 1 11:16:16.071: KA IE 3, length 2, yourseq 23, myseq 23
<following data deleted for brevity>
```

(A) There is a mismatch in the sequence numbers.

(B) The datagram sizes are too small, indicating runts or data corruption.

(C) The DLCI numbers do not match between devices.

(D) There is no apparent issue.

953. You are troubleshooting issues with your Frame Relay connections. Your physical connection is properly in place, but the line protocol is still listed as down. You view the LMI configuration as shown in the figure below. What would you want to verify with your provider?

```
Router#show frame-relay lmi
LMI Statistics for interface Serial1/2 (Frame Relay DTE) LMI TYPE = CISCO
    Invalid Unnumbered info 0        Invalid Prot Disc 0
    Invalid dummy Call Ref 0         Invalid Msg Type 0
    Invalid Status Message 0         Invalid Lock Shift 0
    Invalid Information ID 0         Invalid Report IE Len 0
    Invalid Report Request 0         Invalid Keep IE Len 0
    Num Status Enq. Sent 139         Num Status msgs Rcvd 0
    Num Update Status Rcvd 0         Num Status Timeouts 15
```

(A) Ensure you are using the correct LMI type.

(B) Verify the serial cable is connected to the correct interface.

(C) Correct the MTU size.

(D) Ensure the interface has not been shut down.

954. You are troubleshooting issues with Frame Relay connections. The results of show interface serial identified the interface as up, but the line protocol as down. You issued the command shown in the figure below to further troubleshoot the issue. What is the likely cause of the problem?

```
Router#show frame-relay pvc
PVC Statistics for interface Serial3/0 (Frame Relay DTE)

            Active   Inactive   Deleted   Static
Local        0         0          1         0
Switched     0         0          0         0
Unused       0         0          0         0

DLCI = 105, DLCI USAGE = LOCAL, PVC STATUS = DELETED, INTERFACE = Serial1/0

   input pkts 12        output pkts 3        in bytes 408
   out bytes 102        dropped pkts 0       in FECN pkts 0
   in BECN pkts 0       out FECN pkts 0      out BECN pkts 0
   in DE pkts 0         out DE pkts 0
   out bcast pkts 3     out bcast bytes 102
   5 minute input rate 0 bits/sec, 0 packets/sec
   5 minute output rate 0 bits/sec, 0 packets/sec
   pvc create time 00:21:35, last time pvc status changed 00:21:35
```

(A) The DCLI should always be 100.

(B) The DCLI is not correctly configured.

(C) The line protocol has been deleted.

(D) There is too much variance between input and output packets.

955. What happens when your router does not receive LMI data for 30 seconds?

    (A)   The router will continue to wait for another 60 seconds.

    (B)   The router will consider the link to be failed.

    (C)   The router will automatically restart the interface.

    (D)   Nothing; this is not uncommon when no data is being sent over the connection.

956. You would like to see information about ARP data that is being exchanged with specific DLCIs over the Frame Relay network. What command do you use?

    (A)   `debug frame-relay packet`

    (B)   `debug frame-relay events`

    (C)   `debug frame-relay`

    (D)   `debug frame-relay lmi`

957. When reviewing the PVC status on your switch, you notice that the LMI data is reporting a status of active. Where would you start looking for your troubleshooting?

    (A)   The local side of the connection

    (B)   There is no issue.

    (C)   The remote side of the connection

    (D)   The local serial interface is down.

958. What command would you use to view details about all the data that is crossing the Frame Relay connection?

    (A)   `debug frame-relay events`

    (B)   `debug frame-relay packet`

    (C)   `debug frame-relay lmi`

    (D)   `debug frame-relay data`

959. You are troubleshooting issues with Frame Relay connections. The results of show interface serial are shown in the figure below. What else should be checked during your troubleshooting? (Select two.)

```
Router#show interface serial1/2
Serial1/2 is down, line protocol is down
  Hardware is CD2430 in sync mode
  Internet address is 10.1.1.1/24
  MTU 1500 bytes, BW 128 Kbit, DLY 20000 usec,
     reliability 255/255, txload 1/255, rxload 1/255
  Encapsulation FRAME-RELAY, loopback not set
  Keepalive set (10 sec)
```

(A) Ensure you are using the correct encapsulation type.

(B) Verify the serial cable is correctly connected.

(C) Correct the MTU size.

(D) Ensure the interface has not been shut down.

960. You are troubleshooting issues with Frame Relay connections. The results of show interface serial is shown in the figure below. What else should be checked during your troubleshooting?

```
Router#show interface serial1/2
Serial1/2 is down, line protocol is down
  Hardware is CD2430 in sync mode
  Internet address is 10.1.1.1/24
  MTU 1500 bytes, BW 128 Kbit, DLY 20000 usec,
     reliability 255/255, txload 1/255, rxload 1/255
  Encapsulation FRAME-RELAY, loopback not set
  Keepalive set (10 sec)
```

(A) Correct the MTU size error.

(B) Verify the encapsulation type.

(C) Verify the connection on the far side of the DCE is configured.

(D) Verify you are using the correct DLCI.

961. You are troubleshooting issues with Frame Relay connections. The results of show interface serial is shown in the figure below. What else should be checked during your troubleshooting?

```
Router#show interface serial1/2
Serial1/2 is up, line protocol is down
  Hardware is CD2430 in sync mode
  Internet address is 172.16.1.1/24
  MTU 1500 bytes, BW 128 Kbit, DLY 20000 usec,
     reliability 255/255, txload 1/255, rxload 1/255
  Encapsulation FRAME-RELAY, loopback not set
  Keepalive set (10 sec)
```

(A) Ensure you are using the correct encapsulation type.

(B) Verify the serial cable is correctly connected.

(C) Correct the MTU size.

(D) Ensure the interface has not been shut down.

962. You are able to connect to the Frame Relay cloud, and when you perform show interface serial, you see that your interface and line protocols are both up. You have recently changed the address on the remote network segment and can no longer connect to it. From the command shown in the figure below, what steps could you take to resolve the issue?

```
Router# show frame-relay map
 Serial 1 (up): ip 10.1.1.157 dlci 157 (0x64,0x2C60), dynamic,
 broadcast,
 CISCO
 TCP/IP Header Compression (inherited), passive (inherited)
```

(A) The interface needs to be shut down.

(B) The DLCI is not correct.

(C) The Frame Relay map may need to be cleared.

(D) The encapsulation is not correct.

963. You are having trouble assigning DLCI 1012 to your configuration. What is the likely reason for that?

(A) That is a reserved number.

(B) 1012 is an encapsulation type, and not a DLCI.

(C) DLCIs are always three digits.

(D) DLCI numbers do not go that high.

964. When reviewing the PVC status on your switch, you notice that the LMI data is reporting a status of Inactive. Where would you start looking for your troubleshooting?

(A) The local side of the connection

(B) There is no issue; there is just no data being sent over the connection.

(C) The remote side of the connection

(D) The local serial interface is down.

965. When viewing show frame-relay map output, what information will you see? (Select two.)

(A) PVC Status

(B) Number of BECN packets

(C) Local DLCI

(D) Local IP addresses

Chapter 24

WAN Technologies

The Cisco ICND2 exam will present you with a few questions about configuring your Cisco device in a WAN environment. It is important when preparing for this topic that you review Chapter 15 and also go through this chapter to build on what you learned in ICND1. This chapter presents you with several questions related to configuring and troubleshooting serial ports and WAN configuration.

The Problems You'll Work On

In this chapter, you'll review questions concerning the following topics:

- ✔ Configuring serial ports
- ✔ Understanding frame relay
- ✔ Troubleshooting WAN connections

What to Watch Out For

Don't let common mistakes trip you up; watch for the following when working with these questions:

- ✔ Know that the serial port is used as a connection to your WAN environment. The serial port can be configured with an encapsulation protocol of HDLC if connecting to Cisco routers, or PPP if connecting to other vendors.

- ✔ PPP is an industry-standard serial link protocol that supports authentication, callback, multilink, and compression. PPP can use either PAP or CHAP as the authentication protocol. CHAP should be used because it is more secure.

- ✔ Be sure to know how to configure frame relay on your Cisco router. Know the purpose of the DLCI and how to create the DLCI mappings. Know how to configure a point-to-point sub-interface and its purpose.

- ✔ Know your show commands to troubleshoot WAN connections. You will be tested on commands such as `show interface`, `show ip interface brief`, `show frame-relay PVC`, `show frame-relay lmi`, `show frame-relay map`, and `show controllers`.

Configuring Serial Ports

966–980 Choose the best answer(s).

966. Which of the following devices must configure the clock rate on a point-to-point link?

(A) DTE

(B) DCE

(C) HDLC

(D) PPP

967. Which of the following is the command you would use to set the clock rate on the DCE end of the link?

(A) R1#`clock rate 64000`

(B) R1(config)#`clock rate 64000`

(C) R1(config-if)#`clock rate 64000`

(D) R1>`clock rate 64000`

968. You are connecting a Cisco router to a WAN environment that uses routers from different vendors. What protocol should you use as the encapsulation protocol on the serial link?

(A) PPP

(B) HDLC

(C) PPTP

(D) L2TP

969. Which PPP authentication protocol uses a challenge/response algorithm to perform the authentication?

(A) PAP

(B) HDLC

(C) L2TP

(D) CHAP

970. Which of the following layer-2 protocols supports asynchronous communication and authentication?

(A) HDLC

(B) PPP

(C) PPTP

(D) SNMP

971. Your router has the following ports:

- ✔ AUI
- ✔ BRI
- ✔ Serial
- ✔ Console
- ✔ Fast Ethernet

Which port would you use to connect to a T1 line?

(A) AUI

(B) BRI

(C) Serial

(D) Console

(E) Fast Ethernet

972. Which PPP authentication protocol transfers username and passwords in clear text?

(A) CHAP

(B) MSCHAP

(C) PAP

(D) HDLC

973. Which of the following are true in regards to PPP versus HDLC? (Select two.)

(A) HDLC only supports PAP authentication.

(B) PPP supports authentication.

(C) HDLC is vendor neutral.

(D) PPP is Cisco specific.

(E) PPP is vendor neutral.

974. Which of the following enables CHAP authentication and uses PAP authentication as a backup authentication method?

(A) `authentication ppp chap pap`

(B) `ppp authentication chap backup pap`

(C) `authentication chap backup pap`

(D) `ppp authentication chap pap`

975. You are looking to configure PPP authentication between your two routers. What should you do? (Choose three.)

(A) Set the hostname on each router to the same name.

(B) Set the hostname on each router to a unique name.

(C) Create a username on each router named PPP.

(D) Create a username on each router that matches the hostname of the other router.

(E) Enable PPP authentication on both routers and specify CHAP as the authentication protocol.

(F) Enable PPP authentication on the first router configured and specify either PAP or CHAP as the authentication protocol.

976. Which PPP sub-protocol is responsible for allowing PPP to support multiple network protocols?

(A) LCP

(B) NCP

(C) PPTP

(D) HDLC

977. Which of the following commands would you use to configure your router on a WAN that has non-Cisco routers as well?

(A) Use the following commands:

R1(config-if)#ip address 165.45.1.1 255.255.255.252

R1(config-if)#encapsulation hdlc

R1(config-if)#no shutdown

(B) Use the following commands:

R1(config-if)#ip address 165.45.1.1 255.255.255.252

R1(config-if)#encapsulation ppp

R1(config-if)#shutdown

(C) Use the following commands:

R1(config-if)#ip address 165.45.1.1 255.255.255.252

R1(config-if)#encapsulation ppp

R1(config-if)#no shutdown

(D) Use the following commands:

R1(config-if)#ip address 165.45.1.1 255.255.255.252

R1(config-if)#no shutdown

978. PPP has a number of sub-protocols that perform different functions. Which protocol is responsible for negotiating authentication options?

(A) NCP

(B) LCP

(C) SNMP

(D) HDLC

979. Which of the following serial link protocols can implement multilink for load balancing?

(A) PPP

(B) HDLC

(C) L2TP

(D) PPTP

980. Which of the following are true in regards to WAN technologies? (Select three.)

(A) A router is typically considered a DCE device.

(B) A router is typically considered a DTE device.

(C) A modem is used to connect to an analog line.

(D) A CSU/DSU is used to connect to an analog line.

(E) A CSU/DSU is used to connect to a digital line.

(F) A modem is used to connect to a digital line.

Understanding Frame Relay

981–986 Choose the best answer(s).

981. You have entered the command frame-relay map ip 192.168.5.10 100 broadcast on the router. What is the purpose of the broadcast option in the command?

(A) Ensures the GWLR is shared to other frame relay routers

(B) Allows routing updates to be forwarded across the frame relay PVC

(C) Configures the encapsulation type

(D) Assigns the IP address as the broadcast address of the network

982. Your manager has been reading about frame relay and asks you for two characteristics of frame relay point-to-point sub-interfaces. What are they? (Select two.)

(A) They emulate leased lines.

(B) They must share subnet information.

(C) They must have a unique subnet.

(D) They must share the same DLCI with other sub-interfaces on the router.

983. Which of the following is true of frame relay DLCI?

(A) They must be the same for each router.

(B) They need to increment by 10.

(C) They are locally significant.

(D) They must be odd numbers.

984. What protocol does frame relay use to create a mapping of the layer-3 address to the DLCI?

(A) ARP

(B) DNS

(C) ICMP

(D) Inverse ARP

985. Which of the following would configure a sub-interface for a point-to-point frame relay PVC using DLCI 102 that maps to IP address 192.168.1.2?

(A) Use the following commands:

```
interface s0/1/0.102 point-to-point
ip address 192.168.1.2 255.255.255.0
frame-relay interface-dlci 102
```

(B) Use the following commands:

```
interface s0/1/0
ip address 192.168.1.2 255.255.255.0
frame-relay interface-dlci 102
```

(C) Use the following commands:

```
interface s0/1/0.102 point-to-point
ip address 192.168.1.2 255.255.255.0
```

(D) Use the following commands:

```
interface s0/1/0.102 point-to-point
ip address 192.168.1.2 255.255.255.0
frame-relay interface
```

986. Which of the following commands would you use to map the IP address of 10.0.0.2 to a DLCI of 100?

(A) R1(config-if)#`frame-relay map 100 ip 10.0.0.2`

(B) R1(config)#`frame-relay map ip 10.0.0.2 100`

(C) R1(config-if)#`frame-relay map ip 10.0.0.2 100`

(D) R1(config)#`frame-relay map 100 ip 10.0.0.2`

Troubleshooting WAN Connections

987–1001 Choose the best answer(s).

987. Using the figure below, what is the protocol being used across the WAN link?

```
R1>show interface s0/3/0
Serial0/3/0 is up, line protocol is up (connected)
  Hardware is HD64570
  Internet address is 12.0.0.1/8
  MTU 1500 bytes, BW 1544 Kbit, DLY 20000 usec,
      reliability 255/255, txload 1/255, rxload 1/255
  Encapsulation HDLC, loopback not set, keepalive set (10 sec)
  Last input never, output never, output hang never
  Last clearing of "show interface" counters never
  Input queue: 0/75/0 (size/max/drops); Total output drops: 0
  Queueing strategy: weighted fair
  Output queue: 0/1000/64/0 (size/max total/threshold/drops)
      Conversations  0/0/256 (active/max active/max total)
      Reserved Conversations 0/0 (allocated/max allocated)
      Available Bandwidth 1158 kilobits/sec
```

(A) PPP

(B) L2TP

(C) HDLC

(D) Frame Relay

988. Your Cisco router is having trouble communicating with the 3COM router. While troubleshooting, you use the command in the figure below. What would you do to solve the problem?

```
R1>show interface s0/3/0
Serial0/3/0 is up, line protocol is up (connected)
  Hardware is HD64570
  Internet address is 12.0.0.1/8
  MTU 1500 bytes, BW 1544 Kbit, DLY 20000 usec,
      reliability 255/255, txload 1/255, rxload 1/255
  Encapsulation HDLC, loopback not set, keepalive set (10 sec)
  Last input never, output never, output hang never
  Last clearing of "show interface" counters never
  Input queue: 0/75/0 (size/max/drops); Total output drops: 0
  Queueing strategy: weighted fair
  Output queue: 0/1000/64/0 (size/max total/threshold/drops)
      Conversations  0/0/256 (active/max active/max total)
      Reserved Conversations 0/0 (allocated/max allocated)
      Available Bandwidth 1158 kilobits/sec
```

(A)   Change the encapsulation protocol to HDLC.

(B)   Set the clock rate to 128 000.

(C)   Change the IP address.

(D)   Change the encapsulation protocol to PPP.

989. You wish to determine if your serial port is the DCE or DTE end of a point-to-point link. What command would you use?

(A)   `show controllers s0/0`

(B)   `show interface s0/0`

(C)   `show ip interface brief`

(D)   `show ip protocols`

990. Using the figure below, which of the following is considered layer-2 status information?

```
R1>show interface s0/3/0
Serial0/3/0 is up, line protocol is up (connected)
  Hardware is HD64570
  Internet address is 12.0.0.1/8
  MTU 1500 bytes, BW 1544 Kbit, DLY 20000 usec,
     reliability 255/255, txload 1/255, rxload 1/255
  Encapsulation HDLC, loopback not set, keepalive set (10 sec)
  Last input never, output never, output hang never
  Last clearing of "show interface" counters never
  Input queue: 0/75/0 (size/max/drops); Total output drops: 0
  Queueing strategy: weighted fair
  Output queue: 0/1000/64/0 (size/max total/threshold/drops)
     Conversations  0/0/256 (active/max active/max total)
     Reserved Conversations 0/0 (allocated/max allocated)
     Available Bandwidth 1158 kilobits/sec
```

(A)   Line protocol is up

(B)   Serial0/3/0 is up

(C)   Internet address is 12.0.0.1/8

(D)   RIP routing enabled

991. You have configured the network show in the figure below. Router R1 cannot communicate with router R2. Why not?

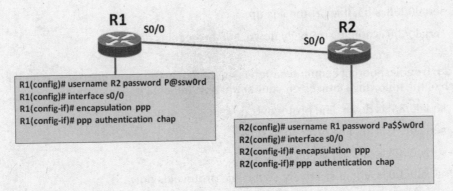

R1(config)# username R2 password P@ssw0rd
R1(config)# interface s0/0
R1(config-if)# encapsulation ppp
R1(config-if)# ppp authentication chap

R2(config)# username R1 password Pa$$w0rd
R2(config)# interface s0/0
R2(config-if)# encapsulation ppp
R2(config-if)# ppp authentication chap

(A) The passwords need to be the same.

(B) The usernames need to be the same.

(C) The wrong interface has been configured.

(D) You should use the PAP authentication protocol.

992. The serial port on your router is showing a status of `Serial0/0 is up, line protocol is down`. What would be two reasons for this status? (Select two.)

(A) The interface has been shut down.

(B) The cable is disconnected.

(C) The clock rate is not set on the DCE device.

(D) The encapsulation protocol is not the same on both ends of the link.

(E) The clock rate is not set on the DTE device.

993. You use the show interfaces command to determine the status of your serial link. Which of the following identifies a layer-1 issue with the serial port?

(A) serial0/3/0 is down, line protocol is down

(B) serial0/3/0 is up, line protocol is down

(C) serial0/3/0 is up, line protocol is up

(D) serial0/3/0 is administratively down, line protocol is down

994. You are troubleshooting why you cannot communicate across the WAN link with serial 0/3/0. Which of the following identifies that the port has been disabled?

(A) serial0/3/0 is down, line protocol is down

(B) serial0/3/0 is up, line protocol is down

(C) serial0/3/0 is up, line protocol is up

(D) serial0/3/0 is administratively down, line protocol is down

995. Which of the following identifies a layer-2 issue with your serial port?

(A) serial0/3/0 is down, line protocol is down

(B) serial0/3/0 is up, line protocol is down

(C) serial0/3/0 is up, line protocol is up

(D) serial0/3/0 is administratively down, line protocol is down

996. You are troubleshooting communication issues and use the show interfaces command. Which of the following statuses on your serial port indicate it is operational?

(A) serial0/3/0 is down, line protocol is down

(B) serial0/3/0 is up, line protocol is down

(C) serial0/3/0 is up, line protocol is up

(D) serial0/3/0 is administratively down, line protocol is down

997. You are looking at options for connecting two autonomous systems together. What routing protocol should you use?

(A) PPTP

(B) RIP

(C) OSPF

(D) BGP

998. You are troubleshooting a frame relay link to non-Cisco frame relay routers. You want to verify whether you are using the Cisco encapsulation protocol or the IETF encapsulation protocol. What command would you use?

(A) `show frame-relay pvc`

(B) `show frame-relay lmi`

(C) `show frame-relay stats`

(D) `show frame-relay map`

999. You are troubleshooting your frame relay link and use the show frame-relay pvc command. The results come back with a "PVC STATUS=INACTIVE". What is the cause of the problem?

(A) Locally you are configured properly, but the other end of the link is misconfigured.

(B) There is a DLCI mismatch.

(C) The link is idle waiting for traffic.

(D) The serial interface is disabled.

1000. Which of the following commands would you use to troubleshoot authentication with PPP?

    (A) `ppp authentication debug`

    (B) `test ppp authentication`

    (C) `log ppp authentication`

    (D) `debug ppp authentication`

1001. Looking at the results of the show frame-relay map command shown in the figure below, what is the meaning of dynamic in the command output?

```
R1#show frame-relay map
Serial1/2 (up): ip 192.168.1.4 dlci 401(0x191,0x6410), dynamic,
        broadcast,, status defined, active
```

    (A) The PVC will forward routing updates.
    (B) The DLCI was manually configured by the administrator.

    (C) The DLCI mapping was learned through Inverse ARP.

    (D) The address in the DLCI mapping was obtained from DHCP.

Part III
The Answers

In this part...

Here you get answers and explanations for all 1,001 questions. As you read the answers, you may realize that you need a little more instruction. The *For Dummies* series offers several excellent resources. The following titles are available at your favorite bookstore or in e-book format:

- Networking For Dummies (Doug Lowe)

- CCENT Certification All-in-One For Dummies (Glen E. Clarke)

- Cisco Networking All-in-One For Dummies (Edward Tetz)

- CCNA Certification All-in-One For Dummies (Silviu Angelescu)

Visit www.dummies.com for more information.

Answers

Answers

1.   **B. NAT**

NAT is responsible for translating the source IP address of a packet to use the IP of the public interface on the NAT device.

2.   **C. DNS**

If you can communicate with a system by the IP address but not the FQDN, it's a classic indication that the name is not able to resolve to an IP address. This is a sign that there is a problem with the DNS.

3.   **A. DHCP**

The DHCP service is responsible for assigning IP addresses automatically to systems on the network.

4.   **B. DNS server**

DNS is responsible for converting the friendly name, such as `www.gleneclarke.com`, to an IP address.

5.   **A. Authentication server**

An authentication server is responsible for verifying the username and passwords of clients wishing to access the network.

6.   **B. FF-FF-FF-FF-FF-FF**

The DHCP discover message is a broadcast message which is used to locate the DHCP server on the network. FF-FF-FF-FF-FF-FF is the layer-2 representation of a broadcast address.

7.   **B. DHCP discover**

The DHCP discover message is the first message sent out by a DHCP client to locate a DHCP server on the network. The DHCP discover message is a broadcast message which has a destination MAC address of FF-FF-FF-FF-FF-FF.

8.   **C. Repeater**

A repeater is a layer-1 device that is responsible for regenerating the signal.

9. **D. Switch**

A switch is a layer-2 device that filters traffic based off the destination MAC address of the frame.

10. **B. Router**

A router is an example of a layer-3 device and is responsible for sending or receiving information to and from the network.

11. **D. Half-duplex**

When a device can send and receive information, but not at the same time, it is known as half-duplex communication. Full duplex is when the device can send and receive at the same time.

12. **D. Broadcast**

A broadcast message is a message sent to all systems on the network. A broadcast message has a destination MAC address of FF-FF-FF-FF-FF-FF.

13. **B. Multicast**

Multicast traffic is traffic that is destined for more than one system, but not all systems.

14. **D. Broadcast domain**

A broadcast domain is a group of systems that can receive one another's broadcast message. You can break your network into multiple broadcast domains by using routers or VLANs.

15. **B. VLANs**

C. Router

You can use VLANs or a router to break the network into multiple broadcast domains.

16. **C. Collision domain**

A collision domain is an area of the network where one system can collide with another system. Each port on a network switch or bridge creates a separate collision domain, whereas all ports on a hub are part of the same collision domain.

17. **D. 2 broadcast domains and 5 collision domains**

Each port on a switch or bridge creates a separate collision domain, whereas each port on the router creates a separate broadcast domain.

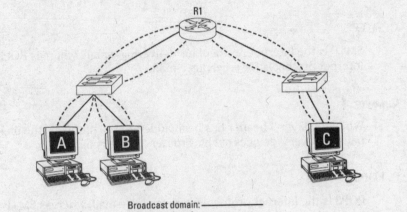

Broadcast domain: ————————
Collision domain: - - - - - - - - - - -

18. **D. 00-AB-0F-2B-3C-4E**

A layer-2 address is the physical address, also known as the MAC address of the system.

19. **B. Physical**

The physical layer of the OSI model deals with physical aspects of the network, such as the cables and connectors. A displayed link light simply means a connection exists.

20. **D. Transport**

The transport layer is responsible for breaking the data into smaller chunks called segments.

21. **A. 192.168.2.200**

A layer-3 address is a logical address that is assigned to the system. An example of a logical address is an IP address.

22. **A. Network**

The network layer is responsible for logical addressing and routing.

23. **A. Bridge**

D. Switch

Both bridges and switches run at layer 2 and are devices that filter traffic by the MAC address.

24. C. Repeater

E. Hub

A hub and a repeater are examples of layer-1 devices. Remember that a layer-1 device works with the electrical signal.

25. C. SMTP

SMTP is the Internet protocol for delivering e-mail, whereas POP3 and IMAP are Internet protocols for receiving e-mail.

26. C. Layer 3

When the layer-3 header has been added to the message, the message is known as a packet. Layer-3 devices such as routers process packets.

27. D. POP3

POP3 is the Internet protocol for receiving e-mail, whereas SMTP is the Internet protocol for delivering e-mail.

28. A. 1000BaseTX

The Gigabit Ethernet standard that uses UTP cabling is 1000BaseTX.

29. C. 10GBaseSR

The 10 Gbps standard that uses multimode fiber-optic cabling is 10GbaseSR. Remember that the S stands for short range, and multimode fiber-optic cabling is used for short distances.

30. A. 24.56.78.10

C. A layer-3 address

Routers use layer-3 addresses to determine where to send a packet.

31. B. Layer 2

Layer 2 of the OSI model works with frames. This means that devices such as bridges and switches process frames because they are considered layer-2 devices. Note that at layer 3 the data being processed is called a packet because it has a layer-3 header, and at layer 4 the data is known as a segment.

32. C. Straight-through

Straight-through cables are used to connect dissimilar devices such as a computer to a switch or a router to a switch.

33. B. Crossover

To connect two systems directly together, you use a crossover cable.

34. **D. 1 and 2 with 3 and 6**

In order to create a crossover cable, you would cross wires 1 and 2 with wires 3 and 6 on one of the ends.

35. **D. The cable type between the switches and routers is incorrect.**

You should use a straight-through cable to connect switches to routers. You use a crossover cable only when connecting similar devices such as a computer to a computer, a switch to a switch, a router to a router, or a computer to a router.

36. **B. Crossover**

This is a strange question because you typically would not do this, but it is on the exam. In this example, the router and workstation are both "hosts" on the network, so you can consider them similar devices; similar devices are connected with a crossover cable.

37. **A. Straight-through**

A straight-through cable is wired the same at both ends of the cable.

38. **A. 568B**

To create a crossover cable, you wire one end of the cable with 568A and the other end of the cable with 568B.

39. **B. 10.35.87.5**

E. 121.59.87.32

Class A addresses have a value in the first octet that ranges from 1 to 127. Class B addresses have a value in the first octet that ranges from 128 to 191. Class C addresses have a value in the first octet that ranges from 192 to 223.

40. **D. 10.55.67.99**

Class A private addresses start with 10.0.0.0. Note that class B private addresses range from 172.16.0.0 up to 172.31.255.255. Class C private addresses range from 192.168.0.0 to 192.168.255.255.

41. **B. 255.255.0.0**

With 189 as the value of the first octet, this address is a class B address, which has a default subnet mask of 255.255.0.0.

42. **C. 255.255.255.0**

The default subnet mask of a class C address is 255.255.255.0.

43. **C. 172.16.45.10**

Class B private addresses range from 172.16.0.0 up to 172.31.255.255. Note that class A private addresses start with 10.0.0.0 and class C private addresses range from 192.168.0.0 to 192.168.255.255.

44.

B. No

Because the IP address starts with 201, it means that it is a class C address. Class C addresses use the first three octets as the network ID, so any system on the same network would have the same first three numbers in the IP address.

45.

C. 190.34.255.255

E. 202.45.6.0

F. 127.87.3.22

You cannot assign an IP address to a system that has all host bits set to 1s or all host bits set to 0. You also cannot have an IP address where the first octet is 127, which is reserved for loopback.

46.

A. 10001001

To convert the decimal number to binary, you would enable the bits that hold the values of 128+8+1=137.

47.

A. Yes

Looking at the first address, you can see that the value of the first octet is 121, which makes the address a class A address. Class A addresses have the network ID as the first octet, so if another system has the same first octet then it is on the same network.

48.

B. 255.255.0.0

Because the value of the first octet is 130, this is a class B address. Class B addresses have a default subnet mask of 255.255.0.0.

49.

C. 131.107.22.15

Because the value of the first octet is 131, it means this system is using a class B address. Class B addresses use 255.255.0.0 as a subnet mask, which means that the first two octets make up the network ID and the last two octets are the host ID. Any system that is going to be on the same network as this system would have to have the first two octets of 131.107.x.y since that is the network ID.

50.

A. 216.83.11.255

D. 131.107.0.0

E. 127.15.34.10

You cannot assign a system an IP address that starts with 127.x.y.z. You also cannot have a system with all host bits set to 1 (which is the case of choice A) or all host bits set to 0 (which is the case of choice D).

51.

B. 109

To convert this binary value to decimal, you take the value of each bit set to 1 and add them together (64+32+8+4+1=109).

52. **C. Class C**

Class C addresses always have the first three bits set to 110. This means that a class C address ranges from 11000000 (192) to 11011111 (223).

53. **B. Class B**

Class B addresses always have the first two bits set to 10. This means that class B addresses range from 10000000 (128) to 10111111 (191).

54. **A. Class A**

Class A addresses always have the first bit of the IP address set to 0. This means that class A addresses range from 00000001 (1) to 01111111 (127).

55. **D. ARP**

Address Resolution Protocol (ARP) is a network layer protocol that converts the IP address (logical address) to a MAC address (physical address).

56. **A. FF-FF-FF-FF-FF-FF**

The ARP request message is a broadcast message and is therefore destined for the broadcast address of FF-FF-FF-FF-FF-FF.

57. **B. SYN, ACK/SYN, ACK**

The TCP three-way handshake starts with a SYN message from computer A to computer B. Computer B then sends an ACK/SYN message, which is then followed by computer A sending an ACK.

58. **C. Sequence numbers and acknowledgements**

TCP assigns each message (known as a segment) a sequence number. When a message is received at the destination, it sends an acknowledgement based on the received sequence number indicating that the message has been received.

59. **B. IP**

The Internet Protocol (IP) protocol is responsible for logical addressing and routing functions. The IP protocol runs at the network layer.

60. **D. UDP**

User Datagram Protocol (UDP) is responsible for unreliable delivery, which means it does not track whether the data has been received at the destination.

61. **C. ICMP**

Internet Control Message Protocol (ICMP) is responsible for error and status reporting and runs at the network layer of the OSI model.

62. **B. Destination IP address**

When a router receives a packet, it compares the destination IP address in the IP header against the routing table to determine where to send the packet.

63. **C. ACK/SYN**

The second phase of the TCP three-way handshake is ACK/SYN, which is a system acknowledging it has received the other system's SYN message but at the same time sending its own SYN message.

64. **C. ACK**

The acknowledgement flag (ACK) is set on a packet to indicate that the message is confirming a previous packet has been received.

65. **B. 8**

ICMP type 8 is used for echo requests, whereas echo reply messages are ICMP type 0.

66. **C. Source IP address**

E. Time to Live

The IP header contains information used by the IP protocol. Things such as the source and destination IP address, along with the TTL, are stored in the IP header. Source and destination port information are stored in the TCP or UDP header, and sequence numbers and acknowledgements are stored in the TCP header.

67. **C. FTP**

FTP is an example of an application layer protocol. IP and ICMP are network layer protocols, whereas TCP is a transport layer protocol. For the CCNA exams, you must know the layers of the OSI model and what protocols run at those layers.

68. **D. TCP**

TCP is responsible for reliable delivery. Note that UDP is a transport layer protocol but it is used for unreliable delivery.

69. **A. 0**

The echo reply message uses ICMP type 0. Note that echo request messages use ICMP type 8.

70. **A. ICMP**

ICMP is the protocol used by the ping command, so to block pings you need to block ICMP.

71. **D. RST**

A reset flag (RST) is used to drop the TCP connection at any time.

72. C. ::1

The IPv6 loopback address is 0000:0000:0000:0000:0000:0000:0000:0001, which can be shortened as ::1. To shorten an address you are allowed to remove leading zeros to make the address 0:0:0:0:0:0:0:1. But then you are allowed to collapse multiple zeros with a colon between them to a double colon (::), which gives you ::1.

73. B. A global address starts with 2000

E. The loopback address is ::1

The loopback address in IPv6 is ::1, whereas global addresses start with 2000. Be sure to know the IPv6 address types for the CCNA exams!

74. B. fe80::f407:622c:a0ce:90cc

Link-local addresses in IPv6 are similar to APIPA addresses in IPv4 and start with FE80. Be sure to study the IPv6 address types for the CCNA exams!

75. B. No broadcast messages

E. Automatic configuration

There are some huge changes with IPv6, and two of those changes are the elimination of broadcast messages and the fact that IPv6 uses automatic configuration.

76. C. Teredo

Teredo is an IPv6 tunneling protocol that can be used to encapsulate IPv6 packets into an IPv4 packet so that it can travel across an IPv4 Internet. Teredo is the only IPv6 tunneling protocol that can be used, when the system is behind a NAT device.

77. B. Translation between IPv6 and IPv4

D. Use of dual-stack routing

E. Use tunneling protocols

When transitioning to IPv6, you can use translation protocols to convert, or proxy, from IPv4 addressing to IPv6 addressing. You also have the capabilities of running IPv4 and IPv6 on the same devices, and can use tunneling protocols to tunnel the data across dissimilar protocol networks.

78. D. Unique local address

A unique local address is similar to an IPv4 private address and starts with FC00.

79. D. TCP 25

SMTP is the Internet protocol for sending e-mail and uses TCP port 25.

80. C. 21

FTP uses TCP ports 21 (to transfer FTP commands) and 20 (to transfer data). Note that SMTP uses TCP port 25, telnet uses TCP port 23, and DNS uses TCP 53 (for zone transfers) and UDP 53 (for DNS queries).

81.

B. 110

POP3 uses TCP port 110. Note that FTP uses TCP 21 and 20, IMAP uses TCP 143, and HTTPS uses TCP 443.

82.

A. FTP uses TCP ports 21 and 20

D. HTTP uses TCP port 80

F. SMTP uses TCP port 25

You must know your ports for CCNA exams. FTP uses TCP ports 21 and 20, HTTP uses TCP port 80, and SMTP uses TCP port 25.

83.

A. DHCP uses UDP 67/68

C. SNMP uses UDP 161

F. DNS uses UDP 53

DHCP uses UDP ports 67 and 68, SNMP uses UDP port 161, and DNS uses UDP port 53.

84.

D. The DHCP server is down.

Sue's system has an IP address that starts with 169.254.x.y, which is known as an Automatic Private IP Address (APIPA) address. A system is assigned an APIPA address when it cannot locate a DHCP server to obtain an address from. This is most likely a DHCP problem.

85.

B. Change his IP address to 192.19.0.79.

In this example, when you look at the IP address and subnet mask you can see that the network ID is 192.19.210.x. The default gateway which references your router must have an IP address within the same network ID.

86.

B. Set all host bits to 1

In order to calculate the broadcast address of a subnet, you set all host bits to 1 and then convert to decimal.

87.

C. 255.255.224.0

To create six new subnets, you need to actually create eight subnets by borrowing three bits from the host ID portion of the subnet mask and converting them to subnet bits.

88.

B. 255.255.240.0

The /20 is the CIDR notation for the number of bits enabled in the subnet mask. This calculates to 255.255.240.0 — which is 11111111.11111111.11110000.00000000 in binary (count the 20 bits set to a 1 value).

89. **A. 255.255.240.0**

In order to get support for 12 subnets you would need to subnet with 4 bits ($2^4 = 16$ networks). Because you started as a class B (the value of the first octet falls between 128 and 191) with a default subnet mask of 255.255.0.0, to add 4 subnet bits you would get a new subnet mask of 255.255.240.0. See below:

11111111.11111111.**1111**0000.00000000

equals

255.   255.   240.   0

90. **B. 10**

The formula to calculate the number of host bits required for a certain number of systems is:

$2^{host\ bits} - 2$

So $2^{10} - 2 = 1{,}024 - 2 = 1{,}022$

This means that with 10 host bits you can support up to 1,022 systems on the network as you have that many valid addresses. Always remember to subtract 2 because you need to take away the addresses reserved for the network ID and the broadcast address.

91. **C. 5**

You need to mask at least 5 bits to create 20 subnets ($2^5 = 32$ subnets). If you try to use 4 bits, you do not have enough subnets ($2^4 = 16$ subnets).

92. **A. Set all host bits to 0.**

The network ID for a subnet can be calculated by having all host bits set to 0 and then converting to decimal.

93. **C. 4,094**

With a subnet mask of /20, 12 bits remain for host bits. You can calculate how many hosts are valid with the formula of $2^{12} = 4{,}096 - 2 = 4{,}094$ valid addresses.

94. **A. 3**

If you were to use only 2 bits to create subnets, you would get 4 of them ($2^2 = 4$). Because that is not enough, you need to add one more bit to get $2^3 = 8$ networks! Three subnet bits are used to create between 5 and 8 networks.

95. **B. ip subnet-zero**

The ip subnet-zero command is a default command on today's Cisco routers, which allows you to use the first and last subnets when subnetting.

96.

A. 255.255.255.224 = /27

The subnet mask of 255.255.255.224 would have 27 bits enabled, which would correspond to /27. The breakdown is shown below:

11111111.11111111.11111111.11100000

equals

255.   255.   255.   224

97.

C. Subnet C does not have enough addresses

D. Computer A is assigned an incorrect address

In the network diagram, you can see that subnet C requires 22 users but is using a subnet mask of /28. A subnet mask of /28 only allows for 4 host bits, and — 4 host bits calculates to only 14 valid addresses ($2^4 - 2 = 14$) for the subnet — not enough addresses to support 22 users.

The second problem is that computer A has an IP address in the wrong subnet. The subnet mask of /25 tells you that the network is subnetted because classful IP addresses use /8, /16, or /24. In this case, you are looking at a class C address broken into two subnets. Note that with a /25 you are dealing with one subnet bit that has an increment of 128 — this means the network IDs are 0 and then 128. The network diagram is showing you that the subnet ID is 202.45.67.0, and therefore all systems on that subnet must be between 1 and 127 (because 128 is the value of the next network ID).

98.

A. 126

There are 126 systems supported on the network. To calculate this you take $2^{host\ bits}$, which for 7 host bits is 128, then take the two illegal addresses (network ID and broadcast addresses) away to get $128 - 2 = 126$ hosts on the network.

99.

B. 4,094

There are 4,094 systems supported on the network. To calculate this, you look at the existing subnet mask in CIDR notation (/20) — meaning 20 bits are used for network bits. You then take that away from the possible 32 bits to calculate the number of host bits and get 12. You then calculate how many hosts (or systems) are supported by using the formula of $2^{12} = 4,096 - 2 = 4,094$. (Remember you need to take two away from the 4,096 because two host addresses are always illegal to use for hosts — the network ID and broadcast address.)

100.

D. 192.168.2.67

The second subnet is the 192.168.2.64 subnet, with the third valid address being 192.168.2.67. Remember that the first address (64) is the network ID, so the first valid address is 65, then 66, and the third valid address is 67.

101.   **B. 255.255.255.128**

In order to support 92 systems, you need 7 host bits ($2^7 = 128 - 2 = 126$ valid addresses). This means your subnet mask in binary looks like this:

11111111.11111111.11111111.10000000

When you convert this to decimal you get:

255.255.255.128

102.   **C. 9**

You would need 9 host bits to support 510 hosts on the network ($2^9 = 512 - 2 = 510$ addresses).

103.   **D. 255.255.224.0**

Because you need to borrow 3 bits from the third octet in order to have each subnet support 8,190 hosts, the new subnet mask is 255.255.224.0.

104.   **B. 30**

With only 5 host bits remaining in the address, you can have 30 hosts on the network ($2^5 = 32 - 2 = 30$ valid IP addresses).

105.   **B. 255.255.255.192**

You would need 6 host bits to support a minimum of 60 hosts ($2^6 = 64 - 2 = 62$ valid IP addresses). This would create the following subnet mask in binary:

11111111.11111111.11111111.11000000

This converts to decimal as 255.255.255.192.

106.   **D. 198.45.6.94**

This is a tricky question, but one you should get familiar with for the ICND1 and ICND2 exams. The question is giving you an IP address to use as a reference, and you need to choose which IP address exists on the same subnet as the IP address in the question.

The first step to figuring out which choice is on the same subnet is to determine how many bits were used to create the subnetted example. In this case, because it is a class C address it should only have a /24 indicating the number of bits enabled in the subnet mask (which is a subnet mask of 255.255.255.0). Because this is a /27, you know that there are 3 additional bits that have been enabled in the subnet mask to create the sub-netted example. Step 2 is to look at the value of the last subnet bit that has been enabled and use this as the "increment" value (in this case, it is 32). Once you know the increment value, the third step is to list out all the subnet network IDs and deter-mine which network the IP address given in the question refers to. In this case, the network IDs are 198.45.6.0, 198.45.6.32, 198.45.6.64, 198.45.6.96, 198.45.6.128, etc. The address given is 198.45.6.87, and because .87 falls between .64 and .96 you know that the address is on the 198.45.6.64 network. So the answer to which IP address would you assign must fall between .64 and .95 (it cannot be .96 because that is the next network ID). The answer cannot actually be .64 because it is reserved for the network ID (all host bits set to 0), and it cannot be .95 because that is the broadcast address for the .64 network. So you need a number from .65 to .94 — and .94 is the only value in the list of choices that is on that subnet.

The figure below shows a visual reference of this explanation.

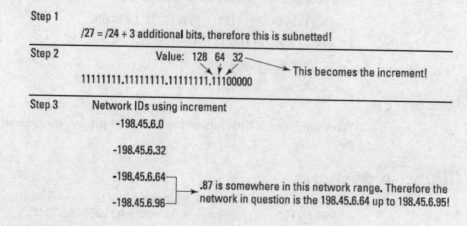

Step 1

/27 = /24 + 3 additional bits, therefore this is subnetted!

Step 2   Value: 128 64 32

11111111.11111111.11111111.11100000   This becomes the increment!

Step 3   Network IDs using increment

-198.45.6.0

-198.45.6.32

-198.45.6.64

-198.45.6.96   .87 is somewhere in this network range. Therefore the network in question is the 198.45.6.64 up to 198.45.6.95!

It is critical that you feel comfortable with this method of calculating the answer, because most of the subnetting questions found on the ICND1 and ICND2 exams can be answered quickly using this technique.

107.   **D. 220.55.66.64**

220.55.66.64 is the network ID of the third subnet. A quick way to figure this out is to determine the increment value of the last bit used to subnet — in this example, it is 32, so the increments are 0, 32, 64, 96, and so on. The third network ID is 64, so you simply add that to 220.55.66.0 to get 220.55.66.64.

108.   **A. 24.32.0.0**

The 24.60.32.20/11 address is located in the 24.32.0.0 network range. A quick way to figure these questions out is to look at the /11 and ask yourself what the increment value supplied by the last bit used to subnet is. It is 32! This means that the network IDs increment by 32, starting with 24.0.0.0, then 24.32.0.0, and then 24.64.0.0. In this question, the address 24.60.32.20 is less than 24.64.0.0, so it must be on the 24.32.0.0 network.

109.   **D. 107.48.0.4**

To figure this question out, you must first determine the subnet range. You can do this by looking at the address first and determining that it is a class A address. Then look at the number of bits used in the network ID (/12) and note that it is 4 bits more than a default class A (/8). This means the network is subnetted. Look at the value of the last subnet bit (the 4th bit), which is 16, and that becomes the increment for you to determine the network IDs. The network IDs are:

107.0.0.0/12

107.16.0.0/12

107.32.0.0/12

107.48.0.0/12

107.64.0.0/12

You then identify where the address in the question falls, and it is between 107.48.0.0 and 107.64.0.0 — this means that the IP address supplied in the question is on the 107.48.0.0 network. Once you identify the network ID, you then count four addresses up from the network ID:

> 107.48.0.1
>
> 107.48.0.2
>
> 107.48.0.3
>
> 107.48.0.4 — this is the answer!

110. **A. 195.34.56.35**

D. 195.34.56.58

In order to create 8 networks, you must use 3 subnet bits ($2^3 = 8$). If you were to subnet with 3 bits, you would get this as a new subnet mask in binary (only the relevant portion is in binary):

> 255.255.255.**111**00000

Next, you look at the value of the last subnet bit to determine the increment value (32) and then calculate your network IDs:

> Network 1: 195.34.56.0
>
> Network 2: 195.34.56.32
>
> Network 3: 195.34.56.64
>
> Network 4: 195.34.56.96
>
> Network 5: 195.34.56.128

You then look at all the choices provided in the question and determine which two addresses fall within the same network. Because Network 3 goes from 195.34.56.64 up to 195.34.56.95, it includes the addresses for choices A (195.34.56.35) and D (195.34.56.58). All choices and their networks are listed below — you are looking for two on the same network:

> A. 195.34.56.35 — Network 2
>
> B. 195.34.56.14 — Network 1
>
> C. 195.34.56.76 — Network 3
>
> D. 195.34.56.58 — Network 2
>
> E. 195.34.56.98 — Network 4
>
> F. 195.34.56.129 — Network 5

111. **C. 199.11.33.128/27**

In order to support a network of 27 systems, you need to use 5 host bits ($2^5 = 32 - 2 = 30$ hosts). This means that your subnet mask would look like this in binary:

> 11111111.11111111.11111111.11100000

This can be written in shorthand CIDR notation as /27, meaning that 27 bits are enabled in the subnet mask and used as network bits (whereas the bits set to 0 are host bits).

112.

D. 190.53.156.0

In this example, a large number of networks is being created because 6 subnet bits are being used. /22 bits minus 16 bits used by default = 6 bits extra are being used.

With 6 bits being used, that makes an increment of 4:

255.255.**11111100**.00000000

Your network IDs are going to increment by 4 starting with:

190.53.0.0 — Network 1

190.53.4.0 — Network 2

190.53.8.0 — Network 3

… continue on to …

190.53.152.0

190.53.156.0

190.53.160.0

The IP address displayed in the question falls before the 190.53.160.0 network, so that means it is part of the 190.53.156.0 network.

113.

C. The network ID of the subnet is 205.56.34.48

F. The network is subnetted

H. The broadcast address of the subnet is 205.56.34.63

In this example, you are dealing with a class C address, so the default subnet mask uses /24. However, this example uses /28. This means that the network has been subnetted with 4 subnet bits.

11111111.11111111.111111111.**1111**0000

The value of the last subnet bit is 16, so you increment the network IDs, giving you 0, 16, 32, 48, 64, etc. The IP address given in the example ends with 53, so you are part of the 48 network:

205.56.34.48 — Network ID

205.56.34.49 — First valid address

205.56.34.62 — Last valid address

205.56.34.63 — Broadcast address

114. **A. 107.63.255.255**

The example address in the question is a class address and by default should use /8 to represent the subnet mask, but this example is using /12 with 4 additional subnet bits, making the subnet mask the /12. The value of the last bit subnetted is 16, which is the increment value. This creates network IDs of 0, 16, 32, 48, 64, etc. So the network IDs are as follows:

107.0.0.0 — Network 1

107.16.0.0 — Network 2

107.32.0.0 — Network 3

107.48.0.0 — Network 4

107.64.0.0 — Network 5

The address in the question falls into network 4, which would have a broadcast address of one less than the next network's network ID — which is 107.63.255.255.

115. **D. 199.45.67.190**

The address in the question is a class C address, so by default it uses /24 for the subnet mask. Since the example uses /26 you know that the network has been subnetted with 2 additional bits in the subnet mask:

11111111.11111111.111111111.11000000

The value of the last bit subnetted is 64, which becomes your increment to calculate the network IDs of 0, 64, 128, and 192. The address in the question ends with 139, an address on the 128 network, which would have a last valid address of 190 (because 191 is the broadcast address in this case).

116. **B. 220.55.66.94**

The last valid address of the 64 subnet in this example is 94. An easy way to figure this out is the next network ID would have 96 as a value and the number before that would be the broadcast address (95), which leaves the last valid address to be 94.

117. **B. 195.34.56.7.30**

E. 195.34.56.7.17

The subnet mask of 255.255.255.240 can be converted to the binary of:

11111111.111111111.111111111.11110000

The value of the last bit is 16, so that becomes the increment for network IDs (0, 16, 32, 48, 64 …). The following lists the networks for each IP in question:

A. 195.34.56.7.14 —Network 1

B. 195.34.56.7.30 — Network 2

C. 195.34.56.7.38 — Network 3

D. 195.34.56.7. 55 — Network 4

E. 195.34.56.7.17 — Network 2

F. 195.34.56.7.69 — Network 5

118.

D. The first valid address of the subnet is 190.88.96.1

F. The network is subnetted

H. The broadcast address of the subnet is 190.88.127.255

The address given is a class B network that has been subnetted (there is a /19 instead of a /16) with 3 subnet bits. Three subnet bits has an increment of 32, so the network IDs for the class B given are:

190.88.0.0 — Network 1

190.88.32.0 — Network 2

190.88.64.0 — Network 3

190.88.96.0 — Network 4

190.88.128.0 — Network 5...and so on.

The IP address in the question falls into the range of network 4, which means the first valid address is 190.88.96.1; the broadcast address is 190.88.127.255; and the last valid address is one less than the broadcast, 190.88.127.254.

119.

C. 255.255.255.252

A WAN link only needs two IP addresses available, so to get two available IP addresses you need 2 host bits ($2^2 = 4 - 2 = 2$ valid IP addresses). This is your subnet mask in binary:

11111111.11111111.11111111.11111100

This converts to the decimal of 255.255.255.252.

120.

C. VLSM

The variable-length subnet masks feature allows you to use different subnet masks for different subnets within your organization.

121.

D. 255.255.255.252

To make the most efficient use of addressing, you should use a subnet mask that supports only the number of addresses needed. In this case, only two IP addresses are needed on the WAN link so you need 2 host bits ($2^2 = 4 - 2 = 2$ valid addresses). If you have 2 host bits, this means you would have 30 network bits, giving you a subnet mask of 255.255.255.252.

122.

B. 199.11.33.0/25

Because this question states that you must make the best use of the address space (IP address allocation), you must look at the subnet in question (New York office) and ensure that you use an IP range and subnet mask that has enough addresses for that office. In this example, the office has 125 users, so you must have 7 host bits available for this network ($2^7 = 128 - 2 = 126$ addresses). If you were to have 7 bits as host bits, that would leave 25 bits as network bits (25 + 7 = 32 bits in total). So B is your answer!

Answers
101–200

123.   **E. 199.11.33.160/30**

Because the WAN link only requires 2 valid addresses for hosts, you only need 2 host bits ($2^2 = 4 - 2 = 2$ valid addresses). The binary format of the mask is:

11111111.111111111.11111111.11111100

This means there are 30 bits enabled in the subnet masks, which is noted as /30 or shown as 255.255.255.252.

124.   **C. To connect to the WAN**

The serial port is typically used to connect to the WAN environment with an external CSU/DSU. You could also use the serial port to connect directly to the serial port of another router for a back-to-back serial link.

125.   **B. f0/0**

E. fa0/0

When working on a router or switch, you can refer to a Fast Ethernet port by using an interface ID such as f0/0 or fa0/0.

126.   **D. Rollover**

The rollover cable, also known as a console cable, is used to connect a system to the console port.

127.   **D. To connect a modem**

The AUX port is used to connect a modem to the router. This modem can be used as a method to remotely connect to the router and fix any problems with the configuration.

128.   **C. AUX**

The AUX port should be configured with a password. If it is not, then it is possible that someone with a local access to your router can connect directly to the AUX port and bypass the security you placed on the console port.

129.   **A. clock rate 64000**

The clock rate command should be configured on the DCE end of a point-to-point serial link. Note that if you are connecting your serial port to the ISP, then they are the DCE end of the communication channel and will configure the clock rate.

130.   **D. Serial0/0/0**

The serial port is used to connect to a WAN environment and is typically connected to an external CSU/DSU if you do not have an integrated CSU/DSU in the router.

131.   **C. WIC**

You can purchase a Wan Interface Card (WIC) and install that in the router to add different ports to your router.

132. **B. The interface type specified does not exist.**

Using the interface ID of "e" means you are referencing an Ethernet port (which is a 10 Mbps port). In this example, Fast Ethernet ports run at 100 Mbps and should be referenced with the ID of "f" or "Fa."

133. **B. VRAM**

The running configuration is stored in volatile RAM (VRAM).

134. **B. POST**

C. Bootstrap

E. ROMMON

ROM memory on a Cisco device is used to store the Power On Self Test (POST) routines, the bootstrap program, and the ROMMON.

135. **D. Flash**

Flash memory holds the Cisco IOS and is typically added to the device with a flash memory card, as shown in the figure.

136. **D. copy running-config startup-config**

E. write

In order to save the running configuration to more permanent memory, use the copy running-config startup-config command or the write command.

137. **D. Flash**

The IOS image file is stored in flash memory and is loaded from flash memory into RAM during the bootup process.

138. **A. NVRAM**

The startup configuration is stored in permanent memory known as nonvolatile RAM (NVRAM).

139. **A. telnet**

You use the telnet command to remotely connect to another switch or router for remote administration on that device.

140. **A. line vty 0 4**

In order to configure remote access to the router, you will need to configure the telnet ports on the router. You can navigate to the telnet ports with the line vty 0 x command, where x is the last telnet port supported by your device.

141. **A. disable**

The disable command is used to move from priv exec mode to user exec mode.

142. **B. ping ?**

You can use the **?** to get help from the Cisco IOS. If you use **?** by itself you will get a list of available commands, and if you use it after the command you get a list of parameters.

143. **A. router>enable**

In order to move to priv exec mode, you use the `enable` command from user exec mode.

144. **B. router(config)#**

Global configuration mode is identified with (config)# in the prompt.

145. **C. router**

The default configuration applied to a new router will have the name router if a name has not been configured.

146. **D. #config terminal**

Once in priv exec mode, you can type the `config terminal` command to navigate to global configuration mode.

147. **B. Disable the interface**

E. Assign an IP address

When you are at an interface prompt (config-if#) you can execute commands that apply to the interface, such as disabling the interface or assigning an IP address.

148. **C. setup**

The initial configuration dialog, also known as the setup mode, can be launched at any time by typing the setup command.

149. **B. When there is no startup-config**

D. When you type setup

The initial configuration dialog, also known as the setup mode, displays when a Cisco device starts up and there is no startup configuration file. The initial configuration dialog also appears when you type the setup command.

150. **C. The option to enter initial configuration**

A brand new router does not have a startup configuration, so it will ask you to enter the initial configuration dialog so that you can configure the router.

151. **C. Verify that hardware is functioning.**

The POST is the first step performed in the boot process and is responsible for verifying that the hardware is functioning.

152. **A. A failure during POST**

When the system LED is displaying an amber light it means that the device had a failure during POST and is not operating properly.

153. **B. The router prompts to enter setup mode.**

When the router cannot find the startup configuration, it prompts you to enter setup mode, also known as the initial configuration dialog. This will then walk you through the basic configuration of a Cisco router without you needing to know the commands.

154. **A. A limited operating system used to troubleshoot startup and password recovery**

ROMMON is a limited operating system that is typically used to recover forgotten passwords. You enter ROMMON by restarting the router and pressing Ctrl-Break.

155. **D. POST; bootstrap loads IOS from flash; apply startup configuration to running config**

When a device boots up, the POST first verifies the hardware, and then the bootstrap program loads the IOS image file from flash memory. Once the IOS has been loaded, the startup configuration is read from NVRAM and copied to the running configuration.

156. **D. Ctrl-Break**

On startup, if you press Ctrl-Break you will interrupt the normal startup of the Cisco device and will be placed in the ROMMON prompt. This process is typically used to recover the password of the Cisco devices.

157. **B. 2**

There are two Fast Ethernet ports on this router. Note that there are 4 serial ports on the router as well.

158. **B. 12.4**

Version 12.4 is the version of the IOS shown in the resulting output of the show version command.

159. **show version**

The show version command displays the types of ports detected on the device and how many of each type of port. Note that it also displays some important information regarding your Cisco device, such as the version of the IOS you are running, the IOS image filename, and the configuration register value.

160. **C. Show version**

The show version command displays some really important information regarding your Cisco device. It displays the version of the IOS you are running, the IOS image filename, the types of ports detected on the device, and the configuration register value.

161. **B. show version**

The show version command displays the current value assigned to the configuration register. The configuration register controls how your device boots.

162. **A. router(config-if)#shutdown**

In order to disable an interface on a router, you must use the shutdown command at the interface prompt.

163. **B. PPP**

D. HDLC

You can configure the serial interfaces of a Cisco router for either the HDLC encapsulation protocol or the PPP protocol.

164. **A. Use the following commands:**

```
R1#config term
R1(config)#interface f0/0
R1(config-if)#duplex full
```

In order to configure full duplex mode on an interface, you must first navigate to the interface and then use the duplex command, followed by the word "full" as a parameter.

165. **C. R1(config-if)#no shutdown**

In order to enable an interface on a Cisco device, you must use the no shutdown command when at the interface prompt.

166. **A. PPP**

D.HDLC

PPP and HDLC are layer-2 protocols used on a serial link. PPP is an industry-standard protocol and should be used when connecting heterogeneous environments, whereas HDLC is used only when connecting Cisco devices together.

167. **C. router(config-if)#ip address 10.0.0.1 255.0.0.0**

In order to assign an IP address to an interface on the router, you must be at the interface prompt for the appropriate interface (using the global configuration interface command). Once at the interface prompt, you can use the IP address command and specify the IP address and subnet mask for the interface.

168. **B. 1**

The syntax to reference an interface is first the type of interface, followed by the slot/port. In this example, the FastEthernet 0/1 is referencing slot 0, but the interface is 1.

169. **D. DCE**

The router with the data communication equipment (DCE) end of the point-to-point serial link is responsible for setting the clock rate. Note that when connecting your router to the WAN environment, this is usually done at the ISP because the ISP is the host to the DCE and you are the data terminal equipment (DTE) in the ISP scenario.

170. **A. clock rate 64000**

C. encapsulation hdlc

When configuring a serial interface that acts as the DCE device, you need to provide the encapsulation protocol and the clock rate.

171. **C. serial0/0 is administratively down, line protocol is down**

Because the serial port has been shut down by the administrator, the first part of the status will display as serial0/0 is administratively down. The second part, which is associated with the layer 2 protocol on the link, will say line protocol down because if the link is not up, the protocol cannot be up.

172. **D. R1(config-if)#ip address dhcp**

In order to assign an IP address to an interface via DHCP, you use the ip address command but pass in the word dhcp as a parameter instead of an actual IP address.

173. **D. router(config)#hostname R1**

In order to change the hostname of the router, you must be in global configuration mode and use the hostname command.

174. **C. enable secret**

The enable secret is an encrypted password within the configuration files by default.

175. **B. exit**

You would first need to exit from the Interface prompt to go back to global configuration mode and then use the hostname command to change the name of the router.

176. **B. Use the following commands:**

```
enable
config term
line con 0
password myConPass
login
```

In order to configure a password for your console port, you must first navigate to priv exec mode with the enable command. You then navigate to global configuration mode with the config term command, and finally navigate to the console port with the line con 0 command. To set the password, use the password command, but then you must use the login command to tell the Cisco device to prompt for login using that password.

177.   **A. r1(config)# username tom password P@ssw0rd**

To configure a username and password on your Cisco device, you must be in global configuration and use the `username` command.

178.   **A. show history**

The `show history` command is used to display a list of recently used commands on the router.

179.   **B. service password-encryption**

To encrypt all passwords in the configuration files on the router, you use the `service password-encryption` command — a great command to be familiar with for exam purposes and the real world!

180.   **C. show running-config**

The `show running-config` command displays the configuration in volatile RAM, which must be saved to nonvolatile RAM (startup-config) if you wish to have the changes persist when the power is lost or the system is rebooted.

181.   **B. no ip domain lookup**

The `no ip domain lookup` command can be used to disable DNS lookups on the Cisco device!

182.   **A. exec-timeout 1 45**

You can use the `exec-timeout` command on the console port to specify a timeout value for the console. When you do this, you specify the duration of inactivity in the format of minutes (space) seconds.

183.   **A. R1#terminal history size 30**

The command to increase the number of commands that are stored in the history buffer is the `terminal history size` command, which is executed from priv exec mode.

184.   **C. r1(config-line)# login local**

To configure the Cisco device to prompt for a username and password when connecting to the console port, you must first navigate to the console port and then use the `login local` command. This command tells the Cisco device to prompt for a username and password and authenticate against the local list of usernames.

185.   **B. MOTD**

The Message Of The Day (MOTD) banner is displayed first. After the MOTD banner, you see the login banner before logging into the device, but after the MOTD banner. Finally, the exec banner displays when the administrator enters user exec mode.

186.   **B. reload**

D. erase startup-config

In order to delete the configuration off your router you would first erase the startup-config and then use the `reload` command to reboot the router. When the router reboots there is no startup-config to apply (so the router will prompt you to enter setup mode).

187.   **C. Use PPP as the serial link protocol.**

The HDLC protocol on Cisco routers is a proprietary implementation of the protocol and can only be used to communicate with other Cisco routers via serial ports. If you have an environment that uses routers from different manufacturers, you will need to use an industry standard serial link protocol such as PPP.

188.   **A. show interfaces**

The `show interfaces` command is used to view all interfaces and their status. You can also use the `show interface <interface ID>` command to view the status of a particular interface.

189.   **D. Enable the interface.**

Because the status of the link shows as administratively down, this is an indication that you have disabled the port or have not enabled the port. You need to enable the port with a no shutdown command.

190.   **C. show ip interface brief**

The `show ip interface brief` command displays a table listing all the interfaces and their settings.

191.   **A. show version**

D. show flash

E. show running-config

To view information on the IOS version that is running on your Cisco device, you can use the `show version` command, the `show flash` command, or the `show running-config` command.

192.   **C. The serial port has the wrong cable connected.**

The figure is showing that router R1 has the DTE end of the serial cable, but it appears as if the router is configured as the DCE end of the link when looking at the output of the show controllers command.

193.   **D. show controllers serial0/0**

The `show controllers` command is used on an interface to display the clock rate on the link and to indicate whether the interface acts as the DTE or DCE device.

194. **C. Check the physical connection.**

When looking at the status of an interface, the output first displays physical layer status (serial0/2/0 is down) followed by a comma, then the layer-2 status (line protocol is down). The layer-2 status relates to the protocol being used to carry data across the link (such as HDLC or PPP). If there is a problem with the physical connection, then the interface will appear as down. It is important to note that when the interface is "down," the line protocol will always be "down." In this case, you should be troubleshooting layer 1, the physical connection. If the interface is up and the line protocol is down, then you know there is a physical link, but there is a problem with the protocol or clock rate.

195. **A. P@ssw0rd**

Because the enable password and enable secret are used, this means that the secret password of P@ssw0rd would be required because the secret takes precedence over enable password. Because there is no additional password on the console port, no other password is required.

196. **B. Layer-2**

When using the show interfaces command, you see the status of the link shown in the format of Serial0/2/0 is up, line protocol is down. The Serial0/2/0 is up part indicates whether there is a link (layer-1), whereas the line protocol down part indicates whether the layer-2 protocol has been configured properly.

197. **A. P@ssw0rd**

The only password required is the secret password (because it takes precedence over the enable password). You are not required to enter the console password, although one is set, because the administrator forgot to use the login command to force authentication on that port! Very important to remember for the exams and the real world!

198. **B. A protocol or clock rate has not been set.**

If the line protocol is down, there is a problem with the configuration of the serial link protocol or the clock rate. Also note that if the protocol has not been configured properly on the other end, the line protocol still displays as down.

199. **D. conpass / P@ssw0rd**

Tom would first need to type the console password of conpass and then, when entering priv exec mode, he would need to input the secret password of P@ssw0rd.

200. **A. TFTP**

TFTP is UDP based and is the protocol Cisco devices use to backup the IOS image and configuration files to a remote server.

201. **B. copy running-config tftp**

In order to back up your configuration, such as the running-config, or your IOS, you can use the copy <source> <destination> command.

202.

D. copy tftp running-config

In order to copy your configuration from a TFTP server to your router, you will use the copy command and specify TFTP as the source, and running-config as the destination. For example:

```
Copy tftp running-config
```

The Cisco device will prompt you for the IP address of the TFTP server to connect to for the configuration.

203.

A. To back up the IOS image to a server

The copy command is used to back up or restore your IOS image or the configuration files of the Cisco device, depending on what you specify as the source and destination parameters. In this example, because flash is used as the source, the command is copying an IOS image from flash memory and the destination is set to a TFTP server. The actual details of the filename to be copied and the IP address of the TFTP server to use will be asked by the Cisco device.

204.

C. Replace the IOS –> copy tftp flash

E. Back up the IOS –> copy flash tftp

Cisco exams will have drag-and-drop questions where you must drag the command onto the appropriate description, so be prepared for questions like this. In this case, the description and corresponding commands that are true in regards to restoring the IOS is the copy tftp flash command. To do the opposite and back up the IOS, you would switch the source and destination parameters on the copy command — copy flash tftp.

205.

C. It is the address of the TFTP server to copy the running configuration to.

Because the format for the copy command is copy <source> <destination>, and the command being typed in the figure is copy running-config tftp, the IP address being supplied is the address of the TFTP server, which is the destination address of where the configuration file is being copied to.

206.

B. show flash

The show flash command can be used to view the contents of flash memory and includes showing you the file name and size of the IOS image.

207.

A. The old IOS file is deleted to make room.

When you copy a new IOS image from a TFTP to flash memory, if there is not enough room the old IOS image is deleted. You will first be asked if it is OK to erase flash memory before the copy operation starts.

208.

D. copy flash tftp

The copy command backs up the Cisco IOS. Because the IOS resides in flash memory and you are sending the copy to the TFTP server, you need to use the copy flash tftp syntax.

209. **B. UDP 69**

TFTP is a connectionless protocol so it uses UDP as its transport layer protocol and runs on port 69. TFTP can be used to transfer IOS images and configuration files to a remote location for backup purposes.

210. **C. boot system**

You can use the boot system command followed by where the boot image can be found, then the filename of the boot image. Syntax is similar to:

```
Boot system <flash/tftp> <filename.bin>
```

211. **A. xmodem**

You cannot use TFTP to restore the IOS image in this case because the router does not have network access. You can connect a computer's serial port to the console port of the router and transfer the IOS image via Xmodem. Keep in mind the transfer rate through the console port is slow and will take much longer than a normal TFTP transfer.

212. **C. boot system flash c2800nm-advipservicesk9-mz.124-15.T1.bin**

In order to specify an image to use that is located in flash memory, you would use the boot system command followed by where the IOS image is stored (in this case, flash memory), followed by the image filename. For example:

```
boot system flash c2800nm-advipservicesk9-mz.124-15.T1.bin
```

213. **C. Cisco Discovery Protocol**

The Cisco Discovery Protocol (CDP) identifies neighboring Cisco devices and gives you information about each device, such as its platform and IP address.

214. **D. R1, R2, SW3**

When you use the show cdp neighbors command to view other devices on the network, you will only see devices that are directly connected. These directly connected devices are known as neighboring devices.

215. **A. CDP is a Cisco proprietary protocol**

D. CDP runs at the data link layer

F. CDP discovers directly connected devices.

CDP is a layer-2 protocol that Cisco created that is designed to discover neighboring (directly connected) Cisco devices and their details.

216. **D. Disable CDP on the interface connected to the Internet.**

In order to stop CDP message from being sent to the Internet, you would disable CDP on the interface connected to the Internet with the no cdp enable command at the interface prompt.

217. **B. show cdp neighbors detail**

You could use the `show cdp neighbors detail` command to view a list of neighboring devices and their details, such as type of device, model, and IP address.

218. **A. show cdp entry NY-SW1**

To display details about a specific neighboring device, use the `show cdp entry` command with the device ID. This displays information about the device, such as the device ID, IP address, and the platform (model).

219. **D. CDP timer**

CDP advertisement messages are sent out every 60 seconds by default. The interval of which messages are sent is known as the CDP timer and can be changed with the cdp timer command.

220. **B. 60 seconds**

CDP advertisements are sent out every 60 seconds by default. The default interval can be modified with the CDP timer command in global configuration mode.

221. **A. show cdp entry * protocol**

The `show cdp entry * protocol` command shows all devices, and their IP addresses — and that's all. Similarly, the show cdp neighbors detail command displays all devices and their IP addresses, but since it also displays additional information, this is an incorrect choice.

222. **D. 180 seconds**

By default, a device stores CDP information for 180 seconds. This is known as the CDP hold timer and can be altered with the `cdp holdtimer` command in global configuration.

223. **C. cdp holdtime**

To alter how long a Cisco device stores CDP advertisement information it receives from other Cisco devices, you would use the `cdp holdtime` command. Note that the default hold timer value is set to 180 seconds.

224. **D. no cdp enable**

To disable CDP on an interface, you need to navigate to that interface and use the `no cdp enable` command.

225. **D. R1(config)#cdp timer 90**

To alter the frequency at which CDP sends out advertisement messages, you would use the `CDP timer` command at the global configuration prompt.

226. **B. no cdp run**

To disable CDP on the router and not just on an interface, use the `no cdp run` command.

Answers
201–300

227.

C. Ctrl-Shift-6, then X

You can temporarily suspend a Telnet session with the `Ctrl-Shift-6`, then X keystroke.

228.

A. telnet

You use the `telnet` command to be able to remotely connect to another device and administer it. When you use the `telnet` command, you are connecting to the telnet ports on the target device, which are also known as the VTY ports.

229.

A. TCP 23

Telnet is an application layer protocol you can use for remote administration of your Cisco devices. Telnet uses TCP port 23. Keep in mind that Telnet is an unsecure protocol and transfers all information in clear text.

230.

D. SSH

SSH is the secure protocol replacement to Telnet and is used to encrypt the communication between your administration system and the Cisco device you are remotely connecting to. SSH can be used to encrypt all communication, including authentication traffic.

231.

F. TCP 22

SSH is the secure replacement protocol for Telnet and uses TCP port 22.

232.

B. Traffic is unencrypted

E. Requires configuration on the destination device

Telnet transfers information in clear text including authentication traffic. By default, you cannot telnet into a device until you configure an IP address and passwords on the telnet ports (VTY ports).

233.

A. For remote management

Switches do not need IP addresses assigned in order to allow hosts connected to the switch to communicate. The only reason to assign an IP address to a switch is to be able to telnet into the switch at a later time for remote administration purposes.

234.

B. resume <Device ID>

In order to resume a suspended Telnet session, you use the `resume` command and specify the device ID as a parameter.

235.

A. show sessions

The `show sessions` command displays a list of suspended Telnet sessions.

236. **C. show users**

In order to view who is connected to your Cisco device, you can use the show users command. It will display any connections, including console connections and remote connection to the device through the VTY ports.

237. **C. Configure a default gateway on the switch.**

In order to remotely manage a switch from a different network, you must have the default gateway setting configured on the switch. A great indication that the default gateway is the problem is that you can telnet into the switch when on the same network. If you were not able to telnet to any of the Boston switches, then it may have been a problem with the New York router.

238. **B. Add the entry to the hostname table**

In order to resolve the name to an IP address, you must add the name and its corresponding IP address to the MAC address table.

239. **D. show hosts**

You can use the show hosts command to display the contents of the hostname table.

240. **A. ip name-server 23.0.0.10**

The ip name-server command configures your router to send name queries to a DNS server.

241. **A. NY-R1(config)#no ip host BOS-R1**

From global configuration, you can use the no ip host BOS-R1 command to remove the entry from the hostname table.

242. **D. ip host BOS-R1 15.10.0.5**

You resolve the name to the IP address by adding the name to the hostname table using the ip host command.

243. **B. show hosts**

Looking at the output in the figure, you can see that it is displaying the hostname table on the router. Note the name BOS-R1 and the IP address on the right.

244. **B. no ip domain lookup**

You can disable domain lookups to stop the router from querying DNS every time you type at the console. You should only do this if you are not using DNS to resolve addresses when doing administration.

245.   **A. ip domain-lookup**

If you have configured your router for a name server, you may have to enable domain lookups if the administrator has disabled domain lookup. Use the ip domain-lookup command from global configuration to enable domain lookups.

246.   **B. NY-R1(dhcp-config)#default-router 23.0.0.1**

You can use the default-router command at the DHCP prompt to configure the DHCP server to hand out the default gateway setting.

247.   **D. service dhcp**

In order to start the DHCP service, you can use the service dhcp command in global configuration.

248.   **B. no service dhcp**

In order to stop the DHCP service, you can use the no service dhcp command from global configuration mode.

249.   **C. Use the following:**

NY-R1(config)#ip dhcp pool NY_Network

NY-R1(dhcp-config)#network 192.168.3.32 255.255.255.224

NY-R1(dhcp-config)#lease 7 0 0

This is a tricky question. It is a subnetting question mixed with a configuration of DHCP question. The first step is to note that the question asks to configure DHCP for the second subnet. With an increment of 32 (/27), the second subnet is 192.168.3.32. Then to create the DHCP pool you first use the ip dhcp pool global configuration command. Then specify the network range and any DHCP options, such as the lease time of 7 days in this case. Note that the syntax to specify the lease time is days hours minutes (7 0 0).

250.   **B. show ip dhcp server statistics**

In order to view statistics on your server, you use the show ip dhcp server statistics command.

251.   **C. show ip dhcp binding**

In order to view the addresses that your DHCP has assigned to clients on the network, you use the show ip dhcp binding command.

252.   **B. show ip dhcp binding**

The show ip dhcp binding command displays the list of addresses that have been leased to clients on the network.

253.   **C. PAT**

NAT overloading is accomplished by port address translation (PAT) along with the address translation feature of NAT.

254.   **D. For publishing an internal system to the Internet**

A common use of static NAT, which is manually associating a single private IP address with a single public IP address, is for publishing an internal system out to the Internet.

255.   **A. NY-R1(config)#Access-list 16 permit 10.0.0.0 0.255.255.255**

In order to create an access list, you use the `access-list` global configuration command. In this case, using a standard access list requires an ID, then a permit/deny, then the IP address and wildcard mask.

256.   **D. NY-R1(config-if)#ip nat outside**

Since the serial port is connected to the WAN, you want to share that IP address with all other systems connected on the LAN. Part of the process to configure NAT is to configure the interfaces as either inside (they are connected to the LAN) or outside (connected to the WAN/Internet).

257.   **D. PAT**

NAT uses port address translation to overload a single IP address to multiple systems inside the network.

258.   **C. NY-R1(config)#ip nat inside source list 1 interface serial 0/0 overload**

You need to configure NAT and specify access list 1 as the inside source list. In the same command, you are specifying serial 0/0 is to overload its IP address.

259.   **A. Overloading**

Overloading is a type of NAT that translates all private addresses on the network to the one public address. Overloading is achieved through port address translation (PAT).

260.   **D. NY-R1(config-if)#ip nat inside**

In this scenario, the Fast Ethernet port should be configured as the inside interface on the NAT device.

261.   **D. show ip nat translations**

To view the translation table of internal addresses to external addresses, you can use the `show ip nat translations` command.

262. **D. Use the following commands:**

NY-R1(config)#Access list 1 permit 192.168.4.64.0.0.0.31

NY-R1(config)#ip nat inside source list 1 interface serial 0/0 overload

NY-R1(config)#interface Serial0/0

NY-R1(config-if)#ip nat outside

NY-R1(config-if)#interface FastEthernet0/1

NY-R1(config-if)#ip nat inside

Notice in the figure that the serial interface is the one connected to the Internet, so it is the outside interface and needs to be overloaded. The Fast Ethernet port should be flagged as the internal interface. You also should note the IP range because this is a subnetted network and use that IP address in an access list as the source list. Note the wildcard mask when creating the access lists – a quick way to calculate the wildcard mask is to subtract the subnet mask from 255.255.255.255.

263. **B. Ctrl-Break**

When trying to bypass a router's password, you interrupt normal boot operations with Ctrl-Break.

264. **C. 0x2102**

Most routers are configured for a default register of 0x2102, which specifies to load an IOS from flash memory and the startup config from NVRAM.

265. **C. show version**

To view the current value of the configuration register on your router, use the show version command. The value of the configuration register is displayed at the bottom of the output.

266. **A. config-register 0x2102**

After you have recovered the password at the global config prompt, you can type the config-register command and use the original configuration register value of 0x2102.

267. **C. 6**

You will enable bit 6 in the configuration registers to skip loading the startup-config from NVRAM.

268. **A. 0x2142**

Once you enable bit 6 to omit loading the startup-config, the new value on the configuration register will be 0x2142.

269. C. 100–199

An extended access lists uses an ID ranging from 100 to 199. Extended access lists allow you to filter traffic by source and destination IP address, source and destination port, and also by the protocol. Since version 12.0.1 of the Cisco IOS, extended access lists can also use numbers of 2000 to 2699.

270. A. Access lists have an implied deny all at the bottom.

It is important to remember that access lists have an implied deny all rule at the bottom of each access list. This means that unless you specify traffic to be allowed, all traffic is disallowed. When creating access lists, if you expect all other traffic to be allowed you must have that as the last rule.

271. B. Standard

A standard access control list allows you to filter traffic by only the source IP address. Standard access lists use an ID ranging from 1 to 99. Since version 12.0.1 of the Cisco IOS, standard access lists can also use number of 1300 to 1999.

272. C. Extended

An extended access lists allows you to filter traffic by the source and destination IP address, source and destination port, and protocol.

273. A. Use the following:

```
access-list 20 permit 216.83.11.64 0.0.0.63
line vty 0 4
access-class 20 in
```

When configuring access lists to control telnet access, you first create the access list. In this case, you have to specify a standard access list that includes the network ID and the wildcard mask to include the system in that network ID. It is important to note when creating the access lists, you do not use the subnet mask. Once the access list is created, you apply it to the telnet ports with the access-class command.

274. A. access-class 20 in

When applying an access list to the telnet ports, you use the access-class command when at the prompt for the port. It is important to note that when assigning an access list to an interface you would use access-group instead of access-class while at the interface prompt.

275. **A. It denies the 192.168.10.50 system from accessing the 192.168.2.0 network, denies the system of 192.168.10.50 from accessing the website on 3.3.3.3, and permits all others.**

The first rule prevents the one single host address of 192.168.10.50 from accessing the 192.168.2.0 network. The use of the wildcard mask in the rule of 0.0.0.255 matches the first octet against the rule (because of 0), matches the second octet (because of the 0), matches the third octet (because of 0), but does not match the fourth octet (because of 255).

The second rule denies the system with the IP address of 192.168.10.50 from accessing the web site on the system with the IP address of 3.3.3.3. Finally, the last rule allows all other traffic. Remember that if the last rule was not there to permit all other traffic, then there is an implied deny all at the end.

276. **D. RAM**

The routing table is stored in volatile memory (VRAM, also known as RAM) and is retained through reboots only because it is rebuilt from the startup-config.

277. **A. The destination IP address is that of Computer B**

E. the destination MAC address is that of router R1.

When traffic is traveling the network, the source and destination IP addresses always stay the same each step of the way so that the big picture is always maintained, but the source and destination MAC addresses are always changing to suit the current phase of the communication.

278. **A. Determines if a destination route exists in the routing table and what the next hop is**

C. Looks at the destination IP address in the packet

When a router receives a packet, it will first look at the destination IP address in the packet to determine where the packet is headed. Then the router will look to its routing table to determine if it has a route to that network.

279. **C. Connected routes**

Connected routes exist by default in your routing table and are routes that are there because the router is connected to those networks.

280. **C. They are manually configured by the router administrator.**

When working with static routing as the network administrator, you are responsible for configuring each individual route on each router. If you work for a company with a large number of subnets/networks, then this could be a huge administrative burden.

281. **B. No network bandwidth is being used by protocols sharing routing tables**

One of the major benefits of static routing is that the administrator configures the routing tables, which means that the routers do not need to generate network traffic and share routing table information in order to build up each other's routing tables.

282. **B. The static route**

Because a static route has a lower administrative distance than a dynamic route, the router will trust and use the static route over the dynamically learned route.

283. **A. Determine if a route exists in the routing table**

D. look at the destination IP address of the packet

When a router receives a packet, it will first look at the destination IP address in the packet to determine where the packet is headed. Then the router will look to its routing table to determine if it has a route to that network.

284. **B. ANDing**

ANDing is the mathematical process the IP protocol uses to determine if two systems are on the same network.

285. **A. no ip route**

You delete a static route using the `no ip route` command. Most Cisco commands can be negated by placing the word no in front of the command.

286. **A. ip routing**

If you want to enable routing on your router, you can use the `ip routing` command. In order to disable routing, you use the `no ip routing` command.

287. **B. Any data destined for the 217.46.33.48/28 network is forwarded to the IP address of 26.10.20.2.**

This command adds a static route for a subnetted network of 217.56.33.48/28 and specifies that traffic destined for that network should be sent to 26.10.20.2.

288. **C. no ip route 27.0.0.0 255.0.0.0 26.0.0.2**

In order to remove a route, you would use the `no ip route` command and then specify the routing information.

289. **D. ip route 35.0.0.0 255.0.0.0 22.0.0.1**

In order to add a static route to the routing table, you use the `ip route` command and then specify the destination network ID, destination subnet mask, and the next hop where the router is to forward information for that network.

290. **D. The administrative distance to the destination network is 10.**

The `IP route` command is used to add a route to the routing table. The syntax is:

```
Ip route <dest_net> <dest_mask> <next_hop> <admin_distance>
```

Therefore, the command shown is setting up a route for the 200.45.7.0 network with an administrative distance of 10. Also note that this question is working with a subnetted scenario, which means that the only addresses that would be routed due to this route are 200.45.7.0 – 200.45.7.31:

291.   **B. Configure the GWLR on both routers to point to one another.**

In order to have each router send data to networks it is unaware of, you can configure the GWLR for each router to reference one another. For example, when RouterA does not know what to do with a packet it could forward to RouterB, and when RouterB does not know what to do with a packet it could be sending to RouterA.

292.   **A. If there is no matching destination network in the routing table, the router will send the packet to 55.12.4.38.**

This command will configure the Gateway of Last Resort (GWLR), also known as a default route, so that if there is no entry in the routing table for the destination network, the router will send the traffic to 55.12.4.38.

293.   **D. ip route 13.0.0.0 255.0.0.0 12.0.0.2**

Routers know about networks they are connected to by default so you need to add a route to the 13.0.0.0 network on router R1 using the IP route command.

294.   **C. Packets destined for 200.45.7.89 will be forwarded to 22.202.33.10.**

In this question, you are adding a static route for a subnetted network. The first step is to determine the range of the subnet. The subnet range is from 200.45.7.64 to 200.45.7.95 (increment of 32). This makes C a correct answer because the explanation falls into that range.

295.   **A. They allow communication to networks not appearing in the routing table**

D. the routing table size is kept to a minimum.

When you configure a default route, you are essentially telling the router where to send the data if the router does not know how to reach a certain network. For example, you could configure a default route on ROUTERA that says "if you do not know of a pathway for a particular network, send the data to ROUTERB and let him figure it out!"

296.   **B. The address that your router will forward a packet to when it does not have a route for that packet.**

The gateway of last resort is a default route that you can add to the router so that it forwards all packets for unknown destinations to a particular router that will then forward the packets on, using its routing table.

297.   **C. The default route is used when there is no other route to the destination.**

You can configure a default route, also known as the gateway of last resort (GWLR), on the router so that when the router receives a packet to a destination network it has no route for, the router will use the default route as a way to deliver the packet.

298.   **D. ip route 0.0.0.0 0.0.0.0 145.66.77.99**

When you configure the Gateway of Last Resort (GWLR), you configure a static route to the 0.0.0.0 network with a subnet mask of 0.0.0.0 and then specify where to send the traffic for unknown destinations.

299.

B. show ip route

The command to view your routing table is the show ip route command.

300.

B. Gateway of last resort

The gateway of last resort shows as an entry in the routing table with the destination network ID of 0.0.0.0.

301.

C. It will be sent out Serial 0/0/0

In this example, the packet is headed to the 26.0.0.0 network, so when the router consults the routing table it will see the 26.0.0.0 network as a destination route and that it can reach that network by sending the data out the serial 0/0/0 interface.

302.

C. interface fa0/0.20

In order to create a sub-interface, you would use the interface command and reference the physical interface followed by a. (dot) and then a unique number to represent the interface. For example:

```
Interface fa0/0.20
```

303.

D. Data will be sent to 26.0.0.2.

Looking at the results of the show ip route command on the router, you can see the routing table. In the routing table, it is showing that there is a static route for the 29.0.0.0 network and traffic is to be sent to 26.0.0.2 to reach that network.

304.

A. Data will be sent out FastEthernet0/1

When looking at the routing table, you can see that there is a connected route for the 25.0.0.0 network (shows with a C on the left side). Looking at that entry, you can see that data destined for the 25.0.0.0 network will be sent out the FastEthernet0/1 port.

305.

B. 5

The hop count is shown after the administrative distance within the [1/5]. In this case, the hop count is 5.

306.

B. Configure F0/12 on SW1 for trunk mode

E. configure sub-interfaces on R1

In order to configure routing between two VLANs with a single router (known as router on a stick), you must create sub-interfaces on the router for the single interface connected to the switch. You also must configure the port on the switch that the router is connected to trunk mode so it carries all VLAN traffic across the link.

307. **C. You need to enable dot1q and specify the VLAN on each interface.**

When setting up each of the sub-interfaces, you need to specify the encapsulation protocol to use for VLAN tagging and the VLAN ID that the interface is part of. The commands should look like this:

```
interface fa0/0.20
encapsulation dot1q 20 #interface responds for VLAN 20
ip address 192.168.20.1 255.255.255.0

interface fa0/0.10
encapsulation dot1q 10 #interface responds to packets for VLAN 20
ip address 192.168.10.1 255.255.255.0
```

308. **B. lowest**

The route with the lowest administrative distance is always used. If there are two routes with the same administrative distance that could be used, the metric value is used.

309. **A. The static route entry**

The static route would take preference over the RIPv2 entry because it has a lower administrative distance value.

310. **C. 120**

The administrative distance, which is trustworthiness value of the route, is 120 for RIPv1 and RIPv2. The lower the administrative distance, the more preference the router puts on that route when there are two routes to the same destination.

311. **D. 0**

The administrative distance of a connected route is the lowest (0) because it is the most trustworthy type of route.

312. **C. RIP**

The RIP routing protocol has an administrative distance of 120.

313. **A. 1**

A static route has an administrative distance of 1, the second-lowest administrative distance next to a connected route, which has an administrative distance of 0.

314. **C. Adds the route to the routing table**

When a router receives a routing table update for a route it does not have in its routing table, it adds that route to the routing table.

315. **B. RIP**

RIP is an open standard distance vector routing protocol that is supported by many different router manufacturers.

316. A. EIGRP

D. OSPF

OSPF and EIGRP are examples of link state routing protocols. OSPF is an open standard link state protocol, while EIGRP is a Cisco protocol that uses link state.

317. C. RIP

The RIP routing protocol is limited to 15 hops so is therefore typically only used on smaller networks.

318. A. Distance vector

A distance vector routing protocol only knows how many hops (routers) away a network is; it does not know if a link is available or how much bandwidth the link has.

319. C. Layer 3

Dynamic routing protocols are routing protocols, so therefore run at layer 3.

320. B. Routers share routing table with neighboring routers

E. Sends entire routing table as an update

Distance vector routing protocols share their routing table with neighboring routers and typically send the entire routing table as an update.

321. A. It is a classless routing protocol

B. Maximum hop count of 15

D. RIPv2 supports authentication

RIPv2 is a classless routing protocol that is limited to 15 hops and also supports authentication. This is different than RIPv1, which is a classful routing protocol and does not support authentication.

322. B. False

RIPv1 is classful, meaning it cannot use variable length subnet masks (VLSM).

323. C. Every 30 seconds

The RIP routing protocol, whether RIPv1 or RIPv2, sends routing updates out every 30 seconds. RIPv2 does send those updates out as multicast traffic instead of broadcast traffic, as is the case with RIPv1.

324. B. Sends periodic updates

C. Updates routing table based on updates received from neighboring routers

Distance vector routing protocols send out periodic updates (based on an interval) and updates the routing table based on routes received from neighboring routers.

325.   **C. Link state**

OSPF is an example of a link state routing protocol.

326.   **A. Routers share routing table information with all other routers on the network**

D. Maintains multiple tables in memory — one for neighboring routers, one to store the entire topology, and final table is the routing table.

Link state routing protocols are aware of the entire network topology because there are multiple tables maintained in memory: a topology table, neighboring routers table, and the routing table. The routing table is shared with all other routers on the network.

327.   **B. OSPF**

Because OSPF has a lower administrative distance than RIP, it would be considered more trustworthy and would be added to the routing table of the router. OSPF has an administrative distance of 110, while RIP has an administrative distance of 120.

328.   **D. Sharing routes learned from one neighbor to other neighboring routers**

Routing protocols such as RIP only shares their routing table with neighboring routers. Once one router shares its routing table with its neighbors, those neighbors will share the routes out to their neighbors, which is how all routers know of all routes on the network (eventually). This is known as routing by rumor.

329.   **A. Convergence time**

Because distance vector routing protocols only share the routing table with neighboring routers, it could take a long time for all routers to know about changes to the routing table. The time it takes for all routers on a network to know of a change is known as convergence time.

330.   **D. Supports VLSM**

RIPv2 has a few benefits. It sends routing updates out via multicast traffic (RIPv1 uses broadcast). Also RIPv2 is classless and supports variable length subnet masks (VLSM).

331.   **B. RIP**

The RIP routing protocol sends routing updates to neighboring routers every 30 seconds.

332.   **D. RouterA#show ip protocols**

To view the current RIP configuration after RIP has been enabled, you can use the `show ip protocols` command.

333.   **A. The entry with code R**

RIP entries found in the routing table display with a code of R.

334. **B. RIPv2**

RIPv2 supports VLSM, which allows the use of different-size subnets.

335. **C. debug ip rip**

You can enable debugging for RIP to view the RIP-related messages, as they are sent and received, to help troubleshoot RIP.

336. **B. Use the following commands:**

R1(config)#`router rip`

R1(config-router)#`network 25.0.0.0`

R1(config-router)#`network 26.0.0.0`

R1(config-router)#`version 2`

In order to configure your router for version 2 of RIP, you must first enter the `router rip` command in global configuration mode. Once at the router prompt, you then specify the networks to run RIP on and then use the `version 2` command to specify you wish to use RIPv2.

337. **C. 120**

RIP uses a default administrative distance of 120.

338. **D. Use the following commands:**

RouterA>`enable`

RouterA#`config term`

RouterA(config)#`router rip`

RouterA(config-router)#`network 27.0.0.0`

RouterA(config-router)#`network 29.0.0.0`

RouterA(config-router)#`version 2`

When specifying the networks for the RIP routing protocol, you need to specify only the classful addresses, even when the address space has been subnetted.

339. **A. You need to enable RIPng on each interface.**

RIPng is the next generation version of RIP for IPv6 and requires you to enable RIPng on each interface.

340. **B. RouterA(config-router)#passive-interface serial 0/1**

To disable sending RIP update messages, you can use the `passive-interface` command at the router prompt.

341. **B. RIP will load-balance the links to that destination.**

When multiple routes to the same destination exist, with RIP, the router will load-balance the multiple routes.

342.

A. 110

OSPF has an administrative distance of 110. Routers will use the route with the lowest administrative distance.

343.

A. Highest IP address assigned to a loopback interface

With OSPF, the router ID is chosen by the highest IP address used by a loopback interface. If there are no loopback interfaces, then the router ID will be that of the highest IP address of the physical interfaces.

344.

D. ABR

An area border router is designed to connect areas together; specifically, it is designed to connect OSPF areas to the backbone area known as area 0.

345.

B. show ip ospf

You can use the `show ip ospf` command to verify your OSPF configuration.

346.

A. Backbone

Area 0 is known as the backbone of your network. When configuring OSPF, you start with the backbone and then create other areas for remote offices.

347.

B. Use the following commands:

router ospf 1

network 192.168.1.0 0.0.0.255 area 0

When configuring OSPF, you must first use the `router ospf <ID>` command in global configuration, where the ID is the process ID you want to assign to the OSPF process. You then specify the network interfaces to run OSPF on by using the `network` command and the wildcard mask (not the subnet mask) while specifying the area.

348.

A. Use the following:

router ospf 1

network 192.168.1.0 0.0.0.255 area 0

In order to configure OSPF as a dynamic routing protocol on your router, you first use the `router ospf 1` command to run an OSPF process as process ID 1 (in this example). You then use the network command to specify what interfaces OSPF will run on. The key point is that the `network` command uses a wildcard mask and not a subnet mask. You also specify the area <ID> for OSPF. Your router will share routing table information to any other OSPF-enabled routers in the same area.

349.

B. show ip protocols

E. show ip ospf neighbor

When troubleshooting OSPF, you can use the `show ip protocols` command to view which routing protocol is loaded and the `show ip ospf neighbor` to verify there are neighboring relationships with other routers.

350. **D. ipv6 router ospf 5**

In order to enabled an OSPFv3 process, you use the `IPv6 router OSPF 5` command. Note that OSPFv3 is OSPF for the IPv6 protocol.

351. **D. Use the following:**

Router ospf 1

Router-id 8.8.8.8

When using OSPF, you can change the router ID by using the `router ospf 1` command to navigate to the OSPF process, and then type `router-id <ip_address>` to signify the ID you wish to use for this router.

352. **D. The port has been disabled.**

If the port has been disabled by an administrator (or automatically shut down through a feature such as port security), the port displays an amber light when a system is connected to the port. You will need to enable the port before you can use it.

353. **A. The system started without problems and is operational.**

When the System LED on the switch displays a solid green light, this means that the system booted without any problems.

354. **D. Data is being transmitted**

When the switch display mode is set to Status, which is the default, a blinking light indicates traffic being sent or received. A solid light would indicate a link is present — both very useful indicators when troubleshooting.

355. **D. There were POST errors.**

When the switch powers on, it performs a POST. If there are problems with the POST, the System LED on the switch displays amber. A successful POST results in a green-lit System LED.

356. **A. Switch the display mode to duplex and watch for a solid green light on the different ports.**

When you toggle the display mode of the switch to duplex, the port LEDs display a green solid light to indicate they are running in full duplex mode. If the port is running in half duplex, no light appears on the port LED.

357. **D. Flashing green**

This could change per switch, but typically, if the port is running at 1 Gbps it displays a flashing green light when the switch display mode is toggled to speed mode.

358. **C. The port is running in half duplex.**

Light indicators and display modes seem to change a little with each Cisco model switch, but in general, when you are in the duplex display mode if the port is running at half duplex then the port LED does not light up.

Answers
301–400

359.   **C. Ports are running at 10 Mbps.**

Although this is potentially different with each model switch, when the display mode is set to speed the port LEDs will not light up if the port is running at 10 Mbps, show a solid green if they are running at 100 Mbps, or display a flashing green if they are running at 1 Gbps.

360.   **B. 2**

Switches are considered layer-2 devices. You can remember this by the fact that they filter traffic by the MAC address, which is a layer-2 address.

361.   **C. STP**

The Spanning Tree Protocol is used to prevent a layer-2 loop between switches.

362.   **A. The destination MAC address**

When a switch receives a frame, it looks at the destination MAC address and then compares that to its MAC address table to determine where to send the frame.

363.   **A. A group of systems that can have their data collide with one another**

A collision domain is a group of systems that can have their data collide with one another. Each network segment is a collision domain, and each port on a switch creates a network segment. Therefore, each port on a switch is a separate collision domain. This means that a system connected to a port can have its data collide with any other system connected to the same port. Systems connected to different ports cannot have their data collide. This is different than a hub device, which has all ports in one collision domain.

364.   **A. filtering and forwarding**

   B. loop avoidance

   E. address learning

The three core services of a switch are filtering and forwarding, loop avoidance, and address learning.

365.   **A. A group of systems that receive one another's broadcast messages**

A broadcast domain is a group of systems that receive one another's broadcast messages. Unless you create VLANs on the switch, all systems connected to a switch are part of the same broadcast domain. To create multiple broadcast domains, you use a router or VLANs.

366.   **D. It forwards the frame to port 12.**

When the switch receives a frame, it compares the destination MAC address that is in the frame to its MAC address table. In the figure, you can see an entry for the destination MAC address of 00d0.bc8a.2766, so the switch forwards the frame to the port associated with that MAC address (port 12).

367.   **B. Floods the frame**

The frame is flooded when the switch is unsure what port to forward the frame to. A flooded frame is destined for a specific MAC address but was sent to all ports on the switch because the location of that MAC address is unknown.

368.   **B. Switches filter traffic and only send the traffic to the destination port, while a hub sends all traffic to all ports.**

A switch offers the benefit of filtering traffic and only sending traffic to the port where the destination system resides. This gives a huge security advantage and bandwidth benefit.

369.   **A. Hub – 1 collision domain / switch – 24 collision domains**

All ports on a network hub are part of a single collision domain, while each port on a switch creates its own collision domain.

370.   **A. The source MAC address of the frame**

In order to dynamically learn which port each system is connected to, the switch uses the source MAC address of a frame as it receives it. Remember for the exam that the switch uses the source MAC address to populate the MAC address table, but uses the destination MAC address of the frame to determine where to send a frame.

371.   **A. 2 broadcast domains, 5 collision domains**

The diagram shows 2 broadcast domains and 5 collision domains. Each interface off the router will create a separate broadcast domain, while each interface is creating a separate network segment, which is a collision domain.

372.   **B. 1**

All switches are part of the same broadcast domain. The only way to get multiple collision domains is by using a router or VLANs on the switch.

373.   **C. Use a crossover cable.**

When connecting similar devices together, such as two switches, you need to use a crossover cable.

374.   **C. Fragment-free**

Fragment-free is the switch operation mode that processes frames by waiting to receive the first 64 bytes before forwarding the frame on.

375.   **A. Frame**

When the data is being processed at layer 2, it is known as a frame. This is important to understand; when talking about a switch and how it processes the data, note that the actual data is known as a frame. If it were a router, then you would use the term "packet" because it works with the layer-3 header instead of the layer-2 header.

376.   **A. Store-and-forward**

The store-and-forward operation mode processes a frame by waiting till the entire frame has been received before forwarding the frame on to its destination.

377.   **C. It will flood the frame.**

When the switch receives a frame, it compares the destination MAC address to the MAC address table. If there is no matching address in the table, the switch floods the frame. Flooding a frame means that the switch sends the frame to all ports on the switch in hopes the frame finds the destination system.

378.   **D. Cut-through**

The cut-through operation mode is used to start forwarding the frame as soon as possible.

379.   **B. Destination IP Address: the_remote_system / Destination MAC Address: your_router**

This is an important question. When the packet is sent from your system to your router, the destination IP address is set to the remote system you are trying to talk to, but the destination MAC address is set to the MAC address of your router.

380.   **B. The destination MAC is that of Computer B**

E. the destination IP address is that of Computer B

G. the source MAC is that of R2

Remember that the source and destination IP addresses in the message stay the same the entire time, so the source and destination IP addresses are that of the two computers. It is the MAC address that changes each step in the conversation, so therefore since the message is traveling at the point between R2 and SW2 in this question, then the source MAC is that of R2 and the destination MAC address is that of Computer B. Note that the switch is not the destination; it would simply forward the message to Computer B (because that is the address in the destination MAC field).

381.   **B. The source IP address is that of Computer A**

C. the source MAC address is that of router R1

E. the destination IP address is that of Computer B

This is an important question for the ICND1 exam; it tests your knowledge of communication pathway. The important part to remember is that the source and destination IP addresses in the message are set to the sender and receiver (in this case, Computer A and Computer B), and never change as the message travels the network. However, the source and destination MAC addresses change each step along the way because the MAC address is used for whatever the current phase of the conversation is. So when the message hits router R1, R1 needs to send the message to R2 so he alters the source and destination MAC addresses to be those of R1 and R2.

382.   **B. Switch(config)#hostname NY-SW1**

In order to change the name of your network device, whether it be a router or a switch, you must use the hostname command from global configuration.

383. **D. Switch# show mac-address-table**

You use the `show mac-address-table` command from priv exec mode to display the MAC address table.

384. **B. No default gateway address assigned on the switch**

If the switch has not been configured for a default gateway address, it cannot send data off the network.

385. **C. Use the following commands:**

NY-SW1(config)#`interface vlan1`

NY-SW1(config-if)#`ip address 23.0.0.25 255.0.0.0`

You configure the switch for an IP address by first navigating to VLAN1 and then assigning the IP address. Note that the switch does not need an IP address to function; you simply configure an IP address so that you can remotely manage the switch.

386. **C. Switch(config)# ip default-gateway 24.0.0.1**

The `IP default-gateway` command is used to configure your switch for a default gateway address. Note that this command is executed from global configuration mode.

387. **D. 300 seconds from last time used**

A dynamic entry in the MAC address table is one that is learned automatically by the switch based off traffic it has received and stays in the MAC address table for 300 seconds since last time it was used (by default).

388. **C. The switch has learned the address based off traffic received.**

A dynamic address in the MAC address table is one that the switch has learned from the source address located in the frames as it received them.

389. **D. mac-address-table aging-time 400**

The amount of time an entry stays in the MAC address table is known as the aging time and is set with the `mac-address-table aging-time` command.

390. **B. Use the following commands:**

Switch#`config term`

Switch(config)#`interface f0/5`

Switch(config-if)#`description File Server Port`

In order to configure settings on an interface, you must first navigate to global configuration and then to the interface you wish to configure. After that, you can change the setting on the interface you would like; in this case, it is the description of the interface using the `description` command.

391. **C. no shutdown**

You first navigate to the port you wish to enable, and then you can use the `no shutdown` command to enable a port.

392. **A. speed auto**

In order to have the switch negotiate the speed with the connecting system, you would configure the speed setting to auto.

393. **D. duplex full**

In order to configure full duplex, you must first navigate to the interface and then use the `duplex full` command.

394. **A. Use the following commands:**

Switch(config)#`interface range f0/1 - 24`

Switch(config-if-range)#`speed 100`

In order to configure settings on multiple ports at one time, you can use the `interface range` command to select the ports, then configure the setting on the port. In this case, after the 24 ports are selected with the interface range command, you then configure the speed to 100 Mbps with the speed 100.

395. **D. switch(config-if)#speed 100**

To modify the port speed on a switch, you first need to navigate to the port interface of the port you wish to configure and then use the `speed` command.

396. **D. Use the interface range command**

To configure any settings on multiple ports at once, you would use the `interface range` command first to select the different ports.

397. **D. Use the following commands:**

Switch(config)#`interface range f0/6 - 12`

Switch(config-if-range)#`shutdown`

In order to disable a port, you must first navigate to those ports from global configuration mode with the `interface range` command. After navigating to the ports, you can use the shutdown command to disable the ports.

398. **D. show mac-address-table**

To display the MAC addresses associated with each port on the switch, you view the MAC address table, which resides in memory on the switch. Use the `show mac-address-table` command.

399. **B. Half duplex**

Looking at the output shown in the figure, which is the result of the show interface command being used, you can see that the port is running in half-duplex mode (third to last line).

400. **D. show interface f0/8**

The output shown in the figure was generated by the show interface f0/8 command. This command is used quite often when troubleshooting issues with a port.

401. **C. show interface f0/5**

In order to view the settings on the port, you must use the show interface command and then the port number.

402. **C. 100 Mbps**

The output in the figure is showing the results of the show interface command being executed, where you can see the port is configured for half duplex at 100 Mbps (third to last line in the output).

403. **B. 24**

Each port on a switch creates a separate collision domain, so a 24-port switch has 24 collision domains. This is different than a network hub, which would use one collision domain for all ports on the hub.

404. **D. 4**

Each VLAN on a switch creates a separate broadcast domain, so there would be 4 broadcast domains in this example.

405. **C. no shutdown**

To enable a port on the switch, you would use the no shutdown command.

406. **A. no shutdown**

Looking at the output of the show interface command, you can see by the top line that the interface is administratively down. This means that the port has been disabled by the administrator and should be enabled with the no shutdown command.

407. **C. 100000 Kbps**

The figure in the question is displaying the results of the show interface command. You can see the bandwidth setting configured on the port (the BW setting); in this case, it is set to 100000 Kbps.

408. **D. You are in a different VLAN than the file server.**

If you find that you can communicate with some systems on the network but not with others, it is possible that you are connected to a port that is part of a VLAN — meaning that you will not be able to communicate with others that are in a different VLAN unless a router is being used.

409. **B. The port is disabled.**

When looking at the interface, if you notice that it says administratively down, you have most likely disabled the port with the shutdown command. You will need to enable the port before it can be used.

410. **B. Port Security**

The Port Security feature allows you to control which systems can connect to the individual ports. You can limit systems that can connect by their MAC address.

411. **C. sticky**

The sticky option is important when configuring Port Security. It allows you to configure a port to allow traffic only from the current or first MAC address (assuming you set the maximum addresses to 1).

412. **D. To prevent unauthorized access to the network**

Port Security is used to control which systems can connect to a port by limiting the MAC addresses that can connect to the port.

413. **B. restrict**

If you configure the address violation to restrict when you configure Port Security, the switch will allow the system with the valid MAC address to communicate over the port, but no other MAC address will be able to.

414. **B. shutdown**

Shutdown is the action you can configure on the switch that tells the switch to disable the port if there is an address violation.

415. **B. show port-security interface f0/6**

The output in the figure is showing the results of the `show port-security interface` command. You can use this command to verify that you have configured Port Security on the interface properly.

416. **A. Access**

Before you can configure Port Security on a port, you must first put the port in access mode by using the port-security mode access command.

417. C. show port-security interface f0/5

To view the Port Security settings on a port, you use the `show port-security interface` command.

418. B. show port-security address

The output shown in the figure is created by using the `show port-security address` command. This command is used to view the Port Security addresses that have been configured on the switch.

419. A. restrict

C. shutdown

E. protect

When configuring Port Security, you can configure one of three actions to be taken upon address violation: restrict, shutdown, or protect.

420. A. To create communication boundaries

VLANs are a great way to create communication boundaries because when a system is part of a VLAN it can only communicate with other systems in the same VLAN by default. It is possible to configure a router to route between the VLANs.

421. D. VLANs

You can use VLANs on a switch to create multiple broadcast domains. Remember that a VLAN is a communication boundary, so that means even broadcast messages cannot go from one VLAN to another by default.

422. B. show vlan

To view a list of VLANs and the ports associated with the different VLANs, use the `show vlan` command.

423. A. show vlan

You can use the `show vlan` command to view a list of VLANs and their associated ports.

424. C. 802.1q

D. ISL

802.1q and ISL are two protocols used to tag VLAN traffic so that the data can be sent to another switch and processed. The receiving switch looks at the VLAN information to determine what ports to send the traffic to.

425. A. switchport mode trunk

You would configure the port in trunk mode in order for it to carry all VLAN traffic across the port to another switch.

426. **D. vlan 2 name Floor1**

To create a VLAN, you can use the VLAN command followed by the VLAN number and the name of the vlan you are creating.

427. **C. Use the following commands:**

Switch(config)#`interface f0/6`

Switch(config-if)#`switchport access vlan 2`

In order to place a port in a VLAN, you must first navigate to the interface (port 6) and then place the port in access mode and associate a VLAN with the port at the same time.

428. **B. The pings were successful.**

When using the ping command on Cisco devices, five ping requests are sent out and for each reply that comes back you will see a ! on the screen. Unsuccessful pings display with a . (period).

429. **A. The pings were unsuccessful.**

In the figure, you can see that there are 5 periods (.), each one indicating a ping reply that was not received.

430. **D. traceroute ip_address**

When trying to identify the point in the communication pathway that is failing, use the `traceroute` command, which sends you status information with each router that is hit on the way to the destination.

431. **D. telnet**

In order to verify that you have configured the VTY ports successfully, you would use `telnet` to connect to the system.

432. **A. 23.0.0.1**

The router would be the first hop in order to send data to a different, or remote, network. In this example, the first hop that a reply comes back from is 23.0.0.1, which is the router on your network.

433. **A. Straight-through**

When connecting a switch to a router, you would ensure you are using a straight-through cable. Watch for questions on the exam that show a network diagram and ask why communication cannot occur. Sometimes you may find the wrong type of cable is being used in the diagram.

434. **D. Verify your cable is connected properly.**

The first thing you should do is check the physical components of the network. Is the network cable connected to the computer properly, and to the switch properly? Do you see link lights on the computer and the switch?

435. **D. Crossover**

When connecting similar devices together, you should use a crossover cable. Watch for scenarios on the exam that describe communication issues and mention the cabling used. You may find that the wrong type of cable was used.

436. **A. Check the physical aspects of the link, such as the cable.**

When an interface shows a status of down and the line protocol is down, you should look to the physical (layer-1) components of the network because the line protocol will not be up unless the interface is up — meaning you don't know if the line protocol is a problem (even though it shows as down) until you fix the problem with the interface.

437. **D. You are connected to a port in a different VLAN than the other system.**

In this scenario, the most likely cause of the problem is you have the port configured for the wrong VLAN. You will need to change the VLAN that the port is a member of.

438. **B. R1**

The ARP request would be sent to router R1 because that is the device Computer A needs to send the data to in order to have the data leave the network.

439. **D. Use straight-through cables to connect switches to routers.**

In this example, the IP address configuration is fine. The wrong cable types are being used to connect the switches to the router. You should be using straight-through cables to connect switches to routers.

440. **B. The network media is attached at both ends of the link**

D. a layer-2 protocol has been loaded and configured at either end of the link.

If the link light on an interface displays green, it indicates that a physical connection is established between the two points, and a data link protocol is configured at either end.

441. **C. Change the IP address on Computer A.**

In this example, the communication problem is occurring because Computer A has been configured for an invalid IP address on that network ID. A subnet mask of /27 means the increment is 32, making the network range for Computer A's network 216.83.11.64 to 216.83.11.95. The IP address assigned to Computer A is outside that range.

442. **C. There is an implied deny all traffic at the end of the ACL.**

In this example, the access control list was created to allow telnet and SMTP traffic to pass through the router. There is an implied deny all other traffic rule at the end of the ACL, so if you expect traffic to pass through the router you must explicitly specify it.

443. **B. Enable trunking on the port connecting the switch to the router.**

After configuring the router with sub-interfaces, you need to ensure that you configure the port on the switch that is connected to the router as a trunk port so that it can carry the VLAN traffic.

444. **A. Computer B's default gateway is invalid.**

In this example, the IP address for the default gateway for Computer B is using the broadcast address for that network, which is invalid. You need to change the IP address of the LAN interface on router R2 and ensure computer B uses that IP address as the default gateway.

445. **D. 0010.11d9.d001**

When looking at the output for the command, you can see that FastEthernet0/0 has the IP address of 23.0.0.1 and its hardware address is 0010.11d9.d001.

446. **B. show ip arp**

The command is displaying the ARP cache on the Cisco device. In order to view the ARP cache, you would use the show ip arp command.

447. **B. show cdp neighbors detail**

Of the commands listed, only the show cdp neighbors detail command displays a list of neighboring devices and their IP addresses.

448. **D. HDLC**

When looking at the show interfaces command, you can see that the serial port is using the encapsulation of HDLC.

449. **A. DCE**

Looking at the output in the figure, you can see that the serial port on the router is configured as the data communication equipment (DCE). The other end of the point-to-point link would be the opposite, data terminal equipment (DTE).

450. **C. no shutdown**

If an interface is shown as administratively down, try to bring the interface up by using the no shutdown command on the interface.

451. **A. show ip arp**

D. show arp

The show ip arp command and the show arp command can be used to view the ARP cache on a Cisco router. The show ip arp command only displays mac addresses that map to the IP Layer 3 protocol, while show arp will display all mac addresses for all Layer 3.

452. **B. 64 Kbps**

You can view the clock rate on a serial link DCE link when using the show controllers command. Note that the clock rate is set to 64000, or 64 Kbps.

453. **C. Check that the data link protocol is configured.**

When the interface status displays as up and the protocol is down, this is an indication that the data link protocol has not been configured properly. With a serial port, check that a layer-2 protocol such as HDLC or PPP has been configured.

454. **D. FastEthernet0/1 has not been configured.**

Looking at the figure, you will notice that serial 0/2/0 is using HDLC and not PPP, Fast Ethernet 0/0 has an IP address assigned, and the bandwidth is 100,000 Kbits. So the only true statement when looking at the status of the interfaces is that the Fast Ethernet 0/1 has no IP address assigned and is currently down: It has not been configured.

455. **A. show ip route**

After you have verified the physical components and the IP addresses, you should verify that there is a route in the routing table to the destination network.

456. **A. show ip interface brief**

C. show protocols

E. show ip route

When answering questions such as this, ask yourself what happens at layer 3 of the OSI model. The answer is the routing and logical addressing (which is handled by the IP protocol). So any commands that relate to routing or the IP protocol would be layer-3 Troubleshooting Commands. Be familiar with each of these show commands for the exam. You will need to use them in different simulators to identify the problem.

457. **B. show controllers serial 0/0**

When troubleshooting your serial port and wanting to verify whether you have configured the interface as the DCE or DTE device, use the show controllers serial slot/port command.

458. **B. show interfaces**

D. show controllers

Layer 1 deals with the physical aspect of the network, such as a link being present, while layer 2 of the OSI model deals with the protocol used to carry frames. The show interfaces command and show controllers command are used to troubleshoot layer 1 and layer 2.

459. **A. Runt**

C. CRC

The runt and CRC count can be viewed on an interface to determine the number of small packets received and the number of packets received that do not have the CRC information matching the calculated checksum. Both of these are an indication of collisions on the network or a bad network card sending garbage packets out on the network.

460. **B. 6**

A runt is a packet that is smaller than the allowable size for the network. With Ethernet networks, that is 64 bytes. Looking at the figure, you can see that there are 6 runt messages received. Runt could be due to collisions or a malfunctioning network card sending garbage packets out on the network.

461. **D. show interfaces**

To view the number of runt packets, which are packets too small for the network, you can use the `show interfaces` command.

462. **C. 87**

When looking at the show interface command, you can see the output of the interface in the last 5 minutes toward the bottom of the output. In this example, notice that there are 87 collisions on the fourth to last line of the output.

463. **D. no debug all**

When you disable debugging, use the `no debug all` command so that you can be sure that all levels of debugging are disabled. Debugging places extra processing load on the router, which means you do not want it running if it is not needed.

464. **A. debug ip rip**

When troubleshooting communication problems, you can use a number of `debug` commands in order to see different activity on the router. In order to view rip message sent and received, you can use the `debug ip rip` command.

465. **D. debug ip packet**

In order to view all packets being sent and received, including their details, you can use the `debug ip packet` command.

466. **B. DoS attack**

A denial of service (DoS) attack is when a system or device is overloaded by the hacker, causing the device or system to crash or to be so busy that it cannot service valid requests on the network.

467. **C. VLANs**

Virtual LANs (VLANs) can be used to control systems that can communicate with one another. By default, a system in one VLAN cannot communicate with a system in another VLAN unless you configure a router to route between them.

468. **A. VPN**

Virtual Private Networks (VPNs) are used to create encrypted tunnels between two points over an untrusted network such as the Internet.

469. **C. Application layer firewall**

An application layer firewall, also known as a proxy server, can filter traffic not only by IP address and port information, but also by analyzing the application data and determining if the packet is allowed through based on the contents of the data.

470. **D. Stateful packet inspection firewall**

A stateful packet inspection firewall is more advanced that a simple packet filtering firewall in the sense that it understands the timing of a packet and whether or not that packet is suited for that part of the communication.

471. **B. Spoofing**

Spoofing is when the hacker alters the source address to make the packet look like it is coming from somewhere else. Common examples of spoofing are MAC spoofing, IP spoofing, and e-mail spoofing.

472. **B. Use a firewall to control access to the device from the Internet**

D. Use SSH to remotely configure the device

You would protect the device by using a firewall to control communication to the device and then ensure that you are using a secure protocol such as SSH for remote management.

473. **B. Lock network equipment in a secure location.**

Network equipment should be stored in a secure room with a limited number of individuals who have access to that room.

474. **B. Passwords are not encrypted**

D. The banner is using inappropriate text.

Passwords should be encrypted in the configuration using the `service password-encryption` command. Also, never use a friendly welcome message as banner text — hackers could use it as their defense that you have welcomed them to your device or network.

475. **D. The login local command should be used.**

When you wish to use the local usernames and passwords configured on the device for authentication to a specific port, you must use the `login local` command on that port. In this case, you should be using `login local` on the line con 0 port.

476. **C. The login command is missing.**

In order to be prompted for authentication on a port, you must configure a password on the port (which has been done in this case), but you must also use the `login` command to indicate to the Cisco device you wish to be prompted for authentication.

477. **A. R1(config)# no ip http server**

In order to disable the internal web server, you would use the `no ip http server` command in global configuration.

478. **B. R1(config)# username Bob privilege 3 password P@ssw0rd**

To create a user with privilege level 3, you need to be in global configuration and use the username command with the privilege 3 option.

479. **D. show privilege**

To display your privilege level, you can use the show privilege command.

480. **B. switch(config-if)#shutdown**

The shutdown command at the interface prompt is used to disable a port.

481. **D. Sticky**

The sticky option should be configured on the port so that the switch configures port security using the MAC address of the currently connected system.

482. **B. Shutdown**

The shutdown option is used when configuring port security to have the port disabled until the administrator enables it.

483. **C. Port security**

Port security is a very important feature of switches that allows you to control what systems can connect to a port on the switch by MAC address.

484. **D. Enable the port.**

In the output displayed, you can see that the port is administratively down because it has been disabled:

```
SW1#show interface f0/5
FastEthernet0/5 is administratively down, line protocol is down (disabled)
```

Therefore, you would need to enable the port with the no shutdown command.

485. **A. SW1(config-if)#switchport port-security mac-address sticky.**

You will need to use the sticky option on the switchport port-security mac-address command within the interface prompt for the interface you are configuring a MAC address for.

486. **C. access**

A port must be placed in access mode before you can configure port security on the port.

487. B. Use the following commands:

SW1(config)#`interface f0/5`

SW1(config-if)#`switchport mode access`

SW1(config-if)#`switchport port-security`

SW1(config-if)#`switchport port-security mac-address 1111.2222.3333`

SW1(config-if)#`switchport port-security maximum 1`

SW1(config-if)#`switchport port-security violation shutdown`

In order to configure port security on a port, you must first navigate to the interface, then place the interface in access mode. You then enable port security and specify the MAC address to associate to the port. Finally, you limit the maximum number of MAC addresses used by the port to 1 and specify your violation mode.

488. A. Connect the monitoring system to port 1 on the switch

D. Configure port mirroring on the switch.

In order to monitor traffic on the network, you will connect your monitoring system to the port on the switch and configure the port mirror to send all traffic to that port.

489. B. router(config-line)#login local

The `login local` command is used on the console port, telnet port, or auxiliary port to ensure a username and password are required.

490. D. router(config)#service password-encryption

The `service password-encryption` command is used in global configuration to ensure that all passwords are encrypted.

491. C. Use the following commands:

ROUTERA(config)#`line con 0`

ROUTERA(config-line)#`password con`

ROUTERA(config-line)#`login.`

You must set the password in the console line prompt but then ensure you use the `login` command to configure the Cisco device to require the password for authentication.

492. D. router(config)#username rebecca password mypass

To create a username and password on the router you can use the `username` command in global configuration mode.

493. A. enable secret P@ssw0rd

To use an encrypted version of a password to enter priv exec mode, you would use the `enable secret` command, which encrypts the password.

494. **D. Login prompts for a password, whereas login local prompts for a username and password.**

The login command is used on a port if you want the device to just prompt you for a password, but if you want the device to prompt you for a username and password when connecting to that port you must use the login local command.

495. **A. The exec banner**

The exec banner is the last banner of the ones listed to display. The exec banner displays after an administrator logs on and as he or she enters user exec mode.

496. **C. Use the following commands:**

R1(config)#banner motd #

R1(config)#This device is for authorized individuals only.

#

In order to create a Message Of The Day banner you must be in global configuration, specify the banner motd command, and include the delimiter that will end the command. The Cisco device knows that you are done typing your banner text when you type the delimiter in.

497. **D. Login**

The login banner displays before the administrator is asked to log in, but after the message of the day (MOTD) banner.

498. **B. router(config-line)#transport input ssh**

To ensure only secure communication is used to remotely connect to the router, you must configure SSH but also configure the VTY ports to use only SSH as the transport protocol.

499. **D. Use the following commands:**

ROUTERA(config)#username bob password pass

ROUTERA(config)#line vty 0 4

ROUTERA(config-line)#login local

The username and password are created in global configuration mode, but then to ensure that anyone connecting through Telnet is prompted for a username and password you must navigate to the Telnet ports and use the login local command.

500. **B. SSH**

You should only remotely manage your Cisco device when using a protocol that encrypts the communication between your system and the device. SSH is the secure protocol that replaces Telnet.

501. **B. There is no Telnet password.**

A part of the default security of a Cisco device is if you do not have proper passwords set, such as a Telnet password, you are unable to remotely connect to the device.

502. **A. Use the following commands:**

R1(config)#crypto key generate rsa

R1(config)#line vty 0 4

R1(config-line)#login local

R1(config-line)#transport input ssh

In order to configure your Cisco device for SSH, you would create a username and password (command not shown, but it is username bob password P@ssw0rd). Then generate a cryptographic key used to secure the communication (crypto key generate rsa). Once you create the key, you would then navigate to the VTY ports (line vty 0 4) and configure the ports to prompt for username and passwords (login local). Finally, you then ensure that the ports only accept SSH communication (transport input ssh).

503. **C. transport input ssh telnet**

To enable both SSH and Telnet access to the device for remote administration, you can use the transport input command on the VTY ports.

504. **D. Ad-hoc**

An ad-hoc wireless network is a wireless network that does not have a wireless access point and the systems connect directly to one another.

505. **B. SSID**

The service set identifier (SSID) is the name of the wireless network.

506. **D. IEEE**

The IEEE is responsible for defining the wireless standards such as 802.11a, 802.11b, 802.11g, and 802.11n.

507. **A. ESS**

An ESS wireless network covers a large area by having multiple access points using the same SSID and different channels. This enables users to roam around within the office and not lose their wireless connection.

508. **B. Cordless phone**

C. Microwave

Wireless networks could experience connectivity issues due to interference from a cordless phone or a microwave.

509.   **D. Change the power levels on the access point.**

In order to ensure that wireless users are within your office environment, you can lower the power levels on the wireless access point so that the signal cannot travel as far — resulting in ensuring that wireless clients are in the building.

510.   **C. BSS**

A Basic Service Set (BSS) is the name used for a wireless network involving clients connecting to an access point to gain network access.

511.   **D. Change the channel on the wireless access point.**

If you are experiencing connectivity issues with a wireless network and you suspect it could be due to interference, then you can change the channel on the wireless access point to change the frequency that it is using.

512.   **B. Infrastructure**

Wireless networks are running in infrastructure mode when connecting to a wireless access point to gain wireless network access. You can also configure wireless networks in ad-hoc mode with one wireless device connecting to another wireless device.

513.   **B. The diagram represents an ESS network with both access points using the same SSID**

D. Each access point is using a different channel.

An ESS wireless network is one that has multiple access points using the same SSID, with each access point using a different channel. An ESS is designed to allow users to roam throughout the building and still have wireless access.

514.   **B. Use multiple access points with the same SSIDs.**

C. Each access point uses a different frequency range.

E. Access points must overlap by 10 percent or greater.

In order to have users roam a wireless network and jump from one access point to another in the ESS, you configure multiple access points with the same SSID, each having a different frequency range (or channel), and they must overlap by at least 10 percent.

515.   **D. FCC**

The Federal Communications Commission (FCC) is responsible for regulating the use of wireless and wireless frequencies. It is the governing body that legalized public use of the 900 MHz, 2.4 GHz, and 5 GHz frequencies.

516.   **B. IBSS**

An independent basic service set (IBSS) is another term for an ad-hoc wireless network. The term comes from the fact that a basic service set (BSS) is a term for a wireless network using an access point.

517. **B. ESS**

You can create an ESS wireless network by using multiple access points with the SSID set the same. This allows you to cover a wide area and support roaming users. You must also set the access points to use different channels.

518. **A. BSS**

The Basic Service Set (BSS) is the type of wireless network that has a single access point with an SSID assigned.

519. **A. Wi-Fi Alliance**

The Wi-Fi alliance would test and certify components for Wi-Fi compliance.

520. **A. BSS**

A single access point creates a BSS wireless network.

521. **D. Ensure that the area of coverage by both access points overlaps by at least 10%.**

In order to support roaming users, you must have multiple access points configured, with each access point overlapping the coverage area by at least 10%.

522. **A. Wi-Fi Alliance**

The Wi-Fi Alliance is responsible for testing and certifying wireless components for Wi-Fi compatibility.

523. **B. 1, 6, 11**

If you want to ensure that your wireless access points are not using overlapping frequencies, you can use channels 1, 6, and 11; they do not overlap with one another.

524. **B. ESS**

Extended Service Set (ESS) is the term used for a wireless network that supports roaming users by having multiple access points use the same SSID. Remember that you must configure each access point to use a different channel, and they must have overlapping coverage of 10 percent or more.

525. **A. Change the SSID**

D. Disable SSID broadcasting

You should change the SSID to one that is not easily guessed and then disable SSID broadcasting so that your wireless does not advertise the newly configured SSID.

526. B. Enable WPA2

D. Enable MAC filtering

F. Disable SSID broadcasting

In order to secure wireless network environments you can follow a number of best practices, such as disable SSID broadcasting to hide the network, enable MAC filtering in order to control what devices can connect to the network, and enable WPA2 to encrypt the communication.

527. A. WEP

WEP is an older wireless encryption protocol that uses the RC4 symmetric encryption algorithm with a static key.

528. B. MAC Filtering

MAC filtering is a feature that allows you to list which MAC addresses can connect to the wireless network.

529. C. SSID

At a minimum, you must configure the SSID so that clients can connect to the wireless network. If you wish to add security, you can configure MAC filtering and WPA2.

530. A. WPA rotates the key with each packet.

WPA uses TKIP as a key rotation protocol. For each packet sent with WPA, TKIP changes the encryption key based off the initial key and its algorithm.

531. A. Personal

WPA personal mode, also known as PSK (for pre-shared key) mode, involves configuring a wireless access point and clients with a WPA key in order to access the network.

532. C. WPA

WPA uses the TKIP protocol as part of the encryption process. TKIP is responsible for changing the pre-shared key with each packet sent.

533. B. Enterprise

WPA enterprise mode is the mode that uses a central authentication server such as a RADIUS server.

534. B. WPA2

WPA2 is the more secure encryption protocol of the three major protocols (WEP, WPA, and WPA2) and uses the Advanced Encryption Standard (AES).

535. C. AES-CCMP

WPA2 uses AES-CCMP as the encryption method. AES is a very strong symmetric encryption algorithm used in many technologies today.

536. B. 802.11b

The IEEE 802.11b standard defines wireless in the 2.4 GHz frequency range that runs at 11 Mbps.

537. D. 802.11n

The 802.11n wireless standard transmits data over 150 Mbps and runs at the 2.4 GHz and 5 GHz frequency ranges.

538. C. 802.11g

802.11g runs at 54 Mbps and is compatible with 802.11b devices because it runs at the same frequency range of 2.4 GHz.

539. A. 802.11a

The 802.11a wireless standard runs at 54 Mbps in the 5 GHz frequency range.

540. D. 802.11

Wireless networking is defined as the IEEE 802.11 standard.

541. D. 802.11n

802.11a and 802.11n both run at the 5 GHz frequency ranges and are therefore compatible. 802.11n also runs at the 2.4 GHz frequency range.

542. A. 1.544 Mbps

A T1 link is made up of twenty-three 64 Kbps data channels, which equates to 1.544 Mbps.

543. A. Leased line

A leased line is a dedicated WAN link that you pay a monthly fee for.

544. C. Circuit switched

A circuit switched network must first establish a communication channel before sending data. This is different than a leased line, which is a dedicated connection the entire time.

545. D. 128 Kbps

A BRI ISDN subscription uses two 64 Kbps data channels, giving you 128 Kbps.

546.   **B. 44.736 Mbps**

A T3 link supports a bandwidth of 44.736 Mbps.

547.   **A. T1**

A T1 or T3 link is considered a dedicated leased line because the connection is always available and dedicated to your company.

548.   **A. 1.544 Mbps**

A PRI ISDN subscription has a bandwidth of 1.544 Mbps.

549.   **C. Circuit switch**

Circuit switching is responsible for creating the circuit, which is the bandwidth and pathway dedicated to the communication until the connection is closed.

550.   **C. Circuit switched**

A circuit switched link is a temporary link that is established when communication is required and then the communication channel is terminated.

551.   **B. ISDN**

ISDN is an example of a circuit switched technology, where the bandwidth is allocated for the duration of the connection.

552.   **C. X.25; Frame relay**

X.25 and frame relay are examples of packet switching technologies where each packet can take a different route.

553.   **C. The DCE device**

The DCE device is responsible for setting the clock rate.

554.   **C. Serial 0/0**

To connect a T1 line to your router, you could connect an external CSU/DSU to the serial port on the router.

555.   **C. Back-to-back serial cable**

A back-to-back serial cable has a DCE end of the cable and a DTE end, and is used to connect two routers together by their serial ports to emulate a WAN link.

556.   **B. Physical layer**

E. Data link layer

When troubleshooting WAN connection issues, you are troubleshooting layer 1 and layer 2. Layer 1 deals with the physical connection, while layer 2 involves troubleshooting the communication protocol.

557. **A. External CSU/DSU**

An external CSU/DSU device would connect to the serial port on a router and then to the service provider's line. An internal CSU/DSU module could be added, but it would not connect to the serial port on the router.

558. **A. The clock rate must be set on the DCE device**

The DCE device must set the clock rate.

559. **D. HDLC**

HDLC is the default encapsulation protocol for serial links on a Cisco router. You can modify this and use the PPP protocol to take advantage of authentication, if you like.

560. **D. encapsulation ppp**

When creating a serial connection to a non-Cisco router, you must use an industry standard protocol such as PPP as the encapsulation protocol.

561. **A. Serial 0/0 is administratively down, line protocol is down**

Because you have disabled the port manually yourself, the port status will display as "administratively down." It is also important to note that if the link is not up (layer 1), then the line protocol will not be up either (layer 2).

562. **A. The encapsulation protocol needs to be set.**

The encapsulation protocol needs to be set to PPP. The default encapsulation protocol on a serial link is HDLC.

563. **B. clock rate 64000**

The DCE device would need to control the communication speed by setting the clock rate. To set the clock rate on the DCE device, navigate to the serial port being used and then type the clock rate command.

564. **C. HDLC**

Looking at the serial port, you can see that the encapsulation protocol is set to HDLC.

565. **D. DCE**

Looking at the output of the show controllers command, you can see that the serial interface is a DCE device.

566. **A. PPP**

The PPP encapsulation protocol is an industry standard available with most router manufacturers and can be used for authentication across router vendors.

567. A. ATM

ATM networks have a fixed length packet size, known as a cell, which is 53 bytes.

568. B. encapsulation hdlc

To utilize the Cisco proprietary version of HDLC, you use the encapsulation hdlc command.

569. B. show interfaces

E. show ip interface brief

In order to verify the status of the serial interface, you can use the show interfaces command and the show ip interface brief command.

570. B. Set the hostname on each router to a unique name

D. create a username on each router that matches the hostname of the other router

E. Enable PPP authentication on both routers and specify either PAP or CHAP as the authentication protocol.

To configure PPP authentication, you set the hostname on each router to a unique name and then create a username on each router that is the hostname of the other router. (Set the passwords to the same value.) Then you enable PPP authentication and specify the authentication protocol of either CHAP or PAP.

571. D. show controllers serial 0/0

You can use the show controllers command to verify whether the serial port is a DCE or DTE device.

572. B. It is the default encapsulation protocol for serial links on Cisco routers

E. it is a Cisco proprietary implementation.

The implementation of HDLC on Cisco routers is a proprietary protocol that can only be used to communicate with other Cisco routers over a serial link. If you are connecting to non-Cisco routers, you will need to specify PPP as your encapsulation protocol.

573. B. Change the encapsulation protocol.

You can see that the link is up, but the line protocol is down. The line protocol being down could be because the clock rate is not set or you are using the wrong encapsulation protocol on the serial interface.

574. D. PPP

Cisco devices can use either HDLC or PPP as the encapsulation protocol, with PPP being the one supporting authentication.

575. A. The link is up

C. communication over the layer-2 protocol is working.

When using the show interfaces command on your serial link, if you see a line protocol is up it means that there is a link and the layer-2 protocol is configured properly.

576. B. Use the following commands:

TOR-R1(config)#username NY-R1 password mypass

TOR-R1(config)#interface serial 0/0

TOR-R1(config-if)#encapsulation ppp

TOR-R1(config-if)#ppp authentication chap

In order to configure PPP authentication, you would first create a username and password on the Toronto router that matches the name of the New York router. You then navigate to the serial interface and enable PPP as the encapsulation protocol and CHAP as the authentication protocol.

577. D. CHAP

CHAP is the more secure PPP authentication protocol because the password is not passed in clear text across the network.

578. D. CHAP

You should use CHAP as the authentication protocol because the username and password are not sent over clear text using that protocol. PAP is the other authentication protocol that could be used, but it sends username and password in clear text.

579. A. ppp authentication chap

To configure CHAP as the authentication protocol, you would use the ppp authentication chap command while at the serial interface.

580. B. Routers increase the number of broadcast domains

C. Switches increase the number of collision domains.

Routers will split up broadcast domains, while switches will split up collision domains but will not affect the broadcast domains.

581. A. Initiate a copy of a file from a TFTP server to flash memory.

After issuing this command, you will be prompted for a TFTP server and file to copy from it, as well as being prompted for the location in flash to save the file.

582. C. Network

The network layer header contains the source and destination address information for the packet. A packet is the term used for the message at layer 3, while a frame is the term used to reference the message when it is at layer 2.

583. **D. Change the crossover to straight-through**

In this example, you are using the wrong type of cable to connect the switches to the routers; you should use straight-through because they are dissimilar devices.

584. **B. Bridge**

C. Switch

Bridges and switches are layer-2 devices.

585. **A. Computer to router**

B. Switch to switch

D. Computer to computer

You use a crossover cable when connecting similar devices together. Watch out for situations where the computer is connecting to the router (unlikely in real world, but is a good exam question).

586. **C. Network**

Logical addressing and routing is handled by layer 3 of the OSI model, also known as the network layer.

587. **D. IEEE**

Institute of Electrical and Electronics Engineers (IEEE) is the organization responsible for Ethernet and many other networking standards.

588. **C. Switch**

E. Bridge

Switches and bridges are layer-2 devices, while routers are layer-3 devices.

589. **C. Console**

E. Straight

The following are the correct cables to use:

A – Straight, B – Straight, C – Console, D – Crossover, E – Straight, and F – Straight

590. **D. exec-timeout 15 30**

The exec-timeout command is used to set a timeout on console and vty ports.

591. **D. Data Link**

CDP is a layer-2 protocol, so the answer is Data Link (layer 2).

592.

A. OUI

D. Vendor assigned values

A 48-bit MAC address is composed of two main pieces, a 24-bit Organizational Unique Identifier (OUI) assigned by the IEEE, and a 24-bit vendor assigned end station address, which is assigned by the network card manufacturer.

593.

A. 802.3ab

The IEEE standard for Gigabit Ethernet on copper wires (1000BaseT) is defined in 802.3ab.

594.

B. TCP

The TCP protocol is responsible for reliable delivery. It does this by using sequence numbers and acknowledgement numbers.

595.

A. ::1

D. 0000:0000:0000:0000:0000:0000:0000:0001

The IPv6 loopback address is known as 0000:0000:0000:0000:0000:0000:0000:0001, or can be abbreviated as ::1.

596.

B. SMTP

D. FTP

SMTP and FTP use TCP as the transport layer protocol. The other protocols use UDP.

597.

B. fe80:d351:3f16:dc41:ed36:317e:410e:3f28

Each character of the IPv6 address can be a value from 0 to 9 or A to F. Any other characters are illegal. Also, there are eight sections to the IPv6 address and you can replace any sections with 0000 that are side by side with a ::, but only once in the address.

598.

B. 172.25.56.10

E. 10.45.3.20

Private addresses are IP addresses that are not routable on the Internet. The following are the private IP address ranges:

- 10.0.0.1 to 10.255.255.255

- 172.16.0.0 to 172.31.255.255

- 192.168.0.0 to 192.168.255.255

599.

A. 255.255.255.224

To create eight networks, you would need to use three subnet bits, which would give you a custom subnet mask of 224.

600. **A. All packets are sent individually.**

D. Packet delivery is not guaranteed.

> UDP is a best effort delivery protocol; as such, data is not guaranteed to arrive in order, or even arrive at all. Each data packet that travels via UDP is treated individually.

601. **C. 128**

> IPv6 addresses are 128 bits in length, while IPv4 addresses are only 32 bits in length.

602. **A. 192.168.15.0/25**

> A subnet mask of 25 bits leaves 7 bits for network hosts. The formula for this is 2^7-2 to calculate the number of possible hosts, or 126 hosts.

603. **B. TCP**

> TCP makes use of windowing as part of its flow control system, which allows it to ensure that all data arrives completely and in order.

604. **B. 172.18.0.0/22**

> The number of bits required to support 545 hosts is 10 bits ($2^{10}-2$), which allows for 1,022 hosts on the network segment. Since you need 10 bits for the host, that leaves 22 bits in the subnet mask.

605. **C. SYN, SYN/ACK, ACK**

> The three-way handshake process starts with a Synchronize request (which sets a sequence value for the sender); this is followed by a dual purpose message from the receiver, which acknowledges the sequence value and sets its own sequence value; and this process is finalized by an acknowledgement from the sender of the receiver's sequence value.

606. **C. 255.255.252.0**

> A mask of 22 bits would be 11111111.11111111.11111100.00000000, or 255.255.252.0.

607. **B. 172.18.0.0/26**

> If you use 26 bits for the subnet mask, that leaves 6 bits available for the hosts. Using the formula 2^6-2, you have support for 62 hosts. While you only need a mask of 27 bits, since that is not available, the next closest valid mask is 26 bits.

608. **D. 216.83.25.127**

> With a /26, the increment value is 64, so that means that the next network ID is 128 – one number before that is the current network's broadcast address.

609. **B. 220.19.36.99**

> /27 means that the increment is 32, so the network ID that the .112 address is in is the 220.19.36.96 – this makes the third valid address of that network, 220.19.36.99.

610.　**C. fe80:d351:3f16:dc41:ed36:317e:410e:3f28**

You can always identify link local addresses because they start with FE80.

611.　**D. OUI**

The first half of the MAC address is a unique identifier assigned to the manufacturer of the network card; this is known as the Organizational Unique Identifier (OUI).

612.　**A. 195.56.78.0/30**

If you have a WAN link that just requires two IP addresses, then you can use the /30 because this leaves 2 bits for the host bits. Two host bits creates four addresses, but two of those are illegal to use (network ID and broadcast address), so that leaves two valid addresses.

613.　**D. Anycast**

Anycast addressing involves sending the information to the closest device that can service the request.

614.　**B. R1#copy running-config tftp**

To back up your configuration to a TFTP server, you use the copy command and specify running-config as the source and tftp as the destination.

615.　**C. show ip route**

In order to view the routing table, you can use the show ip route command.

616.　**C. R1>show sessions**

The show sessions command will display any telnet sessions you have.

617.　**B. R1(config)#ip route 13.0.0.0 255.0.0.0 12.0.0.2**

To add a static route, you use the ip route global configuration mode command and specify the destination network you wish to add to the routing table. This is followed by the subnet mask and the next hop where the router should send data destined for that network.

618.　**A. Use the following commands:**

R1#config term

R1(config)#line con 0

R1(config-line)#password P@ssw0rd

R1(config-line)#login

To configure a password on a console port, you navigate to the port and use the password command. You then use the login command to tell the Cisco device to prompt for the password.

619.   **C. no ip route**

To delete a route on a router, you use the `no ip route` command in global configuration mode.

620.   **C. 10.10.10.0/24**

When choosing a gateway, the router will always choose the entry in the routing table which most closely matches the destination address.

621.   **B. Router**

Routers will reduce the size of broadcast domains, while these domains will stretch across repeaters, bridges, and switches.

622.   **D. Use the following commands:**

R1#`config term`

R1(config)#`interface f0/0`

R1(config-if)#`ip address 14.0.0.1 255.0.0.0`

R1(config-if)#`no shutdown`

In order to assign an IP address to an interface, you must use the `interface` command in global configuration mode to navigate to the interface. You then configure the IP address and use the `no shutdown` command to enable the interface.

623.   **B. Use the following commands:**

R1#`config term`

R1(config)#`interface S0/0`

R1(config-if)#`ip address 14.0.0.1 255.0.0.0`

R1(config-if)#`encapsulation ppp`

R1(config-if)#`clock rate 64000`

R1(config-if)#`no shutdown`

When configuring the DCE end of a serial link, you need to configure the encapsulation protocol and the clock rate for the link.

624.   **D. R1(config)#cdp run**

To enable CDP, you use the `cdp run` command in global configuration.

625.   **B. Static route**

The static route would be placed in the routing table because it has a lower administrative distance than the RIP route.

626. **A. Use the following commands:**

R1#config term

R1(config)#username bob password P@ssw0rd

R1(config)#line vty 0 4

R1(config-line)#login local

After creating the username and password in global configuration, you must navigate to the vty ports and use the `login local` command to force the local usernames and passwords to be used.

627. **D. ip nat inside source list 1 interface serial 0/0 overload**

To configure NAT using the access list, you use the `ip nat inside source list <#>` command and continue by specifying which interface you wish to overload.

628. **D. 2142**

To bypass the password you have forgotten on the Cisco device, you will interrupt the boot process and then change the configuration register value to 2142 in order to not have the startup config applied when you reboot the router.

629. **D. Bandwidth**

OSPF calculates cost using the bandwidth of the link.

630. **C. clock rate 32000**

The correct command to set the clock rate to 32Kb/s is clock rate 32000.

631. **A. OSPF**

EIGRP and IGRP are propriety Cisco protocols, so the choice is between OSPF and RIP v1; but RIP v1 does not support VLSM, leaving OSPF as the only available choice.

632. **B. An excessive number of hosts in a broadcast domain**

D. Broadcast storms

E. Half-duplex interfaces

Half-duplex interfaces only transfer data in one direction at a time; broadcast storms generates excessive traffic, slowing down legitimate traffic; and an excessive number of hosts generates traffic that needs to be processed by other devices in the broadcast domain.

633. **C. OSPF**

D. IS-IS

OSPF and IS-IS are link-state routing protocols, while RIP and IGRP are not.

634.   **D. Switch**

Trunk ports are typically used to connect a switch to another switch; most other devices will typically use access ports. A trunk mode port will pass traffic for all VLANs.

635.   **A. hop count**

B. bandwidth

C. delay

Hop count, bandwidth, and delay are commonly used metrics for routing protocols.

636.   **A. EIGRP**

C. RIP v2

D. OSPF

Only EIGRP, RIP v2, and OSPF support both route summarization and VLSM.

637.   **A. ip nat inside source list 1 interface FastEthernet 0/0 overload**

D. ip nat pool no-overload 192.168.1.2 192.168.1.63 prefix 24

The difference between these two options is based on the final result that you desired. If your goal was to support a PAT configuration, then answer A enables overloading, which would allow your configuration to function, allowing more than one user out; but if you were attempting to perform NAT, then choice D defines a pool of outside addresses and assigns it to be used for NAT.

638.   **C. It changes the function of NAT to PAT.**

Adding overload to your NAT configuration, either with a pool of addresses or with a single external address, changes the function to PAT.

639.   **B. 1**

Directly connected routes have an AD of 0, while static routes have an AD of 1.

640.   **A. RIP v1**

E. IGRP

VLSM is not supported on either RIP v1 or IGRP.

641.

A. Use the following commands:

R1(config)#ip dhcp pool NY_Network

R1(dhcp-config)#network 192.168.1.0 255.255.255.0

R1(dhcp-config)#default-router 192.168.1.1

R1(dhcp-config)#lease 7 0 0

To configure DHCP on your router, use the `ip dhcp pool` command in global configuration mode. You then need to specify the network range that the DHCP service is to have addresses out for, and then you can configure settings such as the `default-router` address and lease time. The lease time is in the days_hours_mins format.

642.

B. You have configured the wrong wildcard mask.

When configuring OSPF networks, you specify the network ID and the wildcard mask – not the subnet mask. The quickest way to calculate the wildcard mask is to take the subnet masks away from 255.255.255.255. For example:

255.255.255.255

-255. 0. 0. 0

———————

0.255.255.255

So, 0.255.255.255 should be the wildcard mask used with the network statement.

643.

D. Configure sub-interfaces on the router.

You can configure sub-interfaces on the router along with the encapsulation protocol used to tag VLAN traffic.

644.

A. R1(config)#access-list 1 permit 192.168.3.0 0.0.0.255

To create a standard access list, you use the `access-list` global configuration command and include the access list number you are creating, with a deny or permit, and then the source network address and wildcard mask.

645.

B. router ospf 3

E. network 192.168.2.0 0.0.0.255 area 0

You use the `route ospf <#>` command to start the OSPF process and give it a process ID. You then use the network command with the wildcard mask and area for the networks you want to enable OSPF on.

646.

D. 2.2.2.2

The router ID that OSPF uses if one has not been configured is the highest IP address assigned to a loopback interface. If a loopback interface does not exist, then it is the highest IP address assigned to a physical interface.

647.   **B. CTRL-SHIFT-6, then X**

To suspend your telnet session, you use the CTRL-SHIFT-6, then press X. You can then resume the session with the resume command.

648.   **B. clear ip nat translations ***

The clear ip nat translations * will remove all NAT associations. You will be able to verify this with the show ip nat translations command.

649.   **D. EIGRP**

Only EIGRP provides support for all three listed protocols.

650.   **C. EIGRP**

This is based on the default administrative distance for each of the routing protocols, which leads to the believability of the routing information. Routing protocols have these administrative distances: OSPF (110), IGRP (100), EIGRP internal (90), and RIP (120). In this case, the protocol offering the lowest distance is EIGRP.

651.   **D. R1(config)#ip default-gateway 23.0.0.1**

You should configure your switch for a default gateway if you're going to telnet into the switch from a different network. Use the `ip default-gateway` global configuration command.

652.   **C. Multiple addresses let you know that the port is connected to another switch or hub.**

If you see multiple MAC addresses associated with a port, it means that there are multiple devices connected to that port on the switch, so the port is likely connected to a switch or hub. When IP telephony is in use, most phones have a two-port switch in them, allowing the desktop computer to be connected to the network through the phone. In this case, the switch port would show two MAC addresses, one for the phone and one for the computer.

653.   **A. Upgrading a hub to a switch**

C. Adding a bridge between two hubs

A collision domain is created when there is no filtering and directing of traffic based on MAC addresses. All ports on a hub will exist in a single collision domain; while each port on a bridge or switch is a separate collision domain. Implementing a bridge or switch to a network will increase the number of collision domains, but reduce the size of each collision domain. If there are fewer collisions on a network, then data will move more efficiently.

654.   **D. Router**

A router is required to allow devices on different VLANs to communicate with each other. If you are using a layer-3 switch, you have router functionality built into the switch.

655. **A. R1(config-if)#switchport port-security mac-address sticky**

Use the sticky option with port security to indicate to the switch you wish it to learn the MAC address of the connected system and configure port security with that address. This saves a lot of typing of MAC addresses!

656. **C. show cdp neighbors**

The figure is showing the output of the show cdp neighbors command. You can use this command to locate network devices that are close to you.

657. **A. show vlan**

To view a list of VLANs, you can use the show vlan command.

658. **D. SW1(config-if-range)#switchport mode access**

To configure multiple ports at once, you use the interface range <port #> command to navigate to multiple ports and then you can use the switchport mode access command at the range prompt.

659. **B. SW1(config-if)#duplex full**

To configure full duplex mode, you navigate to the interface and then use the duplex full command.

660. **C. VTP**

VLAN Trunking Protocol (VTP) is designed to synchronize the VLAN database on all switches on the network or within a VTP domain.

661. **B. Lowest priority**

D. Lowest MAC address

When choosing the root bridge on a STP network, the switches will concatenate their configured priority and MAC address together, and the switch with the lowest value will be chosen as the root bridge.

662. **B. Blocking**

C. Learning

F. Forwarding

When a switch port has a device connected to a port, if the port is configured for STP, then the port will initially enter a Listening state, where the switch will look for and process BPDU data. If the switch determines that it will not cause a network topology loop, the port will enter a Learning state, when the switch will record a list of MAC addresses that exist on a network connected to that port. After a Learning period concludes, the port will enter a Forwarding state, where the port will forward traffic. If the switch (and the STP root bridge) determines that this port will create a loop on the network, then the port will enter a Blocking state.

663. **C. Shutdown**

The shutdown mode specifies to disable the interface till the administrator enables it.

664. **B. 3524XL(vlan)#vlan 2 name MKT**

To create a VLAN, you can navigate to the VLAN database and use the `vlan` command followed by the number and the name.

665. **C. Access**

The port must be configured in access mode before configuring port security on the port.

666. **A. show port-security interface f0/6**

You can verify that port security was configured on an interface by using the `show port-security` command along with the interface.

667. **A. Switch 1 will be root bridge.**

G. Port I will be blocking.

Each switch or bridge has a Bridge ID, which is created by concatenating its priority and MAC address. The switch with the lowest Bridge ID is the root bridge for the network. Each switch then identifies a root port, which will be the least cost path to the root bridge, based on link speeds and types. When there are ties, the port that connects to the bridge with the lowest Bridge ID is used. For Switch 4, that means that the root port will be H, rather than I, because Switch 3 has a lower Bridge ID than Switch 2. Switch 4 is in a loop situation, and it is the farthest point from the root bridge, so Switch 4 will set its non-root port to blocking to resolve the loop.

668. **C. Between 25% and 50%**

If all the LEDs were lit up, then the switch would be using more than 50% of its bandwidth; since there is still one LED that is out, the usage is between 25% and 50%.

669. **C. ping <ip_address>**

In order to verify communication on the network, you use the `ping` command.

670. **A. Ensure that virtual terminal port communication is encrypted**

The set of commands configures the virtual terminal port and more importantly ensures that SSH is used as the protocol to communicate through the virtual terminal ports. This ensures that the communication is encrypted when remoting into the device.

671. **A. Use the secret password.**

When both passwords are set, the enable password is no longer used, and you will only use the secret password.

672. **A. 5**

The output shows 5 input errors and all 5 of those errors are CRC errors. This identifies that the payload data was damaged in transit.

673. **A. Data can be sent only in one direction at a time**

C. There will be an increase in the number of collisions.

Half-duplex settings only allow data to be sent in one direction at a time. This means that even on a port with a single device attached, there is an increased chance that another device will send data to the end node when that end node is attempting to send data, which will yield a collision. Full duplex settings would not have collisions in the same situation.

674. **D. How the system was last restarted**

The version will usually display hardware model, IOS version, compilation date, uptime, what initiated the last restart, the system image filename, the active configuration register, and hardware configuration, such as ports, RAM, and NVRAM.

675. **B. Source IP address**

Standard ACLs are able to filter traffic based only on source IP address.

676. **C. IP route filtering**

ACLs filter IP-based traffic as it passes through the router.

677. **B. service password-encryption**

In order to encrypt all passwords in the configuration file, you can use the `service password-encryption` command.

678. **B. show ip route**

D. show ip protocols

IP runs at layer 3, so any commands that deal with routing or the IP protocol would be used to troubleshoot layer issues.

679. **A. show cdp neighbors detail**

The `show cdp neighbors detail` command will display the IP addresses of neighboring devices.

680. **D. Banners should not welcome someone.**

It is important to note that for legal reasons you should not have a welcome message in your banners.

681. **C. show ip interface brief**

The show ip interface brief command is used to list the interfaces, their IP addresses, and their status.

682. **C. Before routing packets to an outbound interface**

When an inbound ACL is placed on an interface, the ACL is processed when traffic enters the interface, before routing to an outbound interface. If the ACL is placed on an outbound interface, then the traffic is routed through the router before the ACL is processed.

683. **C. interface serial0/0**

no cdp enable

To prevent CDP from being accessed through an interface, you need to execute no cdp enable while in interface mode for the desired interface.

684. **A. Type terminal monitor.**

Typing terminal monitor will copy all console messages over to the SSH or telnet session you are connected on. To stop this from happening, you will type terminal no monitor.

685. **B. Enter rommon**

The first step in the password recovery process is to enter rommon interface at boot, so that you are able to change the configuration register.

686. **C. You did not configure the vty.**

In order to enable ssh, you need to use the commands:

```
line bty 0 4
login local
transport input ssh
```

687. **D. banner motd**

The motd banner is displayed before any other banners.

688. **C. Flash, TFTP server, ROM**

If there is no boot directive in the configuration, which specifies an IOS image to load, the router will search Flash for a valid IOS image. Then it will attempt to locate a TFTP server with an IOS image, and finally will load a mini IOS image that is found in ROM.

689. **C. 54 Mbps**

Wireless networks running 802.11g run at 54 Mbps in the 2.4 GHz frequency range.

690. **D. Infrastructure**

When your wireless network uses access points rather than peer-to-peer networking, it is running in infrastructure mode, while peer-to-peer networks are in ad-hoc mode.

691. **C. 11 Mbps**

802.11b network specifications define 11 Mbps as the maximum speed of the network.

692. **C. 128 Kbps**

ISDN Basic Rate Interface (BRI) subscriptions have 128 Kbps bandwidth.

693. **D. ESS**

The Extended Service Set (ESS) is the term for a wireless network that uses multiple access points with the same SSID.

694. **B. Reflection**

D. Scattering

F. Absorption

RF waves suffer from reflection, scattering, and absorption when they encounter objects in the path of their waves. The exact result will depend on the composition and construction of the encountered object.

695. **C. There are no keepalives on the link**

D. You have set the incorrect encapsulation type.

If there are no keepalives on the link or if you have configured the wrong encapsulation type, then you will see the line protocol down.

696. **B. 3**

When using 802.11 technologies over the 2.4GHz frequencies, channels 1 to 11 have overlapping ranges, yielding a maximum of three non-overlapping choices.

697. **C. CHAP**

Challenge Handshake Authentication Protocol can be used for authentication on PPP links.

698. **A. CSU/DSU**

To connect your router to a T1 line, you either connect a serial port to an external CSU/DSU or use an internal CSU/DSU on the router.

699. **C. encapsulation ppp**

E. authentication chap

Encapsulation and authentication commands are only used when dealing with WAN interfaces.

700. **A. 32,768**

The default STP priority on a switch is 32,768. The priority is joined with the MAC address to create a bridge ID. The switch with the lowest bridge ID is selected as the root bridge and has all of its ports placed in a forwarding state. Note that the priority is changed in increments of 4096.

701. **B. Data Link**

Because RSTP (and STP) are protocols that run on the switch, they are layer-2 protocols (data link).

702. **A. RSTP transitions to a forwarding state faster than STP does.**

Rapid Spanning Tree Protocol (RSTP) introduces new port roles such as alternate so that when a port goes down instead of going through the entire election process again to determine which ports are in a forwarding state and which are in a blocking state, the switch enables the alternate port or the backup port.

703. **B. Converged**

The term used for when the switch has gone through the election process and determined which ports are to be in a forwarding state and which ones are to be in a blocking state is "converged."

704. **D. The switch with the lowest bridge ID**

The switch with the lowest bridge ID is selected as the STP root bridge. The root bridge has all its ports set to a forwarding state. The bridge ID is made up of the priority + MAC address of the switch.

705. **C. Discarding**

Per VLAN Spanning Tree (PVST)+ is based on the IEEE 802.1D standard, but uses only three port states of learning, forwarding, and discarding.

706. **A. Blocking**

B. Listening

D. Forwarding

STP uses port states of blocking, listening, and forwarding. STP does not have a disabled port state.

707. **A. Yes**

When looking at the output of the show spanning-tree command, you can see the bridge ID of the device (the priority and MAC address). Above the bridge ID, you can see the device that was selected as the root bridge. If the address is the same as the existing bridge ID address, then that device was selected as the root bridge. It also says, "This bridge is the root" in the root ID section.

708. **B. Lower the priority.**

In order to force a device to become the root bridge, you would lower the priority of that device so that it has a lower priority than any other device.

709. **C. The port with the lowest cost**

The port with the lowest overall cost to the root bridge is selected as the root port. The cost is determined based off the type of connection. For example, if the link is a 100 Mbps link, it will receive a cost of 19, while a 1 Gbps link has a cost of 4. In this case, the 1 Gbps link would be selected as the root port as it has the lowest cumulative cost.

710. **B. Reduces converging time after a link failure**

D. Uses additional port roles over STP

E. Transitions to a forwarding state faster than STP

Rapid Spanning Tree Protocol (RSTP) is designed to reduce the time it takes for STP to converge. With RSTP, additional port roles such as alternate and backup allow a switch to choose backup ports during conversion. This means that when a link goes down the alternate or backup ports can be used right away because they have already been identified. STP would go through the convergence process again.

711. **B. show spanning-tree**

You can use the `show spanning-tree` command to view which switch is the root bridge.

712. **A. SwitchA**

The switch with the lowest bridge ID will be selected as the root bridge. The bridge ID is made up of the priority+MAC address.

713. **D. show interface fastethernet 0/1 switchport**

The show interface fastethernet 0/1 switchport command can be used to display trunking information such as the operational mode, the encapsulation protocol being used, the trunking VLANs, and the pruning VLANs.

714. **D. Alternate**

Rapid Spanning Tree Protocol designates a backup port known as an alternate port should the root port go down.

715. **A. (config-if)#spanning-tree portfast**

In scenarios where a system reboots a lot and you need it to come online as quickly as possible, you can enable the portfast option on the interface. This dramatically decreases the time it takes for the port to come only due to STP port states.

716. **D. Decrease the priority below 4096.**

To ensure that a switch is selected as a root bridge, you would lower the priority so it is the lowest priority switch. In this case, the existing root bridge has a priority of 4097 so you need to be lower than that.

717. **A. Communication between VLAN requires a router.**

D. Each VLAN requires its own IP subnet.

VLANs are a great way to create communication boundaries on the network. If you have systems in multiple VLANs, you will need a router to route traffic between the VLANs. Each VLAN will need its own IP subnet.

718. **A. ISL**

C. 802.1q

ISL and 802.1q are VLAN tagging protocols. ISL is a Cisco proprietary protocol, while 802.1q is an IEEE standard and is the preferred tagging protocol.

719. **A. Use the following command(s):**

```
vlan 10
name MKT
```

To create a VLAN, use the VLAN command in global configuration and then specify a name for the VLAN.

720. **A. Both sides of the trunk link should use the same native VLAN.**

The native VLAN is the VLAN used on frames that have not been tagged for a particular VLAN. It is critical to set the native VLAN to the same VLAN on both ends of the trunk link.

721. **C. SW1(config-if)#switchport trunk allowed vlan 10,20**

By default, traffic for all VLANs is allowed to pass over a trunk port, but you can specify specific VLANs using the switchport trunk allowed vlan command.

722. **B. F0/0 must be configured with sub-interfaces**

D. F0/0 on R1 and F0/24 on the switch must use the same encapsulation protocol

Looking at the figure, in order to route between the two VLANs you must configure the router as a router on a stick. This involves configuring the interface on the router with sub-interfaces and enabling the connecting port on both the router and switch as a trunk port for the same encapsulation protocol.

723. **A. Systems will not be able to communicate between the two switches.**

In order to have the VLAN traffic travel between the two switches, you must configure the ports that connect the two switches together for trunk mode, not access mode.

724.   **C. Interface f0/0 should be configured as a trunk port.**

When creating a router on a stick scenario, you will need to create the sub-interfaces on the port connected to the switch, but you also need to enable the port on both the router and the switch as a trunk port so that it can carry VLAN traffic. In this case, the router is only asking what you should do with router R1.

725.   **C. Use the following commands:**

sw(config)#interface f0/8

sw(config-if)#switchport access vlan 10

In order to place a port in a VLAN, you must navigate to that interface and then use the switchport access vlan <#> command, where <#> is the VLAN number you wish to place that port in.

726.   **C. 10 Mbps Ethernet**

ISL trunk ports must be above 10 Mbps in order to carry the extra VLAN traffic.

727.   **D. VTP**

The VLAN Trunking Protocol is responsible for deploying VLANs to multiple switches in the enterprise.

728.   **A. Client mode**

If you configure a switch for client mode, then you are not allowed to create VLANs on the switch. The client-mode switch would receive the list of VLANs from the server in the same VTP domain.

729.   **B. VTP pruning**

The VTP pruning feature can be used to filter VTP messages that are destined for VLANs that exist on the switch.

730.   **C. Use the following commands:**

vtp domain glensworld

vtp password P@ssw0rd

vtp mode client

In order to configure a switch to receive VLAN information via VTP, you must configure the switch for the VTP domain and supply the password for that domain. You then must put the switch in client mode so that it receives the list of VLANs from the VTP server.

731.   **C. Transparent mode**

VTP transparent mode allows a switch to create its own VLANs and will forward VTP messages on to other switches it is connected to.

732. **D. Use the following commands:**

```
sw(config-if)#switchport mode trunk

sw(config-if)#switchport trunk encapsulation dot1q
```

When configuring a port as a trunk port, you must first change the mode to trunk mode and then you can specify the encapsulation protocol. In this case, the protocol is to be 802.1q so you would use the dot1q parameter.

733. **D. The VTP domain name is case sensitive.**

When configuring a VTP client, you must specify the VTP domain and the VTP password. It is important to note that the VTP domain is case sensitive.

734. **B. Systems will not be able to communicate between the two switches.**

In order for systems to communicate across switches to other systems in the same VLAN, you need to configure port F0/24 as a trunk port instead of an access port. Configuring F0/24 as a trunk port will allow it to carry VLAN traffic between the two switches.

735. **D. channel-group 1 mode on**

Setting the channel-group mode to on forces the interface to be part of the grouping without any protocol negotiations. If you set the mode to active, then the interface can negotiate with other ports to be part of the grouping. Setting the mode to passive means that the port will not initiate the grouping, and setting it to off means it will not form the grouping.

736. **D. The system with the MAC address of 1111.2222.3333 can connect to port 8 along with two other systems.**

The code example enables the port security feature with a maximum of three MAC addresses to be associated with the port. In the code example, one MAC address is being supplied so the other two MAC addresses can be dynamically learned.

737. **A. The channel cost is increased.**

Because the Etherchannel group has lost some bandwidth, the cost on the grouped link is increased.

738. **C. ROM**

The POST routines on a Cisco device are stored in ROM memory.

739. **B. A central place to upgrade the IOS**

The one benefit of booting from an IOS image located on a TFTP server is that you can have multiple Cisco devices using the IOS image. When you decide to upgrade the IOS image, you simply upgrade the file on the TFTP server with no need to reconfigure each Cisco device or perform the upgrade on each device. The downfall is that if the device cannot communicate with the TFTP server, it will be unable to load the IOS.

740. **C. The IOS is loaded into RAM.**

After the bootstrap program locates the IOS in flash memory, it then copies the IOS into RAM.

741. **B. Ctrl-Break**

You can use the Ctrl-Break keystroke to interrupt the startup of a Cisco device. This is common in password recovery procedures.

742. **C. ROM**

The bootstrap program is stored in ROM memory.

743. **B. NVRAM**

The startup configuration is stored in non-volatile RAM.

744. **A. The device will try to connect to a TFTP server for the configuration.**

If the startup config does not exist, the Cisco device will then try to load a startup configuration from a TFTP server. If a TFTP does not exist, the device will then present the initial configuration dialog to configure the device.

745. **D. config-register 2142**

You would change the configuration register value to 2142 in order to specify that you wish to skip the startup configuration during boot-up.

746. **A. Bootstrap**

The bootstrap, which is located in ROM, is responsible for locating the Cisco IOS and loading it in memory.

747. **B. boot system flash c2800nm-advipservicesk9-mz.124-15.T1.bin**

To configure your Cisco device to boot from a specific IOS located in flash memory, use the boot system flash command followed by the filename of the IOS image located in flash memory.

748. **A. boot config <file>**

To change the configuration file that is applied at startup, you can use the boot config <file> command and then supply the filename with the configuration you wish to use.

749. **D. show boot**

The show boot command is used to display your boot-up (or startup) settings. Note that this command is being replaced by the show bootvar command.

750. **C. ROM**

The bootstrap program is stored in ROM memory.

751. **D. c2800nm-advipservicesk9-mz.124-15.T1.bin**

The Cisco IOS image is located in the bin file and, in this case, the c2800nm-advipservicesk9-mz.124-15.T1.bin file.

752. **A. copy flash tftp**

In order to back up your IOS, you can use the `copy flash tftp` command to copy a file from flash memory to a TFTP server. The Cisco IOS will prompt you for the filename details after the command is issued.

753. **A. If the server is unavailable devices cannot boot up.**

The huge downfall of booting from an IOS located on a TFTP server is if you are unable to communicate with the TFTP server, you will be unable to boot the system.

754. **D. copy tftp flash**

You would use the `copy` command to copy the IOS from the TFTP server to flash memory.

755. **D. show version**

To find out the version of the Cisco IOS you are running, use the `show version` command.

756. **C. boot system tftp <filename.bin>**

To configure the Cisco device to boot from an IOS image located on a TFTP server, you can use the `boot system TFTP <filename>` command.

757. **D. The first image stored in flash**

By default, the first IOS image stored in flash memory is loaded on boot-up.

758. **C. boot bootstrap**

You can use the `boot` command to alter a number of boot preferences, such as specifying a secondary bootstrap image. Use the `boot bootstrap` command to specify the secondary bootstrap image on your Cisco device.

759. **B. show version**

The `show version` command is used to display the IOS version information, filename, and device configuration such as memory and ports that exist in the device.

760. **C. boot system tftp <filename>**

Use the `boot system tftp` command to load the IOS from a TFTP server.

761. **A. delete flash:<filename>**

To delete a file from flash memory, use the `delete` command followed by the type of memory you wish to delete a file from and then the filename.

762. **D. setup**

You can invoke the initial configuration dialog by using the `setup` command. The initial configuration dialog will then walk you through typical configuration of the Cisco device.

763. **D. .bin**

Cisco IOS images use the .bin file extension.

764. **A. boot buffersize**

Older versions of the IOS allowed you to alter how much NVRAM is used for the IFS by using the `boot buffersize` command.

765. **B. show version**

You can use the `show version` command to display the memory installed on a Cisco device. The `show version` command also shows the IOS version and the ports information on the Cisco device.

766. **B. show flash:**

The `show flash:` command was used. Note the top of the output and the types of files listed.

767. **C. show flash**

To view available flash memory, use the `show flash` command. The `show flash` command displays total memory, used memory, and available flash memory.

768. **A. dir nvram:**

To display the contents of NVRAM, you can use the `dir` command followed by the type of memory you wish to do a directory of; in this case, use the `dir nvram:` command.

769. **A. 2800**

When using the show version command, you can see the name of the IOS image that is used by the device. In this case, the IOS file is c2800nm-advipservicesk9-mz.124-15. T1.bin. The platform is displayed first (2800), then the feature set is displayed (advipservices). Following that are any options, such as the m means that the image runs in ram, and the z means that the image is zipped (-mz). After that, you have the version of the IOS; in this case, the version is 12.4 (.124).

770. **D. private-config.text**

The cryptography keys on a Cisco switch are stored in a file called private-config.text. This file is located in flash memory and can be seen with a dir flash command.

771. **B. dir flash:**

You can use the dir flash: command to display the contents of flash memory.

772. **A. 62720 K**

Looking at the results of the show version command, you can see the IOS version, the number of interfaces that exist (and their types), and the memory installed in the device. Looking at the figure in this example, you can see that there are 239 K of NVRAM and 62720 K of flash memory.

773. **C. license clear ipservices**

You can use the clear parameter on the license command to remove a license from your Cisco device.

774. **B. license install flash: r1fs-ips**

After you acquire a new license, you can install it by first copying it to flash memory and then using the license install command to activate the license.

775. **B. show license file**

You can use the show license file command to display the license information on your Cisco device.

776. **B. Is classful**

C. Administrative distance of 120

RIPv1 is a classful protocol, which has an administrative distance of 120. Being classful means that the protocol does not send subnet mask information with the route table.

777. **B. There is no route for the 13.0.0.0 network on router R1.**

Routers know about networks they are connected to by default. In order to ping hosts on the 13.0.0.0 network, router R1 would need to have a route added to its routing table. You could do this by adding a static route or by loading a dynamic routing protocol.

778. **D. They do not send the subnet mask info with the routing update.**

Classful routing protocols do not send the subnet mask information with the routing update, so therefore do not support VLSM; they assume the same subnet mask is used on each network.

779. **C. Administrative distance of 120**

D. Is classless

RIPv2 is a classless routing protocol (support VLSM) and has an administrative distance of 120.

780. **C. Hop count**

Distance vector routing protocols use hop counts as their metric. These protocols are only aware of how far something is away and not aware of bandwidth and availability of the link.

781. **D. 120**

RIP has an administrative distance (AD) of 120.

782. **B. Is vendor-specific**

E. Administrative distance of 90

EIGRP is a Cisco-specific routing protocol, so it could only be used on networks supporting Cisco devices, and has an administrative distance of 90.

783. **A. More secure because the administrator must add the routes**

D. No bandwidth is being used to update the routing tables.

The huge benefit to static routing is that you are not using any network bandwidth to have routing protocols update the routing tables of other routers. Also, static routing is more secure because the administrator must manually add the route versus the router just adding what it hears from others (as is the case with dynamic routing protocols).

784. **E. 1**

A static route has an administrative distance of 1.

785. **A. Elects a DR**

D. Uses cost as its metric

OSPF elects a designated router (DR) that other routers on the OSPF network will exchange routing information with. Also, to calculate the best pathway, OSPF uses cost instead of hop count, as is the case with RIP.

786. **C. 110**

OSPF has an administrative distance of 110.

787. **C. The route of 13.0.0.0 remains on router R1.**

Because you are using static routing, there is no way for router R1 to know that the interface is down on router R2. This means that the route is still valid on router R1 as far as router R1 is concerned.

788.   **B. The EIGRP route**

The route with the lowest administrative distance would be selected in this case. RIP has an administrative distance of 120, OSPF has an administrative distance of 110, and EIGRP has an administrative distance of 90.

789.   **A. It decreases convergence time by sending out an update as soon as there is a change to the network topology.**

Triggered updates are a feature of link state routing protocols and they send out notification immediately when there is a change in the network topology.

790.   **D. Through 12.0.0.2, and through 14.0.0.2**

When looking at the routing table, you can see that the route to the 15.0.0.0 network has two pathways – one going through 12.0.0.2 and the other pathway going through 14.0.0.2. In this case, you will notice that the administrative distance (90) and the cost (2681856) are the same. When the cost is the same, the router will load balance between the routes.

791.   **B. They use more resources as they store multiple tables in memory**

D. Use triggered updates to reduce the time to converge

Link state routing protocols use more resources as they store multiple tables in memory to track the network topology. Link state routing protocols also use triggered updates to notify other routers of a change in the network topology.

792.   **C. Administrative distance**

In order to make the static route a backup route to the one learned by a dynamic routing protocol, you would need to alter the administrative distance of the static route to a number higher than the administrative distance of the dynamic routing protocol.

793.   **A. Topology table**

C. Neighbor table

E. Routing table

Link state routing tables use a topology table identifying the entire network topology, a neighbor table identifying neighboring routers, and a routing table which includes the current routes.

794.   **B. OSPF**

OSPF is the only routing protocol that does not auto summarize routes; you must manually summarize the routes to take advantage of route summarization.

795.   **C. Through R2.**

R1 will send the data through R2 to get to R4 because it will use the route with the lowest administrative distance.

796. **D. ip route 21.0.0.0 255.0.0.0 20.0.0.2 110**

In order to add a static route you use the `ip route` command followed by the route you are adding, subnet mask, and the next hop. By default the administrative distance would be set to 1 so if you want to change it you set the new administrative distance value at the end of the command (such as the 110). You may want to do this so that the static route acts as a backup to a route learned via a routing protocol.

797. **D. ipv6 unicast-routing**

You can enable IPv6 routing on the router by using the `ipv6 unicast-routing` command.

798. **B. Hello messages**

E. LSA from other routers

A link state routing protocol uses hello messages that it sends out to each of its interfaces to discover neighboring routers. The LSA messages are used to announce changes in the network topology.

799. **D. LSA**

When a change occurs to the network topology, a router sends out LSA messages informing other routers on the network of the change. This causes the routers to recalculate routes and update their topology databases.

800. **A. Holddown timer**

The holddown timer is a feature on a router that forces it to retain routing information for a short period of time even after receiving a routing update with conflicting information. Once a route is marked unreachable, the route is held for the duration of the timer before accepting a new route to the destination.

801. **E. Split horizon**

Split horizon is a feature to help prevent routing loops by preventing a router from sending knowledge of a route out the interface it received knowledge of the route through.

802. **B. Poison reverse**

Poison reverse is a routing feature to help reduce routing loops by a router sending an update back to its neighbor for a downed route with an infinite metric.

803. **B. EIGRP**

EIGRP is a Cisco proprietary routing protocol. If you have a network with routers from different vendors, you will need to use an industry standard routing protocol such as RIP or OSPF.

---

804.   **D. To reduce the size of the routing table**

The goal of route summarization is to reduce the size of the routing table by not listing
each different route — you can use route summarization to summarize multiple routes
as one.

805.   **D. 131.107.16.0/22**

If you were to write out the binary of the relevant portions of the network IDs, you
would get the figure below. To create a summary route, you simply identify the
network bits that are the same for each of those networks, in this case, 8+8+6=22 bits

```
131.107.16.0
131.107.17.0
131.107.18.0
131.107.19.0

131.107.00010000.0
131.107.00010001.0
131.107.00010010.0
131.107.00010011.0
```

806.   **B. 172.16.0.0/21**

If you were to write out the binary of the relevant portions of the network IDs, you
would get the figure below. To create a summary route, you simply identify the
network bits that are the same for each of those networks (8+8+5=21).

```
172.16.0.0
172.16.1.0
172.16.2.0
172.16.3.0
172.16.4.0
172.16.5.0
172.16.6.0
172.16.7.0

172.16.00000000.0
172.16.00000001.0
172.16.00000010.0
172.16.00000011.0
172.16.00000100.0
172.16.00000101.0
172.16.00000110.0
172.16.00000111.0
```

807. C. 10.4.0.0/14

If you were to write out the binary of the relevant portions of the network IDs, you would get the figure below. To create a summary route, you simply identify the network bits that are the same for each of those networks (8+6=14).

```
10.4.0.0
10.5.0.0
10.6.0.0
10.7.0.0

10.00000100.0.0
10.00000101.0.0
10.00000110.0.0
10.00000111.0.0
```

808. B. 120.12.0.0/14

If you were to write out the binary of the relevant portions of the network IDs, you would get the figure below. To create a summary route, you simply identify the network bits that are the same for each of those networks (8+6=14).

```
120.12.0.0
120.13.0.0
120.14.0.0
120.15.0.0

120.00001100.0.0
120.00001101.0.0
120.00001110.0.0
120.00001111.0.0
```

809. C. Configure router on a stick

You can configure the router as a router-on-a-stick, which allows the router to route between the VLANs. In order to do this, you must configure the interface on the router that is connected to the switch with sub-interfaces. You must also configure the connected port on the switch for trunking and an encapsulation protocol.

810. A. SW1(config-if)#switchport mode trunk

The port on the switch that is connected to the router on the stick will need to be configured as a trunk port so that it can carry traffic for all VLANs to the router.

811. **A. Configure the interface that is connected to the switch as a trunk port using the same encapsulation protocol.**

D. Configure the interface that is connected to the switch with three sub-interfaces.

In order to create a router-on-a-stick scenario to route between VLANs, you will need to configure three sub-interfaces and ensure that the interfaces are using the same encapsulation protocol as the trunk port on the switch.

812. **B. On R1 perform the following commands:**

```
R1(config)#interface f0/0
R1(config-if)#no shutdown
R1(config)#interface f0/0.10
R1(config-subif)#encapsulation dot1q 10
R1(config-subif)#ip address 192.168.10.1 255.255.255.0
R1(config)#interface f0/0.20
R1(config-subif)#encapsulation dot1q 20
R1(config-subif)#ip address 192.168.20.1 255.255.255.0
```

D. On SW1 perform the following commands:

```
SW1(config)#interface f0/1
SW1(config-if)#switchport mode trunk
```

In order to configure the router on a stick, you need to configure a sub-interface on the router for each VLAN and then enable the encapsulation protocol for that VLAN. You then configure the port on the switch that is connected to the router as a trunk port.

813. **A. Nothing**

Because you are assuming that all configuration is correct, it looks like the sub-interfaces have been created and the trunk port has been set.

814. **B. 120**

RIP has an administrative distance of 120.

815. **C. debug ip rip**

When troubleshooting any routing protocol, you can turn on debugging of that protocol. To enable debugging for rip, you would use the `debug ip rip` command.

816. **B. Version 2**

RIPv2 is a classless routing protocol and supports VLSM.

817. **C. RIPv2 sends updates using multicast communication**

E. RIPv2 supports authentication.

RIPv2 sends routing updates to a multicast address while RIPv1 broadcasts the address. RIPv2 also supports authentication, whereas RIPv1 does not.

818. **B. no auto-summary**

RIPv2 automatically summarizes routes, and if you want to disable that feature you can use the no auto-summary command.

819. **B. Version 1**

Looking at the figure, you can see that the router has received a v1 update, which means version 1. You can also notice that the router is sending updates to the address of 255.255.255.255, which is a broadcast address. RIPv1 broadcasted updates, while RIPv2 multicasted the updates.

820. **A. Every 30 seconds**

All RIP versions send routing updates every 30 seconds by default.

821. **A. R1(config-router)#distance 80**

In order to change the administrative distance of RIP, you can use the distance command at the router prompt. In order to change the administrative distance to a value other than the default, you would not change it to 120, because that is the default value.

822. **A. R1(config-router)#version 2**

To enable RIPv2, you simply use the version 2 command while configuring RIP.

823. **A. 25**

Looking at the figure, you can see that the "Distance" is set to 25, while the default for RIP is 120. In this example, the administrator has modified the administrative distance of RIP from the default.

824. **C. show ip route**

To view the routing table and the routing entries that a routing protocol has added to the routing table, use the show ip route command.

825.

A. Use the following commands:

R1(config)#router rip

R1(config-router)#network 192.168.3.0

R1(config-router)#network 192.168.4.0

In order to configure RIP, you must use the router rip command and then specify the networks you wish to advertise through RIP.

826.

D. 3

Looking at the output of the show ip route command, you can see there are two RIP entries. The one with the destination network of 14.0.0.0 has a hop count of 3.

827.

D. show ip protocols

In order to view information about the routing protocols running on the router, use the show ip protocols.

828.

B. show ip protocols

The show ip protocols command is used to view information about the routing protocols running on a router.

829.

A. Use the following commands:

R1(config)#router rip

R1(config-router)#distance 44

You can change the administrative distance for RIP by navigating to the router prompt and using the distance command.

830.

C. 4

OSPF will load balance between equal cost routes to the same destination. You can have a maximum of 4 equal cost routes to a destination.

831.

C. 110

OSPF has an administrative distance of 110.

832.

C. Cost

OSPF uses cost as a metric.

833.

B. The router with the highest router ID

If the OSPF priority is the same on each router, then the DR is selected based on the router with the highest router ID. The highest router ID is first selected by the highest IP address assigned to a loopback interface. If there are no loopback interfaces then the router ID is the highest IP address assigned to a physical interface.

834. **D. Every 10 seconds**

Hello messages are sent every 10 seconds with OSPF.

835. **B. Area 0**

Area 0 is the identity of the backbone area and all other areas in your autonomous system connect to it.

836. **A. Every 30 seconds**

All RIP versions send routing updates out every 30 seconds by default.

837. **D. All other routers exchange info with the DR to cut down on bandwidth usage.**

The designated router is a router that shares routing information with other routers. Routers on the network share their routing information with the DR and then the DR informs all other routers. This prevents each router from needing to share routing information with all other routers.

838. **A. Set the priority to 0.**

An OSPF router with the priority set to 0 will never become the DR.

839. **C. Every 10 seconds**

Hello messages are sent to discover neighboring routers. Hello messages are sent every 10 seconds.

840. **A. The BDR becomes the DR and an election for a new BDR occurs.**

When the DR fails on the network, the backup designated router (BDR) becomes the DR and a new BDR is elected.

841. **B. Hello and Dead Interval timers are not configured the same on both routers.**

D. The routers are in different areas.

In order for two OSPF routers to create neighboring relations, they must have the same configuration values for the Hello and Dead Interval values. They also must be configured for the same area.

842. **D. The BDR is used when the DR fails.**

The BDR is elected when the DR is elected, and it acts as a backup DR in case the DR fails.

843. **C. It is the process ID for OSPF.**

When enabling OSPF, you specify the process ID you wish to run the instance of OSPF under.

844.

D. The cost

Because the routing protocol is OSPF, the 65 identifies the cost value on the link.

845.

A. 14.0.0.1

If the router-id is not set on the router, the router will use the highest IP address on any loopback interface as the router ID. If there are no loopback interfaces, the router will use the highest IP address on a physical interface as the router ID.

846.

D. 13.0.0.1

The highest IP address assigned to a loopback address would be used as the router ID. If no loopback address is present, then the router will use the highest IP address assigned to a physical interface.

847.

B. router ospf 1

C. network 192.168.5.0 0.0.0.255 area 0

In order to configure OSPF, you must first use the `router ospf <process ID>` command. You then specify the networks you wish to enable OSPF on along with the area you are assigning to that network.

848.

D. ip ospf priority 20

In order to change the priority on the router, you can use the `ip ospf priority` command. The router with the highest OSPF priority will become the DR.

849.

A. Bandwidth

With OSPF, you can calculate the cost of a link by 100 000 000 / bandwidth. For example, if you have a 10 MB link, then the cost is calculated as 100000000/10000000 = 10. The cost on a 10 MB link is 10.

850.

B. R1(config-router)#router-id 13.0.0.1

With OSPF, to change the router ID manually you can use the `router-ID` command at the router prompt when configuring OSPF.

851.

B. 224.0.0.5

OSPF hello messages are multicasted to the address of 224.0.0.5.

852.

B. Feasible successor route

EIGRP determines the best route to a destination which is known as a successor route, and it determines a backup route known as a feasible successor.

853.

D. It is a backup route located in the topology table.

The feasible successor router is a backup route stored in the topology table.

854.

B. It must match on all routers that you want to share routing information.

The autonomous system (AS) value must be the same for all EIGRP routers you wish to share routing information with.

855.

C. It load balances between the two paths.

If EIGRP has calculated equal metric values for multiple routes to the same network, it will load balance between those routes.

856.

C. The autonomous system

The 10 represents the autonomous system number. All routers running EIGRP that you wish to share routes with should use the same AS number.

857.

B. Successor route

The best route is known as the successor route and is placed in the routing table.

858.

A. Topology table

C. Routing table

The successor route is stored in both the routing table and the topology table.

859.

A. A hybrid protocol

EIGRP is considered a hybrid protocol because it uses features of distance vector routing protocols and link state routing protocols.

860.

D. 90

EIGRP has a default administrative distance of 90.

861.

C. Topology table

The feasible successor route is stored in the topology table.

862.

D. The EIGRP route

The EIGRP route would be used because its administrative distance is lower than the others. The metrics come into play when there are multiple routes with the same administrative distance.

863.

B. Quicker convergence

The feasible successor is a backup route that is ready to be promoted to the successor route without the need for update messages and hello packets. This speeds up convergence.

864.

D. Autonomous system number

The routing domain ID is also known as the autonomous system number.

865. **A. Backup route stored in topology table**

The feasible successor routes are backup routes that are stored in the topology table.

866. **A. Is vendor specific**

C. Has a default administrative distance of 90

EIGRP is a Cisco proprietary protocol that has a default administrative distance of 90.

867. **B. Successor routes forward traffic**

C. May have a backup in a feasible successor route.

Successor routes are used to forward traffic to the destination network because those routes are stored in the routing table. The successor route may have a backup route known as a feasible successor route.

868. **D. Primary route stored in routing table**

A successor route is a primary route stored in the routing table. Know that the feasible successor route is a backup route stored in the topology table.

869. **D. Bandwidth**

E. Delay

By default, EIGRP uses bandwidth and delay to calculate its metrics.

870. **B. They are backed by feasible successor routes**

D. They are used to forward traffic to the destination

E. They are stored in the routing table.

Successor routes have backup routes known as feasible successor routes and are stored in the routing table (as well as the topology table). Because the successor route is stored in the routing table, it is used to forward traffic to the destination network.

871. **B. The router sends a multicast message to all adjacent neighbors.**

The EIGRP router will send a multicast query to all adjacent neighbors, asking for available routes to the destination network.

872. **B. Passive**

When looking at the topology table, you can see a status on the left side for each route. If the status displays passive, that is a good thing because it means there have been not changes to the route.

873. **C. R1(config)# router eigrp 5**

You can enable EIGRP by using the router eigrp <AS #>command. The <AS #> is the autonomous system number that is shared by all EIGRP routers you wish to share routing information.

874.

C. R1(config-router)# no auto-summary

EIGRP auto summarizes routes by default; to disable auto summary, you would use the no auto-summary command at the router configuration.

875.

C. Use the following commands:

R1(config)#router eigrp 10

R1(config-router)#network 11.0.0.0 0.255.255.255

R1(config-router)#network 12.0.0.0 0.255.255.255

When enabling EIGRP on a router, you must use the router eigrp <AS> command in global configuration. You then use the network command with the network ID and wildcard mask for all the networks you wish to enable EIGRP on.

876.

D. R1(config-router)#distance eigrp 35 35

In order to change the administrative distance, you can navigate to the EIGRP router prompt and use the distance eigrp <internal_distance> <external_distance> command.

877.

B. Configure the same AS on all routers.

In order for the routers to share routing information with one another, the routers must be configured for the same EIGRP autonomous system number.

878.

C. network 192.168.3.64 0.0.0.31

This is a trick question because it is more of a wildcard mask question. When adding networks to EIGRP, you use the network command with the network ID and then the wildcard mask — not the subnet mask! The quickest method to calculate the wildcard mask is to take the subnet mask away from 255.255.255.255. For example:

255.255.255.255

- 255.255.255.224

---

0.   0.   0. 31

879.

D. network 172.16.16.0 0.0.15.255

Another example wildcard question for you! When adding networks to EIGRP, you use the network command with the network ID and then the wildcard mask – not the subnet mask! The quickest method to calculate the wildcard mask is to take the subnet mask away from 255.255.255.255. For example:

255.255.255.255

- 255.255.240.0

---

0.   0. 15.255

880. B. 0

Looking at the output of the show ip eigrp neighbors command, you can see that the queue count (Q Cnt) is set to 0.

881. A. 10

You can see at the top of the show ip protocols command output that it says "Routing Protocol is eigrp 10". The 10 signifies the autonomous system number.

882. A. show ip eigrp neighbors

The show ip eigrp neighbors command is used to list neighbors, their IP address, and statics on those neighbors.

883. D. show ip eigrp neighbors

To view the IP addresses of neighboring routers with EIGRP, you use the show ip eigrp neighbors command.

884. B. R1 would alternate between 14.0.0.1 and 12.0.0.2.

Because there are two pathways to the 15.0.0.0 network with equal metric values, EIGRP will load balance between them.

885. A. show ip eigrp neighbors

Using the show ip eigrp neighbors command, you can see a list of neighboring devices (adjacent devices) and their statistics, such as the smoothed round trip time (SRTT) and the queue count (Q count).

886. A. 4

Looking at the output of the show ip protocols command, you can see that the maximum paths is set to 4. This means that EIGRP can load-balance between four equal cost routes.

887. A. show ip protocols

D. show ip eigrp topology

You can see the AS number on routers running EIGRP by using the show ip protocols command or the show ip eigrp topology command.

888. D. 40 ms

Looking at the figure, you can see that the Smooth Round Trip Time (SRTT) to R1's neighbor is 40 ms. This is the time it takes for a message to be sent to the neighbor and a reply to come back.

889. **A. show ip protocols**

The show ip protocols command was used in the figure and displays details about the routing protocol, such as the protocol, autonomous system, and the networks that the protocol was enabled on.

890. **D. No changes are required.**

No client changes are required; the new VRRP master router will take over the existing address.

891. **B. GLBP**

D. VRRP

Gateway Load Balancing Protocol (GLBP), Hot Standby Router Protocol (HSRP), and Virtual Router Redundancy Protocol (VRRP) are all high availability options for routing.

892. **B. Two routers**

C. Additional virtual IP address

To implement VRRP on your network, you will require a least two routers, each with its own IP address, and one additional virtual IP, which will be used by one master router and will be taken over by the backup router in the event that the master router goes offline.

893. **A. The router with the highest IP address**

C. The router with the highest priority

When configuring GLBP, routers can be assigned priorities with the glbp priority [1-255] command. The router with the highest priority will be chosen as the new AVG. If all priorities are the same, then the router with the highest IP address will be chosen.

894. **A. 1 second**

The default advertisement timer is 1 second. This is used to send out hello messages, and failure to receive hello data will trigger a failover.

895. **C. GLBP performs Active/Active load balancing.**

Gateway Load Balancing Protocol (GLBP) performs Active/Active load balancing of network traffic.

896. **A. Routers share a common virtual IP address.**

D. Routers have unique virtual MAC addresses.

GLBP routing groups will all share the same IP address, but each will have a separate MAC address. All hosts initially communicate with the AVG, which assigns the session to a router in the group.

897. **B. GLBP**

Since all traffic is already load balanced between several active nodes of the GLBP routing group, device failure in that environment will cause the least user impact. When using VRRP and HSRP (without SSO), there will be a brief interruption in data services (from 3 to 10 seconds) while the secondary router is activated or promoted to the master role.

898. **C. Manages which data will be processed by which router**

The AVG (Active Virtual Gateway) manages the group of routers that are all Active Virtual Forwarders (AVF). The AVG responds to all ARP requests for the virtual IP address and responds with the MAC address of the AVF that it wants to process data for that device.

899. **A. Preserves forwarding path**

While Hot Standby Redundancy Protocol (HSRP) allows for failover between two or more routers, adding Stateful Switchover (SSO) to this configuration allows for preserving forwarding information. It also is less disruptive to the data flow. All three Cisco redundancy options, HSRP, VRRP, and GLBP, make up the First Hop Redundancy Protocol (FHRP) choices. FHRP is a more generic or blanket term.

900. **C. Never.**

GLBP uses the priority option to choose a router to act as the Active Virtual Gateway (AVG). Once a router is running as the AVG, it will continue until it goes offline, when the priority will be used to choose a new AVG. The exception to this behavior is when the command glbp preempt has been added to the configuration, which will cause Router1 to take back the role when it comes online.

901. **E. All routers require matching VRRP primary and secondary IP addresses.**

All routers in a VRRP group are required to use the same primary and secondary addresses. In this case, they are using one primary and one secondary address.

902. **B. debug glbp errors**

D. debug glbp packets

The following are valid debug options for glbp: debug condition glbp, debug glbp errors, debug glbp events, debug glbp packets, and debug glbp terse.

903. **D. Use the following commands:**

Router1(config)#redundancy

Router1(config-red)#mode sso

Router1(config-red)#exit

Router1(config)#no standby sso

Router1(config)#standby sso

To enable SSO mode, you will first set the mode, then clear the current standby settings, and reset standby sso on the device.

904. C. 224.0.0.102, UDP, 3222

GLBP routers communicate with each other using the multicast address of 224.0.0.102 on UDP port 3222.

905. A. Group numbers match

E. Virtual IP addresses match

From the data that is displayed in the output, it is required that the group number and virtual IP addresses match. The other settings do not need to be the same on all members of the group, but it is advisable that all hello times do match to prevent possible issues in communications.

906. C. 256

When working with Ethernet and FDDI, HSRP supports 256 standby groups, while Token Ring supports only 3.

907. D. It depends on the server.

Most syslog servers will separate incoming log data by client IP address, but this varies by syslog server and is usually configurable on the server.

908. B. show logging

To display your logging settings, you will use show logging. The output is shown here:

Router1# show logging

Syslog logging: disabled

    Facility: 20

    Timestamp logging: enable

    Standby logging: disabled

    Debug-trace logging: disabled

    Console logging: disabled

    Monitor logging: disabled

    Buffer logging: disabled

    Trap logging: level warnings, facility 20, 0 messages logged

      Logging to outside 192.168.1.5

    Permit-hostdown logging: disabled

    History logging: disabled

    Device ID: disabled

909. **D. All severity levels**

Although it is configurable, you are able to send all severity messages to your syslog server. The severity levels are:

0 Emergency: System is unusable.

1 Alert: Action must be taken immediately.

2 Critical: Critical conditions.

3 Error: Error conditions.

4 Warning: Warning conditions.

5 Notice: Normal but significant condition.

6 Informational: Informational messages.

7 Debug: Debug-level messages.

910. **D. There was a change in the state of the loopback0 interface.**

Since time is measured in UTC, there is a very small chance that your adjusted date would mean this message was generated on March 5; it does absolutely reference that loopback0 was brought to an Up state.

911. **C. The syslog server is configured for a non-standard port.**

By default, syslog services run on UDP port 514. If your syslog server has been configured for a different port, you need to use a command with this format: logging host 10.1.8.50 transport udp port <port number>.

912. **B. UDP 514**

The default port for syslog servers is UDP 514.

913. **A. Time**

C. Severity

A syslog message from an IOS device will contain the following components:

- Facility: The IOS component source for the message.
- Severity: The importance of the message.
- Hostname: The name of the device generating the message.
- Timestamp: When the message was generated at the device.
- Message: The test string which contains the details of the event or message.

The format of the syslog message would be like this:

mm/dd/yyy:hh/mm/ss:facility-severity-MNEMONIC:Message-text

A sample message would look like this:

- Mar 6 22:48:34.452 UTC:%LINEPROTO-5-UPDOWN: Line protocol on Interface Loopback0,

changed state to up

914. **C. Syslog**

Since all kernel and system messages that occur on the router are passed to the syslog server, this is the best option for capturing data and system messages that lead up to the lockup of the router, if not the actual messages that reflect the lockup or lack of responsiveness. There is a possibility that although you are not able to manage the router, the syslog service may still be running.

915. **D. Trap**

When SNMP generates an alert to be sent to a management server via SNMP, the alert is called a trap.

916. **A. HP Openview**

C. Nagios

Cisco does not create a server to receive traps, so it is left to third-party manufacturers. HP Openview and Nagios both represent server and device monitoring software, which integrate SNMP trap receiving into their product suites.

917. **D. OID**

SNMP structure and data object names are stored in a Management Information Base (MIB), while each piece of data that is stored in SNMP is called an Object Identifier (OID).

918. **D. UDP 161**

The default port for SNMP is UDP 161.

919. **B. MIB**

The Management Information Base (MIB) stores a documented list of OIDs for a product.

920. **D. Security password**

The community name in SNMP is a password used to secure access to the OID information.

921. **A. User authentication**

D. Data encryption

The two major advantages that SNMP v3 provides are user authentication and data encryption.

922. **B. Read**

C. Write

The two default permission types in SNMP are read-only (ro) and read-write (rw).

923. **C. Implement access lists**

The best method to restrict access to poll SNMP data is to implement an access list and allow only read-only (ro) access, using a set of commands like these:

Router1(config)# `access-list 10 allow 10.1.1.0 0.0.0.255`

Router1(config)# `snmp-server community comsecret ro 10`

924. **A. Using secure community names**

B. Restricting access to read-only

D. Implementing access lists

Using non-standard community names, setting communities to read-only, and implementing access lists to restrict the devices that can communicate with the router using SNMP are all valid options for securing traffic to your router. In addition, since SNMP v3 supports user authentication and data encryption, using version 3 over previous versions provides greater security.

925. **A. The IP address of the collector**

C. The port the collector is using

The two pieces of information that you will need to configure a device to send data to a NetFlow collector are the IP address of the collector and the port that it is receiving data on. The default port for NetFlow is UDP 9996.

926. **C. NetFlow-enabled device**

D. NetFlow collector

The two main components required for NetFlow to function are a NetFlow-enabled device (which will send system counters to a NetFlow collector) and a NetFlow collector. Several collectors are available, including Cisco NetFlow Collector, and third-party tools, such as Fluke Networks, SolarWinds, and NTOP.

927. **A. The collector is configured for a non-default port.**

C. The collector is using a different version.

The NetFlow version that is being used can be 1 (default), 5, or 9. The default port is UDP 9996. If the collector is not matching the default values, then the router configuration commands will need to provide these options.

928. **B. DTE**

D. DCE

DTE (Data Terminal Equipment) and DCE (Data Communication Equipment) are the two pieces of equipment that will be used on a frame relay connection. Your router, via the serial connection, will represent the DTE side of the device, while a device from your telco will represent the DCE device.

929.

A. PVC

D. SVC

The two circuit types used on a Frame Relay network are Permanent Virtual Circuits (PVC), which are always connected, and Switched Virtual Circuits (SVC), which establish connections when data needs to be transmitted.

930.

B. SVC

Switched Virtual Circuits (SVC) will destroy or close the session when the data transmission has been completed.

931.

A. Full Mesh

C. Partial Mesh

D. Star

Frame relay network connections between a multiple site wide area network could be configured as a full mesh, partial mesh, or star configuration, depending on required flow of data on the network.

932.

B. A local identifier between the local router and local frame relay switch

The DLCI is used by your router to identify the local end of the Frame Relay switch.

933.

B. Signaling standard between the router (DTE) and Frame Relay switch (DCE)

LMI is a signaling standard to allow management information, such as the status of Virtual Circuits, between the DTE and DCE.

934.

B. 10

To create a fully meshed network, you would require $n(n-1)/2$ links, where n is the number of sites, or 10 links.

935.

B. CIR

CIR, or Committed Information Rate, is the amount of bandwidth that the Frame Relay client is guaranteed.

936.

D. Inverse Address Resolution Protocol

The Inverse Address Resolution Protocol (Inverse ARP) is used to discover the network addresses of devices over the Frame Relay connection.

937.

C. Local Access Rate

The Local Access Rate (LAR) is the Frame Relay component which is the clock speed of the Frame Relay cloud.

938. **C. static map commands**

Static map commands can be used in the interface configuration using the following format:

Router1(config-if)# frame-relay map protocol protocol-address dlci [broadcast] [ietf | cisco | payload-compress packet-by-packet]

A static map command would be:

Router1(config-if)# frame-relay map ip 10.1.1.8 110 broadcast

939. **B. All excess traffic is marked as discard eligible.**

When the CIR is exceeded, the excess traffic is marked as Discard Eligible (DE) and will be discarded when traversing the Frame Relay network if there is congestion on the network.

940. **A. Matching DTEs**

The DTEs that will be communicating with each other need to agree upon the encapsulation type, while the DCEs they communicate through will not care; they will pass any properly formatted traffic.

941. **C. 60 seconds**

An Inverse ARP is sent every 60 seconds to ensure all DLCIs are online.

942. **B. 10 seconds**

LMI information is exchanged every 10 seconds.

943. **B. It connects a router to a Frame Relay switch.**

The CSU/DSU represents a DCE at many client premises when using Frame Relay. It is the device to which their router (DTE) is connected. Some routers have integrated CSU/DSUs or have them added through a WAN Interface Card (WIC) expansion slot.

944. **A. Partial Mesh**

The Partial Mesh supports additional or redundant connections between sites, but stops short of a Full Mesh, which has every site connected to every other site.

945. **A. CIR**

The Committed Information Rate (CIR) is the highest average data rate which is allowed on the Frame Relay network.

946. **A. ANSI**

D. Q.993A

Three LMI types can be used for Frame Relay network: ANSI, Q.993A, and Cisco.

947. **C. DLCI**

The DLCI is used to define the local end of the VC — specifically, the connection from the router to the Frame Relay switch.

948. **C. Identifies the DCLI to be used for traffic being sent to 192.168.155.2**

The map command will statically associate an IP address with a DLCI.

949. **D. Assigning a DCLI to a local serial sub-interface**

The `interface-dlci` command is used to assign a DCLI to the Frame Relay sub-interface on a router.

950. **D. Implement your configuration on sub-interfaces on the serial connection.**

In order to support multiple Frame-Relay links over a single serial interface, you will implement your configuration using sub-interfaces. The following is an example.

interface Serial1

  no ip address

  encapsulation frame-relay

interface Serial1.100 point-to-point

  ip address 10.1.100.1 255.255.255.0

  bandwidth 64

  frame-relay interface-dlci 100

interface Serial1.110 point-to-point

  ip address 10.1.110.1 255.255.255.0

  bandwidth 64

  frame-relay interface-dlci 110

951. **C. 10**

When using point-to-point configuration, you will require one subnet for each VC. You can figure out the VCs for this fully meshed network using the formula 5(5-1)/2 VCs, or 10.

952. **D. There is no apparent issue.**

This output does not show any apparent issue with LMI. You would want to verify that the out packet (on the second line) references your sequence number (myseq) as one higher than the last sequence number seen by the other router. Additionally, you would expect the returning in packet (starting on the 6th line and completing on the 8th line) shows that both routers have seen and are using the same sequence number.

953. **A. Ensure you are using the correct LMI type.**

Since you have been sending LMI information, but not receiving any LMI information back, ensure you are using the same LMI type as the other device.

954. **B. The DCLI is not correctly configured.**

Since the line protocol is listed as down, there is a data link issue, which can be caused by an incorrect DCLI being used on either end of the connection.

955. **B. The router will consider the link to be failed.**

LMI data is automatically exchanged every 10 seconds. When 3 intervals are missed (which is 30 seconds), then the link is considered to be failed. This will repair itself if it then receives LMI data exchanges.

956. **B. debug frame-relay events**

The debug frame-relay events show information about Inverse ARP packets that are exchanged between your router and other devices on the Frame Relay network.

957. **B. There is no issue.**

An Active status indicates that your connection is up and actively transferring data, so there is no need to troubleshoot the connection.

958. **B. debug frame-relay packet**

The debug frame-relay packet command will display information about all frame-relay packets that are received on the interface.

959. **B. Verify the serial cable is correctly connected.**

D. Ensure the interface has not been shut down.

Since the interface is down, you would want to ensure that the cable has been correctly connected and that the interface has not been administratively shut down.

960. **D. Verify you are using the correct DLCI.**

You can verify the DLCI you are using with the command show frame-relay pvc. Ensure that this DLCI matches the one configured on the DCE. Since the serial interface is not up, the issue is between your router and the DCE.

961. **B. Verify the serial cable is correctly connected.**

Since the line protocol is down, there is likely a data link issue with the connection. Verify the physical connections.

962. **C. The Frame Relay map may need to be cleared.**

If the DLCI or encapsulation were not correct, then the line protocol would be down. Since this connection worked prior to changing the remote address, and since the Frame-Relay map is set to dynamic, it is likely that the map entries are out of date. You can have the router rebuild the inverse ARP cache by issuing the clear frame-relay-inarp command.

963.   **A. That is a reserved number.**

There is a set of DLCIs which are reserved, and it includes 1-15 and 1008-1023.

964.   **C. The remote side of the connection**

An Inactive status indicates that your connection to the DCE is proper, so the likely source of the issue is on the remote end of the connection.

965.   **A. PVC Status**

C. Local DLCI

The map output will include the status the PVCs and the local DLCI that is used for them.

966.   **B. DCE**

The DCE device controls the communication and should have the clock rate set.

967.   **C. R1(config-if)#clock rate 64000**

In order to configure the clock rate, you would navigate to the serial interface that is the DCE end of the link and use the `clock rate` command.

968.   **A. PPP**

If connecting to router that is not a Cisco router, you will need to use PPP as the encapsulation protocol because it is a vendor-neutral protocol.

969.   **D. CHAP**

The Challenge Handshake Authentication Protocol (CHAP) securely transmits the authentication traffic by using a three-way handshake.

970.   **B. PPP**

PPP is a layer-2 protocol that is vendor neutral, supports authentication, and is used on serial links as an asynchronous communication protocol.

971.   **C. Serial**

You would use a serial port to connect to an external CSU/DSU that would connect to the T1 line.

972.   **C. PAP**

When configuring PPP authentication, you should stay away from PAP because the username and password are sent in clear text. Use CHAP instead!

973.   **B. PPP supports authentication.**

E. PPP is vendor neutral.

PPP is an industry-standard serial link protocol that supports features such as compression and authentication.

974.

D. ppp authentication chap pap

To enable PPP authentication, you use the `PPP authentication` command and then list the primary protocol and the secondary protocols to use.

975.

B. Set the hostname on each router to a unique name.

D. Create a username on each router that matches the hostname of the other router.

E. Enable PPP authentication on both routers and specify CHAP as the authentication protocol.

To configure PPP authentication, you set the hostname on each router to a unique name and then create a username on each router that is the hostname of the other router. Ensure that the password for both usernames is the same value. Then you enable PPP authentication and specify CHAP as the authentication protocol. CHAP is the more secure than PAP because it encrypts the username and password while PAP transmits usernames and passwords in clear text.

976.

B. NCP

The NCP protocol allows PPP to function with different network protocols, such as IP or IPX.

977.

C. Use the following commands:

R1(config-if)#ip address 165.45.1.1 255.255.255.252

R1(config-if)#encapsulation ppp

R1(config-if)#no shutdown

If connecting to non-Cisco devices, you need to use industry standard protocols. In this case, the encapsulation protocol on your serial link must be PPP.

978.

B. LCP

PPP uses the Link Control Protocol (LCP) to negotiate settings such as compression, callback, multilink, and authentication.

979.

A. PPP

PPP is an industry-standard protocol used on serial ports that has features such as authentication, compression, multilink, and callback.

980.

B. A router is typically considered a DTE device.

C. A modem is used to connect to an analog line.

E. A CSU/DSU is used to connect to a digital line.

In most situations, your router is the DTE end of the communication link while the service provider is the DCE end of the WAN link. CSU/DSU are used to connect to a digital network such as a leased line, while modems are used to connect to an analog network.

981. **B. Allows routing updates to be forwarded across the frame relay PVC**

Using the broadcast option on the `frame-relay` command allows routing updates to be sent across the virtual circuit.

982. **A. They emulate leased lines**

C. They must have a unique subnet.

Frame relay point-to-point sub-interfaces are used to emulate a leased line and must be using a unique subnet and local DLCI.

983. **C. They are locally significant.**

The DLCI is a locally unique value that represents the frame relay link.

984. **D. Inverse ARP**

Frame relay uses inverse ARP to create mapping of the IP address to the DLCI value.

985. **A. Use the following commands:**

interface s0/1/0.102 point-to-point

ip address 192.168.1.2 255.255.255.0

frame-relay interface-dlci 102

When configuring the sub-interface with frame relay, you use the `interface` command to create the point-to-point link and then assign the IP address to the interface. You then use the `frame-relay interface-dlci <num>` to associate the DLCI number with the sub-interface.

986. **C. R1(config-if)#frame-relay map ip 10.0.0.2 100**

In order to create the frame relay mapping of the IP address to the DLCI, you would use the `frame-relay map ip <IP> <DLCI>` command.

987. **C. HDLC**

Looking at the output of the show interface command, you can see that the encapsulation protocol being used is the HDLC protocol.

988. **D. Change the encapsulation protocol to PPP.**

If your router is communicating with another router over a point-to-point link, then you must use a protocol supported by both routers. In this case, the Cisco router is communicating with a 3COM router so you must use a vendor-neutral encapsulation protocol such as PPP.

989. **A. show controllers s0/0**

The `show controllers` command will show if you are at the DCE or DTE end of the link.

990. **A. Line protocol is up**

When looking at the `show interface` command output, the "line protocol is up" section is identifying the layer-2 status information.

991. **A. The passwords need to be the same.**

When configuring PPP authentication, you need to ensure that the user accounts created have the same password.

992. **C. The clock rate is not set on the DCE device**

D. The encapsulation protocol is not the same on both ends of the link.

If the line protocol is down, this indicates a layer-2 issue which relates to the layer-2 protocol on the device. You may have loaded the wrong layer-2 protocol or may not have the clock rate set on the DCE device.

993. **A. serial0/3/0 is down, line protocol is down**

Serial0/3/0 is down indicates that there is a layer-1 issue with the serial port.

994. **D. serial0/3/0 is administratively down, line protocol is down**

When a port has been disabled, the status will show as administratively down when you use the show interface command or the show ip interface brief command. In order to use the interface, you must issue the no shutdown command on the interface.

995. **B. serial0/3/0 is up, line protocol is down**

When viewing the status of an interface, layer-2 issues are identified with "line protocol is down" status. Although choice A has a line protocol is down status, it is because the interface is down (layer-1 issue). So when the interface is up and the line protocol is down, that is a layer-2 problem.

996. **C. serial0/3/0 is up, line protocol is up**

If the interface is operational, it will show serial0/3/0 is up, line protocol is up.

997. **D. BGP**

The Border Gateway Protocol (BGP) is used to connect two different autonomous systems together.

998. **D. show frame-relay map**

When troubleshooting frame relay connections to non-Cisco devices, you want to ensure that the encapsulation protocol is using IETF. You can verify the encapsulation protocol with the `show frame-relay map` command.

999. **A. Locally you are configured properly, but the other end of the link is misconfigured.**

When viewing the PVC status, you can have any of the following three status messages:

- Active: The PVC is operational and all is good!
- Inactive: There is a problem on the remote end of the PVC.
- Deleted: There is a problem with the PVC at the provider. Contact the provider to verify the link.

1000. **D. debug ppp authentication**

In order to troubleshoot PPP authentication, you would turn on debugging for PPP authentication with the debug ppp authentication command.

1001. **C. The DLCI mapping was learned through Inverse ARP.**

The term dynamic in the frame relay mappings indicates that the mapping of Layer 3 to DLCI was learned by the Inverse ARP protocol.

Index

• *X* •

Workspace

Workspace

Workspace

Workspace

Workspace

About the Authors

Glen E. Clarke (CCNA, MCITP, MCSE, MCSD, MCDBA, MCT, CEH, CHFI, Security+) is an independent trainer and consultant who specializes in networking and network security. Glen spends most of his time delivering certified courses on Windows Server, Exchange Server, SQL Server, SharePoint Server, Visual Basic .NET, and ASP.NET. Glen also teaches a number of security-related courses covering topics such as ethical hacking and countermeasures, computer forensics and investigations, vulnerability testing, firewall design, and packet analysis.

Glen is an experienced author and technical editor who has worked on more than 20 certification books. Glen designed and authored the *CCENT Certification All-In-One For Dummies* and designed and coauthored the award nominated *A+ Certification Bible*. Glen has coauthored the *A+ Certification All-In-One For Dummies,* 3rd Edition, and authored many other books, such as *CompTIA Security+ Certification Study Guide* and *CompTIA Network+ Certification Study Guide,* 5th Edition.

When Glen is not working, Glen loves to spend quality time with his wife, Tanya, and their four children — Sara, Brendon, Ashlyn, and Rebecca. You can visit Glen online at www.gleneclarke.com, or contact him at glenclarke@accesswave.ca.

Edward Tetz graduated in 1990 from Saint Lawrence College in Cornwall, Ontario, with a degree in Business Administration. He spent a short time in computer sales and support. In 1994, he added training to his repertoire. Since 2002, Edward has been a computer consultant for a value-added reseller, specializing in enterprise infrastructure in Halifax, Nova Scotia. Edward has earned multiple industry certifications that recognize his commitment to continually bolster his knowledge and skills.

Some of the certifications Edward holds include Cisco Certified Network Associate (CCNA), VMWare Certified Professional (VCP), A+, ITIL Foundations Certificate in IT Service Management (IT Infrastructure Library), Microsoft Certified Trainer (MCT), Microsoft Certified Systems Engineer (MCSE), Microsoft Certified Database Administrator (MCDBA), and Chauncey Group's Certified Technical Trainer (CTT). During his work experience, Edward has supported Apple Macintosh, IBM OS/2, Linux, Novell NetWare, and all Microsoft operating systems from MS-DOS to Windows 8, as well as hardware from most of the major vendors.

Edward has designed and coauthored the award-nominated *CompTIA A+ Certification All-In-One For Dummies* and has worked on certification titles involving topics such as Windows and Cisco certifications.

Dedication

During the writing of this book, I spent two months at the hospital with my son as doctors and nurses helped him walk again. Being at the hospital for that long, I really got to see (and appreciate) how doctors and nurses treat and interact with our children.

This book is dedicated to all the doctors and nurses at the IWK Children's Hospital who work long hours with our children to help them recover from illness. —Glen

Author's Acknowledgments

I want to thank the people at Wiley for their hard work and continued support. A special thank-you goes to acquisitions editor Connie Santisteban for asking me to write this book and for her patience as I worked through the chapters. I also want to thank the project editor, Christopher Morris, for his work and quick responses to my e-mails. Much appreciation goes to copy editor Debbye Butler for an outstanding job on the edits in this book. I also want to thank Ed Tetz and Dan Lachance for doing another great job as technical editors! A special thanks to Ed Tetz for helping with the authoring of a few of the chapters! It is always a pleasure to work with you!

I also want to thank the folks at Tim Horton's for not kicking me out when I occupied a table for hours at a time, and for keeping the coffee *always fresh!*

A special thank-you goes to my four children, Sara, Brendon, Ashlyn, and Rebecca, for giving me the opportunity to sit down and participate in kid's time with them! It is the best time in the world! A needed thank-you goes to my wife, Tanya, for all her support and patience — thank you!

Publisher's Acknowledgments

Acquisitions Editor: Connie Santisteban

Sr. Project Editor: Christopher Morris

Copy Editor: Debbye Butler

Technical Editors: E

Editorial Assistant:

Sr. Editorial Assista

Project Coordinator: Sheree Montgomery

Project Manager: Laura Moss-Hollister

Cover Image: ©iStockphoto.com/Petrovich9

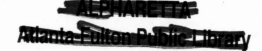